"Despite his significant role in the development of Anabaptism in Hesse, Melchior Rinck has received much less attention than other early Anabaptist leaders. This important book, based on the most recent scholarship, provides the first full biography of this creative theologian and missionary, along with English translations of all Rinck's extant writings. Stuart Murray's incisive assessment of Rinck's contributions—particularly on baptism, civil authority, and the centrality of love in all human relationships—makes this book essential reading for anyone interested in the Anabaptist movement."

—**JOHN D. ROTH**, project director of Anabaptism at 500

"This book is long overdue and a welcome addition to Anabaptist literature. Stuart Murray has given us a comprehensive and cogent account of the life and teachings of Melchior Rinck, the early Anabaptist leader in Hesse. Known to his contemporaries as 'the Greek' because of his learning, Rinck was routinely listed as an Anabaptist founder along with Hans Hut, Balthasar Hubmaier, Hans Denck, and others. Surprisingly, Murray's excellent study is the first book-length study of Rinck and his teachings. Accompanying the clear historical and theological narrative is a welcome translation of surviving texts documenting the Rinck story."

—**C. ARNOLD SNYDER**, professor emeritus of history at Conrad Grebel University College, University of Waterloo

"We are indebted to Stuart Murray, Leonard Gross, and Ellen Yutzy Glebe for recovering the sixteenth-century witness and theological legacy of Melchior Rinck. Long overlooked, Rinck now takes his place as an incisive critic of Christendom and an ardent advocate for personal discipleship, social righteousness, and understanding God as love."

—**STEVEN M. NOLT**, senior scholar at the Young Center for Anabaptist and Pietist Studies at Elizabethtown College

"Anyone interested in early Anabaptist history will love this book. Short enough to read in an evening, Stuart Murray's biography of Melchior Rinck doesn't solve the puzzle of Rinck's absence in Anabaptist historiography, but it does make that absence much less likely in the future. The primary documents at the back are a welcome addition, themselves worth the price of the book."

—**DAVID WEAVER-ZERCHER**, professor of American religious history at Messiah University

"Stuart Murray agrees with close observers of Anabaptism from the sixteenth century: Melchior Rinck's influence should not be underestimated. Murray's thorough biographical and theological analyses, alongside Leonard Gross's and Ellen Yutzy Glebe's translations, make a convincing case for the enduring importance of Rinck's legacy as a wandering evangelist who just may have changed the course of church history."

—**JAMIE PITTS**, associate professor of Anabaptist Studies at Anabaptist Mennonite Biblical Seminary and director of the Institute of Mennonite Studies

"Though less well known than his contemporaries in Switzerland/South Germany and the Low Countries, Melchior Rinck was an important figure among the Radical Reformers of the early sixteenth century. This fascinating volume, which is written in a refreshingly accessible style, introduces readers to Rinck's life and thought and provides translations of his extant writings. It is to be recommended to anyone interested in early Anabaptist history."

—**MARK L. LOUDEN**, Alfred L. Shoemaker, J. William Frey, and Don Yoder Professor of Germanic Linguistics at University of Wisconsin–Madison

"As do other Christian communities, Anabaptists tend to intertwine their movement's origin stories with the biographies of influential leaders: Conrad Grebel, Michael Sattler, Jacob Amman, Menno Simons. In *The Legacy of Melchior Rinck*, Stuart Murray introduces us to yet another such movement builder and argues persuasively for his inclusion in the pantheon. Through careful analysis of the first complete English-language translation of extant writings by and about Rinck, Murray persuasively makes the case that this Reformer offered a distinctive theological vision that shaped early Anabaptism in South Germany and, ultimately, beyond."

—**DEVIN MANZULLO-THOMAS**, assistant professor of American religious history and interdisciplinary studies, director of the Sider Institute for Anabaptist, Pietist, and Wesleyan Studies, and director of archives at Messiah University

THE LEGACY OF Melchior Rinck

Anabaptist Pioneer in Hesse

MELCHIOR. RINCK.

Stuart Murray

Leonard Gross and Ellen Yutzy Glebe, translators

Harrisonburg, Virginia

Herald Press
PO Box 866, Harrisonburg, Virginia 22803
www.HeraldPress.com

Library of Congress Cataloging-in-Publication Data
Names: Murray, Stuart, 1956- author. | Rinck, Melchior, 1492 or 1493-, author. | Gross, Leonard, 1931 November 17- translator. | Glebe, Ellen Yutzy, translator.
Title: The legacy of Melchior Rinck : Anabaptist pioneer in Hesse / Stuart Murray. ; translators, Leonard Gross and Ellen Yutzy Glebe
Description: Harrisonburg, Virginia : Herald Press, 2022. | Summary: "The first comprehensive introduction to the life, ministry and newly translated writings of an under-valued Anabaptist pioneer. It offers fresh insights into the diversity of the early Anabaptist movement and an opportunity to reflect on a less heroic expression of Anabaptism"—Provided by publisher.
Identifiers: LCCN 2022002981 | ISBN 9781513809809 (paperback)
Subjects: LCSH: Anabaptists—Germany—Hesse—History—16th century. | Rinck, Melchior, 1492 or 1493- | Anabaptists—Germany—Hesse—Biography. | Hesse (Germany)—Church history. | BISAC: RELIGION / Christian Church / History | RELIGION / History
Classification: LCC BX4933.G3 M88 2022 | DDC 284/.3094341—dc23/eng/20220325
LC record available at https://lccn.loc.gov/2022002981

Study guides are available for many Herald Press titles at www.HeraldPress.com.

THE LEGACY OF MELCHIOR RINCK

Library of Congress Control Number: 2022002981
International Standard Book Number: 978-0-8361-0980-9
Printed in United States of America
Cover and interior design by Merrill Miller
Cover and title page engravings of Melchior Rinck by Christoff van Sichem

26 25 24 23 22 10 9 8 7 6 5 4 3 2 1

In grateful memory of Alan Kreider,
friend, colleague, and mentor

Contents

Foreword

THE ANABAPTIST STORY is a complex and pluralistic drama, with a large cast of characters acting from diverse motivations. Perhaps the only common thread of purpose that unites the colorful quilt of Anabaptist dissent in the early sixteenth century is devotion to *Nachfolge*—following after Jesus Christ in life.

When ordinary people decided to conform their lives to the way of Jesus Christ as they understood it, they often also emerged from obscurity to become visible on the stage of history—and thus we find them in the song collections, martyrologies, and archival records that document the Radical Reformation. During the past century, a renaissance of Anabaptist studies has amplified the voices of these characters who acted creatively, spoke courageously, and challenged the conventions of Christendom with new forms of life.

One such character is Melchior Rinck, whose life and ministry unfolded in the central German principality of Hesse during the social and religious upheavals of the early Protestant Reformation. Reflecting the spiritual journey of numerous Anabaptist leaders, his ministry began as a Catholic parish priest, continued through his conversion to Protestant teachings, and concluded with his imprisonment as a heretic. For a few short years as a Radical Reformer, he took up the social justice concerns that led to the German Peasants' Revolt of 1525, engaged in a critical public theological disputation at the University of Marburg, served as an evangelist and church planter in Thuringia and Hesse, and published several tracts on such topics as baptism, civil authority, and marriage.

In this biography and primary source collection, Stuart Murray—an Anabaptist church planter and scholar from our own time—has gathered together the key primary sources detailing Rinck's life and work, including writings by and about Rinck that have been translated into English for the first time. Murray's work makes available to English readers a valuable perspective on the Anabaptist movement from the complicated and fleeting contexts of early modern radical reform, through the eyes of a neglected yet significant Anabaptist evangelist.

The picture that emerges from the shadows is of a passionate and persistent spiritual leader, whose deeply held views continued to change and whose influence supported the more flexible and generous forms of Anabaptist community found in central Germany. Rinck clearly understood that communities conformed to the way of Jesus Christ would challenge social and political orders organized by the privileges of worldly power—for "the Lamb is Lord of all lords." With his own marriage on the rocks, Rinck embraced baptism as a more profoundly defining marriage ceremony by which the "devout church commits and binds itself to Christ as [the] true bridegroom." Much of what we know about Rinck's convictions and actions show us a Christ follower whose devotion took concrete form amid the conflicts precipitated by a hostile magistracy and a broken marriage.

The volume in hand reflects the nearly one-hundred-year-old commitment of Studies in Anabaptist and Mennonite History to reliable scholarship that makes the fascinating and inspiring details of the Anabaptist movement available to the church and the academy for edification and understanding. As we approach the five hundredth anniversary of Anabaptist beginnings that took place in a clandestine baptism ceremony in a small Zurich apartment on January 21, 1525, this new biography of Melchior Rinck supplies a fitting introduction to one of the many colorful characters on the dramatic stage of Anabaptist history.

Gerald J. Mast, Series Editor
Studies in Anabaptist and Mennonite History

Preface

THIS IS NOT A book I intended to write. I did intend to research the life of Melchior Rinck, but this research was no more than a spare time project that developed in unexpected ways.

I encountered Rinck many years ago as I read about the early Anabaptists. For some reason, his name stuck in my mind. Although he seemed to have been an influential first-generation leader, it was not easy to discover much about his ministry, and most accounts of Anabaptism in Germany paid only passing attention to him. Every so often I thought about investigating further, but I was daunted by what appeared to be quite limited resources in English and my inability to read German.

Then in 2014, following the gift of the library formerly housed at the London Mennonite Centre to Bristol Baptist College, I was invited to become the founding director of the Centre for Anabaptist Studies in Bristol. Now that I was responsible for designing and teaching post-graduate modules on Anabaptism and supervising research students, I decided I really ought to do some further historical research myself (having not done much since studying for a PhD in Anabaptist hermeneutics over twenty-five years ago). So I turned again to Melchior Rinck.

My initial investigations suggested that Mennonite scholars had not given much attention to Rinck, with only passing references to him in their books or occasional articles about him in the *Mennonite Quarterly*

Review. This encouraged me to look further but also indicated that I might struggle to find enough resources. However, the discovery of recent studies by Ellen Yutzy Glebe and Kat Hill that concentrated on the region in which Rinck lived and operated was timely, not least because these studies also included resources on Rinck's life that I had not found elsewhere. They also alerted me to resources in German that contained primary sources that had not, as far as I could tell, ever been translated into English—writings by Rinck himself, letters about him, and accounts of interrogations of Rinck and his followers and colleagues.

I am grateful to Michael Brealey, the Bristol Baptist College librarian, for his help in tracking down some obscure books and articles. And I am grateful to Silke Chatfield, a member of the Anabaptist study group in Bristol and a native German speaker, who spent many hours poring over these resources and providing rough translations so that I had some idea of what they contained. Her translations were never intended to be publishable, but they convinced me that there were enough resources to pursue my research and that they might throw fresh light on Rinck's career, theology, and legacy.

Over the next few months, as I wrote up my findings, I discovered that I had written nearly 55,000 words, and I began to wonder if others might be interested in this. An exchange of emails with John Roth, director of the Mennonite Historical Library in Goshen, Indiana, and editor of the *Mennonite Quarterly Review*, encouraged me to consider this more seriously. Both he and Gerald Mast, professor of communication at Bluffton University and editor of the Studies in Anabaptist and Mennonite History series, suggested I might submit the manuscript for possible publication. I am grateful to them for encouraging me to do this.

What I still needed, however, was someone able to produce a publishable translation of texts by or about Rinck that had not previously appeared in English. After a number of false starts and disappointments, my friend Eleanor Kreider put me in touch with Leonard Gross, who responded enthusiastically to my invitation to translate this material and has produced all but two of the translations in this book. He has also read the full manuscript, offered corrective comments, and shared additional insights. I am very grateful for his partnership in this project. And I am grateful, too, to Ellen Yutzy Glebe, a professional translator, who reviewed the translations and offered suggestions for improving them.

The story of Rinck and the Anabaptists of Hesse is less heroic and more mundane than that of many other branches of early Anabaptism. A combination of factors, internal and external, led to the relatively early demise of this movement and an unusual number of Anabaptists deciding to return to the state churches. But it is a story worth telling and pondering if we are to understand the range of contexts within which Anabaptism arose and the range of ways in which it flourished and declined.

Rinck's writings and the records of his debates offer distinctive perspectives. Although he shares and endorses convictions held in other branches of the Anabaptist movement, he presents his own insights and interpretations. His critique of infant baptism is more trenchant, multifaceted, and sustained than almost any other Anabaptist leader; and his insistence on the primacy of the love of God is especially powerful and winsome.

INTRODUCTION

Rediscovering Melchior Rinck

ACCORDING TO JAMES STAYER, in his study of the peasants' movement in Germany and its impact on the early Anabaptist movement, Melchior Rinck "played an important role as a zealous Anabaptist apostle in Middle Germany in 1527 and later. Hans Hut and Melchior Rinck, together with Hans Denck, were the major leaders of early Anabaptism in south and central Germany and Austria."[1]

Mention of Hans Hut and Hans Denck comes as no surprise to students of Anabaptism—both have received considerable scholarly attention and both are known, at least by name, even in popular circles. Hut is celebrated as a passionate evangelist; Denck's statement that "no one can know Christ unless he follows after him in life"[2] is one of the classic aphorisms of early Anabaptism. But Melchior Rinck? Was he really significant enough to be bracketed with the others?

Not all historians have apparently thought so. William Estep makes no mention of Rinck in his book *The Anabaptist Story*.[3] There is only a brief reference in *The Anabaptists* by Hans-Jürgen Goertz.[4] And Cornelius Dyck devotes just one page of *An Introduction to Mennonite History* to Rinck.[5] These three overviews of early Anabaptism imply that Rinck was, at best, a marginal figure. Even Werner Packull's introduction to South German–Austrian Anabaptism, the region in which Rinck lived, mentions him only twice.[6] Nor does any extract from Rinck's writings appear in the representative selection of early Anabaptist literature in Walter Klaassen's *Anabaptism in Outline.*

However, evidence from Rinck's contemporaries—both opponents and colleagues—suggests that Stayer's assessment of his influence may be closer to the mark than what is implied in recent historiography. An intriguing reference to Rinck appears in a recently unearthed Hutterite document entitled "Beginnings of the Congregation of God in German Lands."[7] This document identifies seven founders of the Anabaptist movement. It omits some of the early leaders we might have expected to find, such as the Swiss Anabaptists Conrad Grebel, Felix Manz, and George Blaurock, and it surprisingly includes Thomas Müntzer and Lienhart Kaiser, neither of them Anabaptists. Yet whatever the criteria for selection (Werner Packull, who discovered this document, suggests various possibilities), it is noteworthy that Melchior Rinck not only appears in the list of seven founders but is the only one accorded this status while still alive. The Hutterites, who had connections with Rinck's followers in both Hesse and Moravia, evidently regarded Rinck as an important first-generation Anabaptist pioneer.

Obbe Philips, in his *Recollections of the Years 1533–1536*, named Rinck as a significant Anabaptist leader, along with Hubmaier, Hut, Denck, Haetzer, Müntzer, and Hofmann.[8]

Sebastian Franck featured a very similar list in his *Chronica* (1531), naming Hubmaier, Rinck, Hut, Denck, and Haetzer as the leading Anabaptists. Martin Bucer, the reformer invited to debate with Anabaptists in Hesse, where Rinck had operated until sentenced to life imprisonment, esteemed him highly enough to ask for the harsh conditions of his imprisonment to be improved.[9] And the Amtmann of the Wartburg castle near Eisenach, Eberhard von der Tann, insisted that Rinck should not be released because he was the "main instigator" of the Anabaptists.[10] These four testimonies come from his opponents or those who were critical of Anabaptism—they disagreed with Rinck but acknowledged him to be an important Anabaptist leader. Perhaps most remarkably, in 1538 Philip, Landgrave of Hesse, summoned this supposedly insignificant Anabaptist to a personal audience in his hunting lodge in order to hear and understand his teaching. Furthermore, evidence from the interrogation of Anabaptists in the area in which he was operating testify to his impact and the respect with which he was regarded. Court records identify Rinck as the author of many of the theological and ecclesial convictions held by the defendants.[11]

Why, then, has Rinck received so little attention from historians of early Anabaptism?

One reason might be that few of Rinck's writings have survived. Although it is possible that undiscovered manuscripts might yet come to light in European archives, currently we have limited resources from which to discern and assess Rinck's theological emphases, ecclesial convictions, and missional passions. But paucity of surviving written documents has not prevented some other early Anabaptists from receiving rather more attention than Rinck. We have little from the pen of Hans Denck, for example, but he is much better known to posterity.

A second reason for the relative neglect of Rinck might be his uncertain legacy. Although Hans Hut bequeathed no lasting movement of the kind that the Swiss Brethren or Dutch Mennonites founded, his evangelistic passion is legendary, with baptized converts reported to number many hundreds. Rinck was also an evangelist, on the move much of the time, but the nature of the converts he made and the congregations he helped establish did not, as we will see, commend themselves so obviously to historians of German Anabaptism.

A third possible reason for Rinck's marginality is his somewhat anomalous position and the difficulty of locating him within the various branches of the Anabaptist movement. He operated in the central German territories of Hesse, Saxony, and Thuringia, and so was associated with German Anabaptism, but he appears to have developed theological and ecclesial views that were closer to the Swiss Brethren. C. Arnold Snyder, who accords greater significance to Rinck in his *Anabaptist History and Theology* than most other historians of Anabaptism, points to his biblicism and ethical orientation as evidence that, although Rinck was involved in the uprising led by Thomas Müntzer, knew Hans Hut, and was probably baptized by Hans Denck, "his Anabaptism looks more Swiss than South German."[12]

And a fourth reason why historians may have neglected Rinck is that his character and behavior were at times open to serious criticism. There is no doubt that his marriage was unhappy and that contemporaries, including his wife's family, were critical of Rinck's treatment of his wife.

Furthermore, evaluations of his personality and conduct are quite variable, with some characterizing him as irascible and intemperate.[13]

Any attempt to rediscover and reappraise Rinck's ministry and significance within the early Anabaptist movement will be hindered by the limited evidence from his own writings, but it is not apparent why the other reasons should preclude this attempt. He was not the only Anabaptist leader to experience marital disharmony or to be charged with intemperate language, and what evidence we have suggests that there is much to be said in his defense on both issues. His legacy may be less satisfactory to the minds of some historians than that of other early Anabaptists, but it is no less interesting, especially if we are to fill out the story of the movement in all its diversity. And the difficulty of fitting him neatly into established categories or geographical boundaries may add to his significance rather than diminishing it. As Snyder comments, Rinck is an example of the capacity of "strong leaders to 'shape' Anabaptist essentials according to their own understanding and predispositions, regardless of who baptized them."[14] Examining his own extant writings and what others wrote about him offers an opportunity to discover the ways in which Rinck shaped these essentials.

Rinck is not, of course, the only significant figure from the early Anabaptist movement to slip out of sight in the intervening centuries. Pilgram Marpeck, a highly influential leader among the Austrian and German Anabaptists, whose impact was felt also in Moravia and among the Swiss Brethren, was almost unknown to historians until the twentieth century. He is now widely known and respected, and "Marpeck studies" is a recognizable branch of Anabaptist history.[15] There is no likelihood of discovering a body of writings by Rinck that is in any way comparable to the prolific Marpeck, but the rehabilitation of the latter holds out hope that other early leaders might also receive greater attention.

While Rinck himself has yet to receive much attention, primary sources relating to his life have been accessible for many years, and a great deal has been written about the sociopolitical, theological, and ecclesial context in which he operated. Many of the sources—his writings, records of debates, interrogations of Rinck and his followers, and several letters about Rinck—have been reproduced verbatim in German. Early twentieth-century historian Paul Wappler collected numerous source materials in his overview of Anabaptism (which he described as a heresy) in Hesse and Thuringia. These were published in *Die Stellung Kursachsens und des Landgrafen Philip von Hessen zur Täuferbewegung* and *Die Täuferbewegung in Thüringen von 1526 bis 1584.*[16] Additional sources by or about Rinck appeared in the 1951 source collection *Urkundliche Quellen zur hessischen Reformationsgeschichte: Volume IV: Wiedertäuferakten, 1527–1626*, edited by Günther Franz, Eckhart Franz, and others.[17]

Drawing heavily on these sources, John Oyer provides important information about Rinck's life and some examples of his teaching in his *Lutheran Reformers against Anabaptists: Luther, Melanchthon and Menius and the Anabaptists of Central Germany*, which charts the course of the Anabaptist movement in Hesse and the surrounding territories. Rinck was not Oyer's main interest, but he concludes that this branch of Anabaptism "displayed a vitality not always found elsewhere, primarily because of the ability of its first great leader, Melchior Rinck."[18]

More recently some dissertations, examining Anabaptism in Hesse and the surrounding territories, have given further credence to Stayer's claim regarding Rinck's significance as an Anabaptist leader, even though their primary focus has been on other historical figures or the wider context. Ellen Yutzy Glebe's dissertation, "Anabaptists in their Hearts? Religious Dissidence and the Reformation in the Landgraviate of Hesse," explores the impact of the Reformation in the region. She focuses on the distinctive characteristics of the Anabaptist communities in this area, what motivated people to join and sometimes leave these communities, and what issues were of primary concern. In her study, Rinck emerges as an influential Anabaptist leader in this region and so his life, teaching, and influence receive considerable attention.[19] Kat Hill's *Baptism, Brotherhood, and Belief in Reformation Germany: Anabaptism and Lutheranism, 1525–1585* examines the same geographical area, drawing on additional primary sources. Like Glebe, Hill was interested in the beliefs, practices, and interactions of both the Lutheran and Anabaptist communities, and her work refers frequently to Rinck as a leading Anabaptist and a conversation partner with both Martin Bucer and Landgrave Philip.[20]

The unusual ways in which Anabaptism was expressed in this region owe much to the character and policies of the landgrave. Philip was a staunch convert to the Protestant cause and a leading figure in the alliance formed to resist the assaults of the Holy Roman Empire on Protestant territories. He responded vigorously and stubbornly to any military or political challenge to his authority, but he respected the religious views of those with whom he disagreed and resisted calls to execute them. He seems to have been politically and temperamentally disinclined to persecute religious dissent as long as this posed no apparent threat to his governance. David Whitford's *A Reformation Life: The European Reformation through the Eyes of Philipp of Hesse* is a biography of the landgrave that explores his interaction with the leading political and religious figures of his day. It sets the scene for any study of Rinck's life and influence, and it includes references to Rinck and his treatment by Philip.[21]

Some of Rinck's writings have already been translated into English. John Wenger translated his tract on baptism and a short letter.[22] Frank Friesen and Walter Klaassen included his tract on marriage in their collection of sixteenth-century documents.[23] Glebe offers translations of many statements by Rinck's followers under interrogation. And other scholars include translations of snippets from documents by or about Rinck. I am grateful for permission to reprint Friesen and Klaassen's translation of Rinck's tract on marriage and the translation of a letter from the Hutterites about Rinck in *The Chronicle of the Hutterian Brethren*.[24] And I am especially grateful to Leonard Gross (with advice from Ellen Yutzy Glebe) for translating all the other documents. These include a fresh translation of Rinck's tract on baptism. This book contains translations of the first complete collection of extant writings by and about Rinck, enabling us to understand more fully his theological and ecclesial convictions. These texts, which are quoted throughout the book, are collected in Primary Sources at the back of this volume. Cross-references to these texts are indicated in the notes using a letter-and-number system.

Many gaps remain in any attempt to provide a reasonably comprehensive account of the life and teaching of Melchior Rinck. In some periods of his life his activities and whereabouts are unknown, and many of his writings have not survived. But studies of his political and ecclesial context and the policies and writings of those with whom he interacted, together with this collection of source materials, provide enough for at least a partial rediscovery.

ONE

Disturbances in Hesse

MELCHIOR RINCK SPENT most of his life in the central German landgraviate of Hesse. He traveled beyond this region, to Worms and elsewhere, and spent time also in the neighboring territory of Electoral Saxony. The history and geography of this area, which was originally known as Thuringia, is quite complex, with fluctuating boundaries, allegiances, and political arrangements. Mark Greengrass describes it as "an agglomeration of previously separate counties."[1]

The relationship of Hesse to Saxony and other neighboring principalities, as Ellen Yutzy Glebe notes, was a significant factor in the history of Anabaptism in this region. The jurisdictions of the secular authorities were complicated and competitive, allowing Anabaptists to avoid arrest and find new places in which to settle if banished from one of the territories.[2]

In 1247 the War of the Thuringian Succession broke out after the death of the last of the Ludowingian counts and landgraves. This war dragged on until 1264, at which point the western half of the region became independent, adopted the name Hesse, and became a landgraviate within the Holy Roman Empire. Hesse had 138 towns, many of which had been chartered during the Middle Ages. Only fifteen had more than two thousand inhabitants, of which Frankfurt with twenty thousand inhabitants was the largest. The rest of the region initially came under the control of the margraviate of Meissen and then, when the ruling Wettin dynasty in 1485 followed Saxon custom by dividing its territory between different

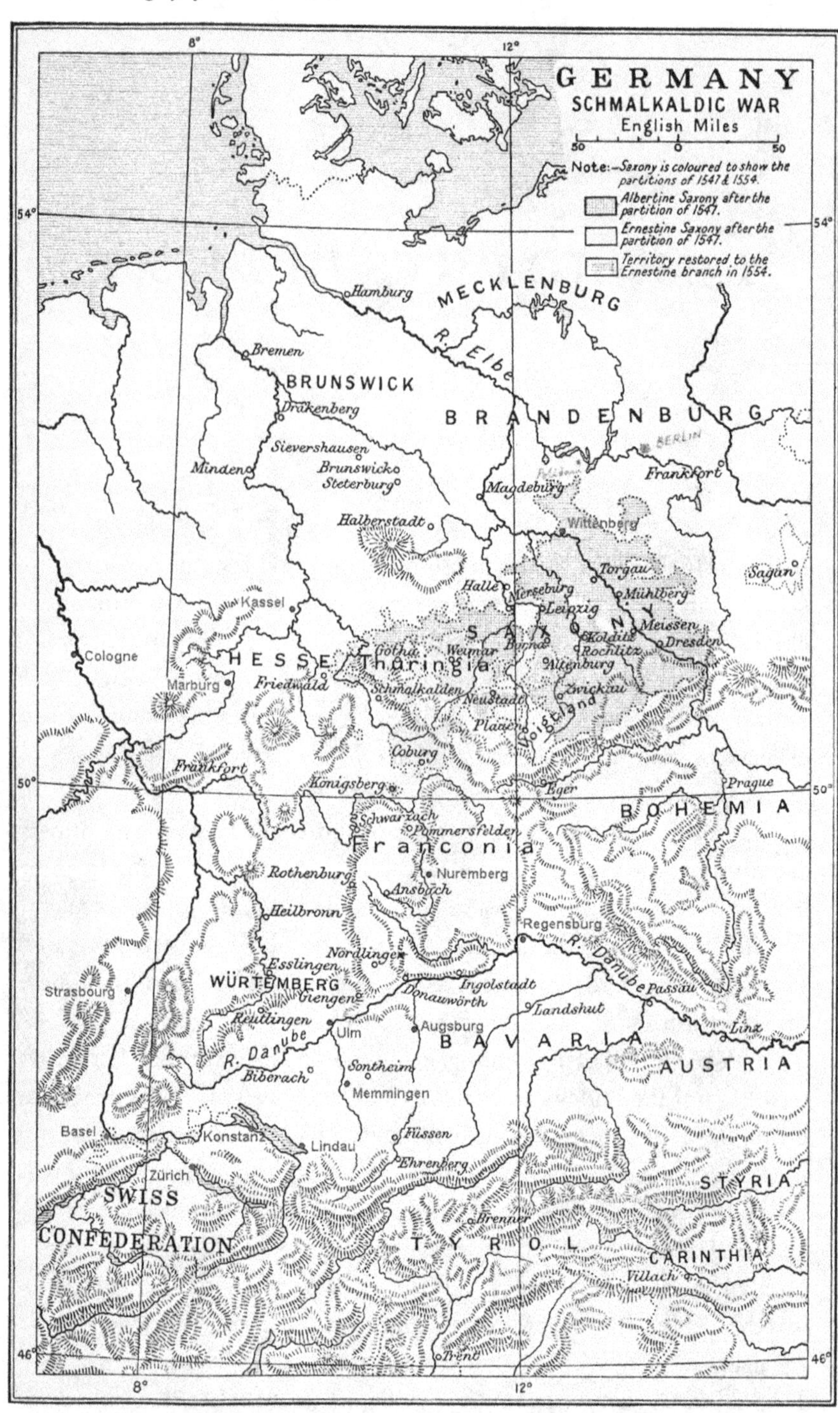

Hesse and Saxony, mid-sixteenth century. From *The Cambridge Modern History Atlas* (1912), Map 14.

branches of the family, the remnant of Thuringia passed into the hands of the Electorate of Saxony. Some ecclesiastical territories, including Fulda and Würtzburg, also enjoyed a measure of autonomy.

PHILIP, LANDGRAVE OF HESSE (1519–67)

Hesse, together with the rest of the region still known generally as Thuringia, embraced the Reformation early and enthusiastically under the auspices of its young landgrave, Philip I of Hesse.[3] Philip, who at the age of fourteen succeeded his father after his mother's regency, first met Luther in 1521 at the Diet of Worms, and by 1524 he was advocating his teachings throughout his realm, despite opposition from the clergy and members of his own family and the absence of any sizable popular movement for reform. Introducing the Reformation officially into Hesse in 1526 at a combined diet and synod in Homberg, his passion for the Protestant cause increased further after a meeting with Philip Melanchthon in 1527, and he founded the first Protestant university in Marburg. Measures were introduced to suppress Roman Catholicism, including the destruction of churches and monasteries and exile of priests who refused to abandon traditional ways. The Roman Catholic faith survived only in the Eichsfeld district, which was governed by the Archbishop of Mainz, and in Erfurt and its vicinity.

Philip emerged as one of the leading figures in German Protestantism. He "dominated the Reformation within his own land in a way in which few other rulers did, due to both his longevity as a ruler and the lack of native Hessian theologians with an imperial profile."[4] In 1526 he forged an alliance with Elector John (1525–32) of neighboring Saxony in order to defend the Protestant states from imperial interference, and in 1529 at the Diet of Speyer he argued strongly for freedom for Protestant preachers.

Irenic in character and known both to his contemporaries and to historians as "Philip the Magnanimous," throughout his long reign he tried to foster unity among the Protestant states and theologians. Eager to avoid division over the Lord's Supper, he invited the Swiss reformer Ulrich Zwingli to Germany and subsequently proposed that a general council should be called to make decisions in relation to differences among the reformers. Accused of being too favorable toward Zwingli, he was cold-shouldered by Luther at the Diet of Augsburg in 1530 and felt obliged to confirm his commitment to the Lutheran position, but he insisted that no undue pressure should be put on the Swiss. He found a kindred spirit in the reformer Martin Bucer, who also advocated compromise on the issue of the Lord's Supper, rather than division and hostility. And he succeeded in creating the Schmalkald League, a broad alliance of Protestant rulers formed to defend them against imperial political and religious interference.

Philip also acknowledged the value of discussions with Anabaptists and Spiritualists[5], to the chagrin of those who wished he would suppress

Philip, Landgrave of Hesse. Portrait by Hans Krell (1534).

them. In 1531, for example, an Anabaptist from Fulda successfully appealed to him to intercede on his behalf with the abbot.[6] Philip regarded Anabaptists as in error but held that true faith was a gift from God and so regarded them as misled and not to be punished severely. He also respected their courage and their upright living, acknowledging sadly that their way of life often compared favorably with that of Lutheran church members. He admitted: "I see more improvement of conduct among those whom we call fanatics than among those who are Lutheran."[7] He also explained to Elector John why Anabaptists were not to be executed for their beliefs: "For if we were to hold to such an opinion, we then would not be able to tolerate Jews or Papists, who blaspheme Christ to the highest degree, but would need to judge them in the same manner."[8] Philip might also have been very conscious of his own reprehensible conduct as a serial adulterer from an early age and eventually a bigamist—conduct to which Luther and Melanchthon, after initial protests, effectively turned a blind eye.

Glebe suggests several other reasons for Philip's reluctance to impose the death penalty for religious heterodoxy. First, he did not want to give Catholic rulers a precedent for executing Protestants. Second, he recognized that making Anabaptists into martyrs often served to make others more resolute. Third, his exegesis of Scripture led him to believe such executions were unjustified. Fourth, he wanted to avoid the risk of being responsible for the death of someone who might have been won over by proper instruction. Fifth, "he discounted the ability of the 'common man'—i.e. 'the poor, irrational laity'—to reach an independent religious conviction, and thus he felt impelled to grant clemency to those who had been 'misled' by Anabaptist teachers." She concludes: "Philip took the spread of Anabaptism among his subjects to be at least in part a sign of his own failing rather than an expression of his subjects' spiritual independence."[9] Elsewhere, she notes the mix of pragmatic, ethical, psychological, and paternalistic factors in Philip's stance.[10]

In fact, Philip may have realized that the Anabaptists were advocating practices that had been considered, but not introduced, in the synod at Homberg in 1526. The *Reformatio Ecclesiarum Hassiae*, produced by this meeting, proposed congregationalism, the use of the ban, the removal of images and superfluous altars, the power to choose and dismiss pastors, aid for the poor, communion in both kinds, church services in the vernacular, the limited use of organs and church bells, the reduction of religious holidays, and abolition of the monasteries. The synod had proposed a more radical reformation than Luther had been prepared to allow; and now the Anabaptists were arguing for the same measures that Philip had considered but Luther had vetoed.[11]

The landgrave resisted the persistent demands of Elector John and his successors for more severe punishment, ruling that the Anabaptists should suffer no more than having "their hearth fire extinguished"—in other words, banishment. This evidently frustrated some of his officials, including Eberhard von der Tann, whose report in December 1531 complained: "This same pernicious sect will flare up if it is not forcefully confronted, with those who persist in their error to be punished bodily, unto death, as our Gracious Lord has decreed in the most recent newly-issued constitution and order, as is also implied in the common law . . . . But their Gracious Lord would have scruples against mistreating these individuals bodily."[12]

The Anabaptist takeover of Münster in 1534–35 gave Philip's opponents an opportunity to put pressure on the landgrave to harden his policy, but he continued to urge instruction rather than punishment. During and after the siege of the city, he sent four of his own theologians (Theodor Fabricius, Johann Lening, Antonius Corvinus, and Johann Kymeus) to try to persuade the rebels to repent. Despite the failure of these efforts, in the following year he issued a further mandate against Anabaptists that was still remarkably lenient. The first step was for the Protestant clergy to summon and instruct them. If they refused to recant, they would be required to sell their possessions within two weeks and leave the country with their families. Those who complied should be helped to do this; but the houses of those who resisted should be barricaded, and they should be banished. However, those who recanted and returned to the church should be warmly welcomed and admonished to avoid "harm and disadvantage" in the future.[13]

Anyone who harbored or helped the Anabaptists would risk the same punishment. Some of their family members or neighbors were undoubtedly unsympathetic toward them and ready to cooperate with the authorities by denouncing them. But there is evidence from various sources that neighbors were surprisingly often supportive of them and willing to risk severe punishment by harboring them. This may be testimony to the exemplary lives of many Anabaptists, which so perturbed their interrogators, or simply to the loyalty of longtime neighbors in the face of official interference. Claims that were often made by Anabaptists in hearings (such as that at Sorga in 1531) that they had little contact with their non-Anabaptist neighbors may not imply disdain or separatism. Rather, this limited contact was likely to prevent their neighbors being pursued by the authorities as those who had harbored Anabaptists.

In 1536, concerned that the numbers of Anabaptists were increasing, perhaps because of this tolerant policy, Philip appealed for advice on how to deal with them, especially those who refused to remain in exile.[14] In 1537, a further mandate was issued that urged action in the state churches to suppress vices that provoked Anabaptist outrage but also imposed more severe forms of punishment for Anabaptists, especially those from other territories or who had returned from exile. These included being beaten with rods, having a sign burned into their cheeks, and the threat of execution. However, Philip insisted that "no Anabaptist shall be put to death, even after the sentence has been passed, without previously notifying us."[15] And in 1540 he wrote that no such death sentence had ever been carried out.[16] Alton Hancock notes that after this the landgrave "was tempted many times to violate his early principles and alter his procedure, but he remained faithful."[17]

Philip maintained this tolerant stance throughout his long reign as Saxon Electors came and went. In a letter to Elector John Friedrich in 1544, he referred to the parable about allowing the weeds to grow until the end of the age (Matt 13:24–30), although this did not apparently preclude lesser forms of punishment. He was also well aware that not all Anabaptists were the same (something the authorities often failed to recognize or at least acknowledge). Writing to Elector Augustus in 1559, he explained his thinking on this issue:

> Many Anabaptists have an unchristian evil sect, as was shown at Münster and elsewhere; but they are not alike. Some are simple, pious folk; they should be dealt with in moderation. Anabaptists who deal with the sword may rightly also be punished with the sword. But those who err in faith should be dealt with leniently, and shall be instructed

> in accord with the principle of love to one's neighbor, and no effort shall be spared, also they shall be heard, and if they will not accept the truth and scatter error like a harmful seed among Christians, they shall be expelled and their preaching abolished. But to punish them with death, as happens in some countries, when they have done nothing more than err in faith and have not acted seditiously, cannot be reconciled with the Gospel.[18]

Christian Hege concludes that Philip "looked upon Anabaptism as only an 'erring child of the Reformation.'"[19] And George Williams summarizes Philip's approach as a "lenient and constructive policy of orderly, unvindictive emigration, of suasion and disputation, firmed up by an occasional life sentence for the defiantly obdurate," noting that this was accompanied by "renewed efforts at moral reform in the state church."[20] The encouraging results of this policy, as some Anabaptists eventually returned to the state churches in Hesse, seem in time to have persuaded other rulers in central Germany to adopt a similarly lenient approach.

THE PEASANTS' MOVEMENT

Philip was much less tolerant of threats to public order, as is evident from his response to the movement known to historians as the Peasants' War, which broke out in 1524 and disturbed the authorities across German-speaking Europe, including Hesse. When this movement appeared in his territory, in Alsfeld, Fulda, and Hersfeld, he acted swiftly and executed the ringleaders, but refrained from the indiscriminate slaughter of peasants that took place elsewhere. He then joined the other Protestant princes at Frankenhausen. His response to the Anabaptist uprising in Münster was equally robust, and he was concerned about reports of Anabaptists supposedly planning arson attacks in his own territory. But Hesse was less affected by revolutionary incidents and political dissent than most areas, giving Philip little need to clamp down on dissidents.

In Hesse and elsewhere, many early Anabaptist leaders and members of congregations had been involved in the peasants' movement and had been deeply influenced by the ambitions of Thomas Müntzer. Müntzer, formerly a colleague of Martin Luther, had become increasingly disenchanted with the progress of the Reformation and its failure to engage with issues of social justice. After a brief pastorate in Zwickau, from which he was expelled for his radical views, and a visit to Prague, from which he was also exiled, he returned to Thuringia, where he was born, and became pastor in Allstedt. In December 1523, he produced the first completely German liturgy, the "Order of German Church Service," and on 13 July 1524, he delivered his infamous "Sermon to

Thomas Müntzer. Engraving by Christoffel Van Sichem.

the Princes," which resulted in him being summoned to defend his views before Elector John in Weimar.[21] Müntzer fled.

In August 1524, Müntzer became one of the leaders of the peasants' movement, which was calling for economic and social reforms and was spreading rapidly, albeit largely nonviolently. The peasants anticipated support from Luther for what they regarded as another dimension of the reform movement, but Luther rejected their claims and urged the authorities to suppress them.[22] Philip approved of Luther's position, declaring that this was not an intended or desired outcome of the Reformation and that the peasants needed to be stopped.

Moving by mid-September to the imperial city of Mühlhausen in Thuringia, Müntzer and his associate Heinrich Pfeiffer produced the eleven "Mühlhausen Articles," which called for the dissolution of the existing town council and the formation of an "eternal council" based on divine justice and the Word of God. Unsurprisingly, they were both expelled from Mühlhausen, but in mid-February 1525 Müntzer returned, and in March the citizens voted out the old council and a new "Eternal League of God" was formed, composed of a cross-section of the male population and some former councilors.

On 15 May, convinced that God would intervene on their side, Müntzer led a group of about eight thousand peasants at the Battle of Frankenhausen, also in Thuringia. The outcome was a massacre, the capture and execution of Müntzer, and the suppression of the peasants' movement.[23]

An unanticipated and, to the authorities, unwelcome further outcome was the emergence of Anabaptist communities in areas affected by the peasants' movement. Many of those involved in that movement, including several leaders, turned to Anabaptism as another way to pursue their goals of reforming church and society. Disappointed by the failure of the peasants' movement, rejecting the violence espoused by Müntzer, and outraged by Luther's failure to support them or acknowledge the legitimacy of their concerns, they saw little prospect of progress in the state churches in light of the conservative position adopted by the reformers.

Although the authorities evidently feared that the professed nonviolence of Anabaptism was a ruse and that violence was very likely to break out again if the movement was left unchecked, these fears proved largely unfounded in most areas. Many of those who had participated in the peasants' movement, which began as a nonviolent uprising, may have been motivated by concern for social and economic justice and did not support the turn to violence. For them, Anabaptism was an authentic heir of that original uprising, offering an opportunity to pursue their concerns within a community committed to nonviolence.[24] This might explain the ambivalence and evasiveness of many interrogated Anabaptists when asked for their view of the peasants' movement.

ANABAPTISTS IN HESSE (1526–40)

Anabaptists were active in Hesse and Saxony from at least 1526. Several different strands can be detected. Franconian Anabaptists were initially involved in spreading the movement, finding many receptive to their message in the region of Mühlhausen and elsewhere. In this area Hans Römer, a comrade of Müntzer, initiated a movement that began peacefully but turned to violence, inspired by eschatological fervor. A plot to attack the city of Erfurt in January 1528 was discovered and thwarted. Elsewhere, more moderate movements emerged. In central and western Hesse, the influence of Melchior Hofmann, the leading figure in north German Anabaptism, was apparent, although this influence seems to have faded quite soon. Hutterite missionaries from Moravia, including Christoph Gschall and Jörg Zaunring, were also operating in the area.

Three distinct, though interconnected, Anabaptist movements seem to have coalesced in Hesse. One, centered on Marburg and influenced by Hofmann's teaching and that of the Dutch Anabaptists associated with David Joris, was led by Peter Tasch, Jörg Schnabel, and Hermann Bastian. Another was the result of work by several Moravian missionaries, including Peter Riedemann, in eastern Hesse and later also in western Hesse. The third was led by Rinck and centered on the villages of Sorga and Vacha, near Hersfeld on the eastern border with Saxony.[25] Rinck's congregations seem to have had only limited connections with Anabaptists in western Hesse. And Hessian Anabaptism as a whole did not interact much with South German Anabaptism.

In a variation on the long-running debate about the origins of Anabaptism across Europe, characterized by the terms *monogenesis* and *polygenesis,* Glebe has proposed *pangenesis* for the origins of Hessian Anabaptism, suggesting that it arose from "simple piety rather than external teaching," and that it had no single leader or source.[26]

Kat Hill, though disagreeing in some respects with Glebe's analysis, also describes a rather amorphous movement, less defined than in other regions, with "no clear leaders, no printed books or even manuscripts to spread ideas, no settled hubs of activity in major towns or cities." She suggests that Hessian Anabaptists were reacting against various aspects of Lutheran theology and finding inspiration from the preaching of Hans Hut, Melchior Rinck, and others.[27]

Anabaptists in the region were first discovered by the authorities in 1528 and a number were arrested. Some recanted but continued as Anabaptists and were arrested again near the cloister of Reinhardsbrunn, south of Gotha. Friedrich Myconius, the Lutheran superintendent of Gotha, conducted a hearing. Six prisoners refused to recant and were executed by order of the Elector of Saxony. Most of the remaining Anabaptists then moved from Saxony to Hessian territory, or at least to Amt Hausbreitenbach, which was under joint Hessian and Saxon administration. These executions, however, seem to have strengthened the resolve of the movement and to have provoked negative reactions in the wider community as some questioned why those who were heterodox but not seditious should be executed. Myconius was disconcerted by this reaction, especially as the number of Anabaptists increased.

Justus Menius, the Lutheran superintendent at Eisenach, wrote a book to justify this harsh treatment of Anabaptists.[28] His description of the Anabaptists is very hostile but offers an unintended testimony to their way of life, once his vitriol is extracted:

> The rabble rousers lodge only with the poor and their greeting is: "The peace of God be with you." They preach that they belong only to the poor, to whom God has sent them out, and wherever they go they pretend special piety with peculiar prayers and read the Gospel to the poor people. But what they teach is only good works, such as that one must help his neighbor with gifts and loans and that goods should be held in common, one should injure no one, but conduct oneself friendly and brotherly among each other, none should rule over another, but all should be brethren and sisters alike.[29]

Menius was an unrelenting opponent, playing an active role in searching for Anabaptists, interrogating them, and urging the authorities to take firm action against them. Much to his evident frustration, those he interrogated refused to divulge the names of those who had taught or baptized them, so he struggled to identify their leaders. In common with other opponents of the Anabaptists, he assumed that if he could find the leaders and remove them, the movement would disintegrate. Only slowly did it become apparent in Hesse and elsewhere that this was not a guaranteed outcome. This was especially the case in Hesse, where Anabaptism was essentially a peasants' movement, which attracted none of the nobility or political leaders and few educated people.

Justus Menius. Artist unknown.

From his encounters with the Anabaptists, Menius constructed a list of their supposed errors. Unlike several other reformers, who had little direct contact with Anabaptists, Menius had met and questioned many of them, including Melchior Rinck. Nevertheless, this list is a mixture of authentic Anabaptist convictions, misunderstandings, deliberate misrepresentations, and views held by only specific Anabaptists:

> (1) The Word of God shall be preached to none but those who are in the Anabaptist order and are sealed with the sign of the covenant. (2) Faith in Jesus Christ alone, without our good works and suffering, makes one neither pious nor blessed before God. (3) Infant baptism is against God and a sin, neither useful nor necessary for children; therefore, only the adults and the aged should be baptized. (4) The bread and wine of communion are not the real body and blood of our Lord Jesus Christ. (5) Jesus is not the actual and true Son of God. (6) All the damned and ungodly and even the devil himself will finally be saved.[30]

The heart of the movement

The area in which Anabaptism flourished during the late 1520s and 1530s included the southwest of Electoral Saxony, southeast Hesse and the northeast part of the Fulda holdings. This was a strip of territory roughly 13 miles from north to south and from Eisenach in the east to Hersfeld in the west. Anabaptism was more strongly represented here than elsewhere in central Germany. According to Georg Witzel, every town and village between Fulda and Erfurt had been "infected" with Anabaptism. Many Anabaptist leaders in neighboring regions originated here or had contacts with Anabaptist groups in this area. It is not coincidental that these were the communities in which many had been receptive to the message of those who galvanized the peasants' movement. The spiritual heart of the movement was the congregation at Sorga, three miles east of Hersfeld, which was also the center of Rinck's activities, and probably where he lived.

Rinck's brief active ministry lasted from 1527 to 1532 (though he was in prison for two years in this period), but the movement associated with him persisted beyond this time. Another significant figure, though not a recognized leader, was Fritz Erbe. Arrested at Hausbreitenbach in

October 1531 with five others, Erbe was interrogated by Menius. He recanted and was released. Two years later he was arrested again for refusing to allow his child to be baptized and was imprisoned. Despite efforts to persuade Erbe to recant, he refused and remained in prison until his death in 1548, his resistance becoming an inspiration to many Anabaptists.[31]

Not all his followers were able to remain so steadfast. Rinck was arrested in Vacha in November 1531 with twelve others, several of whom agreed to receive instruction, recant, and return to the state churches (although, for some of these, much to the irritation of the authorities, recanting and then returning to the Anabaptist community seems to have been simply to avoid punishment rather than indicating any genuine change in their beliefs).

In the following month, Philip issued an Ordinance, instructing his officials and pastors of the state churches about their treatment of suspected or convicted Anabaptists. A clear procedure was spelled out, starting with the instruction of first-time offenders by the local pastor, then (if this was not effective) instruction by the superintendent of the district and "two or three learned pastors." Second-time offenders were required to recant publicly in the state church and promise not to consort with Anabaptists in future. This was the first requirement for third-time offenders, too, but they were further required to sell half their possessions and donate the proceeds into a poor fund. Those who refused to comply with this procedure, if they were leaders in the Anabaptist community, were to be banished and not allowed to return until they were prepared to publicly recant. Other Anabaptists would forfeit property rights until they repented. The Ordinance concludes with a threat to any who returned without recanting that they would face the secular authorities.[32]

The temporary and insincere recantations of those arrested in Vacha demonstrated that this procedure could not guarantee lasting changes of belief and allegiance. However, there are instances of more successful interventions by the authorities. In July 1533, for example, a small group of Anabaptists, mostly followers of Rinck, were discovered and arrested in Hausbreitenbach. Philip dispatched Balthasar Raidt, "by now a specialist in reconversion," and he apparently managed to persuade them all to recant.

Others were more stubborn. In the same year and month, nineteen suspected Anabaptists were interrogated in Berka by officials from both Hesse and Saxony.[33] Raidt was again present and reported on the proceedings to the landgrave. It seems that all the local residents were summoned and ordered to denounce any who were Anabaptists among them. The nineteen who were identified as Anabaptists were Heintz Cleue, Hans and Margret Kessel, Peter Leinweber, Anna Leinweber, Gela and Hans Zwingen, Hans Heylman, Barbara and Hermann Adam, Lentz Rüdiger, a man called Tyle, Jung-Hans Zwingen, Margret Schneider (but not her husband, Casper), Könne Wilhelm (but not her husband, Hans), Margret Garköchen, Elsa Erben (but not her husband, Fritz), Alheit Wagener (but not her husband, Simplicious), and Katharina Young (but not her husband, Hans-Paul). Some refused to disclose the names of others who had attended Anabaptist gatherings, but others named those who had baptized them or had been present.

This list is interesting for the number of women under interrogation, some of them with their husbands, but others without their husbands. Anabaptist convictions had evidently divided households in some cases: Margret Schneider claimed to know nothing about the baptism or otherwise of her husband; Könne Wilhelm reported that her husband was not in agreement with her "errors" and had beaten her because of her views; and Katharina Young acknowledged that she had been baptized without her husband's consent. Even when husband and wife shared Anabaptist views, pressure from the authorities might result in separation. Jung-Hans Zwingen testified that his wife had left him three years earlier, leaving behind her baby, in order to escape arrest. She had been drawn toward the Anabaptists before him, but he now shared her beliefs.

The nineteen prisoners were questioned about their beliefs on four key issues: baptism, communion, economics, and civic authority. Seventeen of them admitted that they had been baptized. Interestingly, when asked who had baptized them, only one (Margret Garköchen) named Rinck, despite the fact that he was the leading Anabaptist teacher in the area. Others named Moravian missionaries—Jörg Zaunring and Christoffel Rudolf—or local men—Jörgen Zwinck, Jacob Schmidt, Jacob Schneider, and Claus Schreiber. Rinck's influence, even in the area in which he lived and spent much of his time, evidently did not preclude members of the congregation from learning from others or taking their own initiatives.

Several of those questioned had been in trouble before but had been released after either denying they were Anabaptists or recanting. Hans Zwingen had recanted twice, but said that his conscience impelled him to confess his Anabaptist beliefs and to refuse to recant on this occasion. Tyle from Rengers had also recanted twice when arrested previously in Eisenach. Margret Garköchen had been banished but had returned to Hesse. And Hermann Adam was one of those who had recanted at Vacha but had returned to the Anabaptist congregation.

All nineteen were ordered to attend the parish church on the Sunday after the hearing, in order to be instructed by Raidt, but none did so, insisting that God did not live in temples made by human hands. Some of them had expressed criticisms of the local pastor with, it seems, some justification, in that Raidt urged his replacement after this hearing. And almost all of them declared that they would continue in their Anabaptist convictions.

One month later, in August 1533, Raidt was involved in a further hearing of suspected Anabaptists in Sorga.[34] Some were residents of Sorga; some were from other places but had settled there, perhaps in order to join the Anabaptist community. The record names those who were interrogated: Elsa and Hans Koch, Greta and Hans Plat, Elsa and Hans Zisen, Heinz and Konne Hutter, Catharina and Heinrich Lutz, a couple named Groschen and Margarethe, Hen Schmidt, Endres Lober, Herda and Marx Baumgart, Hermann Stalpf, Heinz and Osanna Bill, Else and Hen Lutz, Cunz and Gele Hutter, and a tailor called Gilg and his wife, Anna. Their surname is not recorded but it might have been Schneider, since a man with this name is mentioned later as one of those who led a group from Sorga to Moravia. Gilg had been baptized by Rinck and was identified by Hans Kessel and Peter Leinweber in the Berka hearing as one of the Sorga leaders. Several of these men and women paid tribute to the teaching of Rinck as they responded to the questions they were asked. The report of the interrogation identifies Hans Plat, Hans Koch, Hans Zisen, and Heinz Hutter as the main leaders alongside Gilg, who was dismissed as "purely a layperson who is unable to write or read."

This hearing was organized by the abbot of Hersfeld, who was increasingly concerned about the influence of Anabaptism in the region and the failure of previous attempts to stem the flow of the movement. Several articles were presented, to which the prisoners were required to give answers. These covered various topics: the obligation of Christians to support and obey the magistrates; the right of the authorities to demand interest and taxes; doing military service, including killing enemies to defend the fatherland, and paying war taxes; their views on the peasants' movement; attendance at the local church and participation in the communion service; and whether Christians could seize the possessions of others in case of need or own possessions themselves.

"Get rid of these people"

Johann Feige, the Hessian chancellor, wrote to Landgrave Philip two days after the end of the hearing, summarizing his interpretation of the evidence he had heard. Although he may have misunderstood or misrepresented some of what those interrogated had said and he was not slow to ascribe their concerns to "hate and self-will," overall this appears to be an accurate and measured summary. He acknowledged that on some issues, especially the peasants' rebellion and community of goods, their answers were reassuring. However, he did not accept the Anabaptists' criticisms of the state churches, the preachers, and the practice of infant baptism; and he was troubled by their limited allegiance to the civic authorities and their refusal to defend Hesse against its enemies. He wrote:

> Although we earnestly sought to instruct them for the better, we instead found them to be obstinate and determined people who know nothing, or at least almost nothing, of Scripture. They can provide no evidence of our preachers' wrongdoing and must admit that their teachings are correct, but despise them nevertheless. They openly denounce them, stating that they do not practice what they preach. And when asked why they believe this, they can only point to the fact that fruits do not appear among the listeners.

His letter concluded: "I am of the firm opinion that it will be necessary to get rid of these people, for it is impossible to dissuade them once they latch onto their opinions, otherwise than with the sword."[35] Feige acknowledged that the abbot of Hersfeld and the local preachers were demanding severe punishment for the Anabaptists (although not execution), but he assured Philip that he was abiding by the landgrave's instruction to deal with them as compassionately as possible. However, several of them had recanted and then returned to their Anabaptist convictions, so firm treatment was required. The crucial issues, in his opinion, were their unwillingness to defend the fatherland and their refusal to attend the state churches. They could not, therefore, be allowed to remain, so they had been given three weeks to dispose of their possessions before being banished from Hesse. Many of them, it seems, headed for Moravia.

Further arrests and interrogations followed. In December 1535, two other reformers, Philip Melanchthon and Caspar Cruciger, had an opportunity to investigate Anabaptist beliefs as they interrogated four Anabaptist prisoners arrested in a raid in Kleineutersdorf while meeting in the house of a miller, Hans Peissker, who had been baptized by Rinck. These included Heinz Kraut from Esperstedt near Frankenhausen, who had become a leader among the Thuringian Anabaptists in 1533 after the execution of Alexander, who had baptized him.[36]

Then, in May 1536, Jörg Schnabel, Peter Loese, Hermann Bastian, Leonhard Fälber, and nearly thirty other Anabaptists were apprehended while worshiping very late at night in an abandoned church in the Cassel district near Gemünden on the Wohra, probably at Lindenborn. The mayor of Marburg reported to the landgrave on 18 June: "Anabaptists from many different towns and villages assembled . . . and there carried on their discussions and counsels and also baptized several persons."[37] This was a small but very significant regional gathering. They were imprisoned at Wolkersdorf, where they were treated very leniently. The landgrave requested opinions from theologians elsewhere, asking what he should do about the continuing Anabaptist presence in his territory. He received mixed advice, with some urging execution, others more tolerant measures. He then convened a meeting at Kassel on 7 August with his own theologians, inviting their comments on the advice he had received.

Only one of these, Justus Winther of Rothenburg, favored execution. Several recognized weaknesses in the state churches that were provoking the Anabaptists and urged reform in the hope that the Anabaptists might then be willing to return to the churches. Johann Lening of Melsungen said: "We should pray to God that the people change their manner of life, and admonish the Anabaptists kindly and lovingly, and even if everything which the Anabaptists teach is wicked, yet we must use caution and use every means to convert them before we reach for the sword."[38] Dionysius Melander added: "The Anabaptist sect represents an affliction from God; for this reason, general prayer should be ordained, the preachers ought diligently to preach against sectarians, the people should be admonished to improve their lives and should be told that sins will not remain unpunished, in order that the Anabaptists will find no cause in us to establish a new church. It is the duty of the authorities to punish all the evils and to punish each according to the degree of his sin."[39]

The consultation at Kassel resulted in a Visitation Order, issued in 1537, which outlawed the views and practices associated with Anabaptism, but also recognized the legitimacy of some of the Anabaptist criticisms and urged reform. Hege comments wryly: "What the Anabaptists sought to attain out of inner conviction, namely a pure life, this the state church should try to accomplish in its members by pressure from the authorities."[40] The Anabaptists, led by Jörg Schnabel, wrote a response to this order, entitled *Verantwortung und Widerlegung der Artikel, so jetzund im land zu Hessen über die armen Davider, die man Wiedertäufer nent, ausgangen sind*, in 1538. In this response, among other things, they denied the accusations that they practiced community of goods, rejected civil authority, and had strange ideas about marriage.[41] A further attempt was made by two Lutheran theologians to persuade the imprisoned Anabaptists to recant, but this made no impression on them.

Despite the arrests, interrogations, and banishments (it has been estimated that well over one hundred Anabaptists had been arrested by this time), the authorities realized that this problem was not being resolved. John Stalnaker summarizes the situation the authorities faced: "No sooner had the numbers and morale of the sectarians in eastern Hesse apparently diminished, after several years of persistent harassment, than Hessian officials discovered that Anabaptists in the center and west were more numerous and widespread than had previously been believed."[42] Evidence of the continuing growth of the movement, revealed in an intercepted letter to Jörg Schnabel from Peter Tasch, provoked further concern and resulted in Landgrave Philip and the Elector of Saxony writing to Protestant princes across Europe (including Henry VIII, since the letter mentioned Anabaptists in England) to warn them to watch out for Anabaptists in their territories.[43]

Landgrave Philip wrote to the prisoners personally, too, telling them that he would send a "God-fearing man" to them and urging them to listen to him, because "he shall show you the right way, so that you may come to the true knowledge of divine truth, which we would most heartily like to see and would rather hear than to proceed against you with rigor, as is our right, since you refuse to desist from your unchristian sect."[44] This man was the reformer Martin Bucer, who was then based in Strasbourg.[45] Continuing to seek help to address this persistent dissent, Landgrave Philip invited Bucer to Hesse. His concern was not only to control the Anabaptists but to confront problems in the state churches that provoked and exacerbated such dissent.

A turning point

A very significant turning point in the story of Anabaptism in Hesse was the Marburg disputation, held between 30 October and 3 November 1538 (ten years after Rinck's disputation with Balthasar Raidt in Marburg—see chapter 2). Martin Bucer and several Hessian theologians engaged in dialogue with Schnabel and several other Anabaptists, including Leonard Fälber, Peter Tasch, Herman Bastian, and Peter Loese. These were all primarily associated with the stream of Anabaptism in Hesse that had been influenced by Melchior Hofmann. Franklin Littell has provided a translation of the report of this debate written by the secretary, Valentin Breul.[46]

The first part of the debate involved a dialogue between Bucer and Schnabel. It focused on the two reasons Schnabel gave to explain why he was dissatisfied with the pastor of his local state church and had stopped attending: the lack of church discipline and the acceptance of usury (lending money at unreasonable rates of interest). Despite his experience in Strasbourg, where church discipline was high on the agenda in his debates with the Anabaptists, Bucer seemed surprised to be discussing these topics and asked if these were the only issues that had provoked the Anabaptists to separate from the state churches. Schnabel acknowledged that there were others but said that for him these were the most important. This does not imply that this was so for all those present (Schnabel had already insisted that each person must speak for himself), but rather that these had been the presenting issues in Schnabel's own case. Postponing discussion on usury until later, Bucer tried repeatedly to persuade Schnabel that he had no biblical warrant for separating himself from the church and that he was misapplying Matt 18. Schnabel insisted that the church was failing to exercise proper church discipline and left him no choice but to withdraw from it.

Toward the end of the first day and into the following day, Bucer and Schnabel explored the question of what constituted a true church. Schnabel quoted Luther's statement that he did not have the people to build a true Christian church[47] and continued to criticize the low moral standards in the state churches, claiming that behavior there was worse than it had been when these were Catholic churches, and concluding that "the papists have kept better order than we."[48] Bucer acknowledged that the state churches were far from perfect but insisted that they were still true churches. Adopting a longstanding interpretation of the parable of the tares, he argued that these defects must be left until the harvest at the end of the age unless they could be rooted out without damaging the wheat. But Schnabel responded that the lack of church discipline was the root of the problem.

The debate then returned to the issue of usury. Bucer's surprise that Schnabel had raised this issue is an example of the authorities not always being attuned to the concerns of the Anabaptists. But Anabaptists were concerned about ethical as well as ecclesial and ritual matters. Bucer defended the financial practices of the state churches and their teaching, arguing that "it isn't the fault of the teaching that people don't do it." Schnabel was not impressed, telling Bucer that he had spoken well but "the actualities must be dealt with."[49]

The discussion moved on to the issue of baptism, in which the familiar arguments for and against the baptizing of infants were rehearsed, with neither man being able to persuade the other. Three other topics were much more briefly discussed: civil government, the humanity of

Christ, and absolution. Bucer concluded this part of the debate by inviting Schnabel to consider returning to the state church. Schnabel agreed to think it over. The rest of the debate involved Bucer in conversation with Fälber, Bastian, and, very briefly, Loese. The record says that Loese gave "such flippant and light-hearted answer that the audience laughed loudly; and therefore, since he answered so contemptuously and despicably, nothing special was discussed with him."[50] Thus,

Martin Bucer. Portrait by Jean-Jacques Boissard. Original in *Icones quinquagintavirorum*, held in the British Library, London.

the debate ended inconclusively and on a less than serious note, but both sides had actually made a significant impression on the other.

In truth, Bucer was taken aback by the Anabaptists' complaints about the state churches and recognized the need for significant reform. Although he believed they should only be used sparingly, he accepted the need for disciplinary procedures in the church. And while he continued to support infant baptism, he advocated the rite of confirmation so that those baptized as infants could affirm their faith publicly at a later date. He also acknowledged that religious instruction needed to be more prominent in the state churches. Despite disagreeing with them on several issues, Bucer was impressed by the Anabaptists, writing to Landgrave Philip: "There are more Anabaptists in your grace's lands than I ever would have thought, and among them many good-hearted people."[51]

In the aftermath of this disputation, Bucer encouraged the landgrave to introduce some measures in the churches that would address the Anabaptists' main concerns—especially church discipline and Christian education for those who had been baptized as children. Philip was very receptive to this suggestion, having recently received a letter from two interrogators of arrested Anabaptists, in which they wrote: "This error of rebaptism is caused primarily by the incompetence of the preachers, and that they are uneducated, so that they are not able to contradict the Anabaptists."[52] At a synod held in Ziegenhain in November 1538, Bucer's proposal was agreed, and the measures were introduced in the *Ziegenhainer Zuchtordnung*.

Impressed by this, the Anabaptists presented a confession of faith (entitled *Bekenntnis oder Antwort einiger Fragestücke oder Artikeln der gefangenen Täufer und anderer im Land zu Hessen*) to the landgrave on 11 December 1538, offering to compromise on various matters, and about two hundred Anabaptists, led by Peter Tasch, decided to return to the state churches.[53] The Lutheran clergy responded positively and welcomed them. At Bucer's suggestion, these returning Anabaptists were encouraged to urge others to return, with considerable success. Williams comments: "Each side . . . was perhaps more open to the insight and more responsive to the convictions of the other than in any other debate of the Reformation era thus far recounted."[54] Stalnaker describes the outcome as "a brilliant piece of diplomacy, facilitated by limited changes in the practices and structure of the Hessian church" and "a sixteenth-century rarity, successful religious compromise."[55]

Initial indications were encouraging to the authorities. Between mid-1537 and mid-1538, there seem to have been no reports at all of Anabaptists in Hesse. But the compromise was not welcomed by all the Anabaptists, many of whom remained steadfast in their convictions and resistant to being co-opted. Because the Anabaptist community in Hesse was not uniform but was influenced by at least three streams of teaching, this is unsurprising. Tasch represented a different stream from the followers of Rinck, even if there were evidently connections between them. Within months it became clear that the authorities' success was only temporary. Sizable Anabaptist communities were found in several districts and in the main cities of the region. It was also evident that many who were not themselves Anabaptists were sympathetic toward them and reluctant to betray them to the authorities. By the end of 1538, the limited impact of the authorities' actions was evident.[56]

That may have been the case in 1538, but the reprieve for the Anabaptist movement was short-lived. On 22 January 1544, Landgrave Philip wrote that he intended "to drive out of the country the Anabaptists who were not willing to accept the articles which had been accepted by Schnabel, Tasch, and others."[57] On 7–8 February 1544, a large Anabaptist interrogation was held at Berka, an indication of the increasing determination of the authorities to pursue Anabaptists throughout the region.

Anabaptists were present in Hesse until the Thirty Years' War (1618–48). However, the movement had begun to decline from around 1540. There were various reasons for this, not least the landgrave's tolerant approach, which seemed to undercut the need for radical dissent, and Bucer's persuasiveness. The movement was further weakened by emigration to Moravia and elsewhere, and suffered from a lack of effective leadership (especially after some of its more educated leaders rejoined the state churches), with a consequent lack of discipline and cohesion in the congregations.

There were still significant leaders, although we know very little about them. Matthias Hasenhan, about whose teaching and activities we have scant information, was clearly an influential figure in the late

1530s, mentioned in the correspondence between Peter Tasch and Jörg Schnabel, and consulted by the Hutterites in their debate over doctrine with Hans Both.[58] They described him as "zealous for God" and applauded his "piety and fear of God." It seems that he recanted briefly after the Marburg debate under the influence of Peter Tasch but reappears in official documents in 1544 as an Anabaptist teacher.

But the movement lacked consistency. John Oyer contrasts the views of Köhler and Scheffer (surnames unknown), two Anabaptists arrested in 1537, and three others in 1539. All had connections to Fritz Erbe, perhaps, after Rinck, the most influential Anabaptist leader in this period. Köhler and Scheffer adopted a biblicist approach and rejected any use of force; but the other group gave evidence of Spiritualist and revolutionary ideas.[59] Anabaptism in Hesse could not thrive, or survive for long, without greater cohesion. Nevertheless, this short-lived movement left a significant legacy. This legacy, and the unusual combination of factors that resulted in the gradual demise of Anabaptism in this area, are explored in the subsequent chapters.

TWO

Melchior Rinck: Reformer, Revolutionary, Anabaptist

LITTLE IS KNOWN about the first thirty years of Melchior Rinck's life. He was born in 1492 or 1493 in the territory of Hesse, either in the town of Marburg or perhaps in a village on the River Lumda about nine miles away called Allendorf.[1] It seems that he grew up in a peasant home and that the family name was Schnabel.[2] Despite this humble background, he evidently showed academic promise and received a good education at the University of Leipzig—and possibly also at the University of Erfurt—where he excelled in the classical languages, earning him a nickname, "the Greek," which appears in various sources.[3]

In 1516 he published a book of poems in Latin, the quality of which was apparently not great, in which he gave some personal information. In the preface, he paid tribute to his tutor, John Lange of Lowenburg, expressing gratitude for being exempted from tuition fees. He also said he attended the lectures of the Franconian humanist Coelius Aubanus. He described himself as having earned a bachelor of arts in the College of the University of Leipzig. His name is not to be found in the matriculation records, but the family name Schnabel is. A memorandum written by some Württemberg theologians in 1536 to advise on actions to be taken against Anabaptists, refers to one "Melchior

Schnabel, called Reick," described as "a famed Anabaptist," who was by then in prison but had lectured on the Greek poet Hesiod at the University of Erfurt, before becoming a parish priest.[4] Georg Witzel later described him as a learned man, and those who debated with him recognized that they were dealing with someone who was thoughtful and articulate. Beyond this, nothing is known about his activities or his whereabouts until 1523.

REFORMER

Rinck reappeared in 1523 as a chaplain in Hersfeld. Following the lead of the Hersfeld pastor, Heinrich Fuchs, Rinck began to embrace the reformed faith and to preach against corruption in the Catholic Church. Fuchs and Rinck denounced the tithing system as it was administered and the immorality, drunkenness, and profanity of the local Franciscan monks. Their views quickly gained popular support, not least as an excuse to withhold tithe payments. Their teaching also seems to have mocked the eucharist and the crucifix. This stirred up considerable controversy, with breaches of the peace on both sides.

The controversy also precipitated a dispute over jurisdiction. Although the local abbot, whose name was Krafft, was sympathetic to the reform agenda at this point, the canons caught and beat Fuchs and complained to the city council about the views that he and Rinck were expressing. The council initially ordered Fuchs and Rinck to exercise restraint and not to accuse anyone personally in their sermons, but then voted by a majority to issue a decree, ordering monks in illicit unions either to marry or to leave the city within two weeks. This was strongly worded and included the following:

> The Word of God, according to the rules of the Old and New Testaments, condemns very strongly and does not tolerate whoredom and those who live in concubinage, but rather it seeks to harry them from the land—be they clergy or laity. Similarly, no public sin which is against the commandment of God shall be tolerated, like blasphemy in word and deed, the shameful and disgraceful drunkards who daily lie about publicly and in the taverns and do not work. Accordingly, the secular authorities must act according to God's command, for they must answer to God for the damage to the souls.[5]

Fuchs was instructed to read this decree from his pulpit on the third Sunday in Advent, 1523. Those implicated in this measure complained to Abbot Krafft, who regarded this decree as an unwarranted intrusion by the secular authorities into ecclesiastical affairs and a usurpation of his authority. He abandoned his tolerant attitude toward reform and reasserted his ecclesiastical jurisdiction, forbidding the council to issue this mandate. The following day he decreed a "mandate and plaint" against Fuchs and Rinck and announced to the council that they had both been dismissed from their positions and must leave the city within two weeks. They would be allowed to give a farewell sermon on 27 December 1523.

Fuchs and Rinck wrote to the council, asking to be shown from the Scriptures in a public disputation that they had spoken wrongly. When the council ignored their demand, both men spoke from the pulpit on 17 December (sooner than expected), explaining that they were being driven out of the city without legal recourse—and no doubt explaining the reasons for the opposition to them, which had thus far not been made public. This resulted in a riot in which supporters of the reform movement demanded the reinstatement of Fuchs and Rinck. When the city council—which had been conflicted over whether to issue the decree in the first place—ignored this demand, the reform supporters stormed and destroyed the office of the chancellor of the imperial monastery. They then surrounded the monastery but, unable to gain access, instead plundered the homes of ten priests in the city who had concubines and expelled these women. Wolfgang Breul explains that this outburst of popular indignation "tapped deeper sources of resentment. Looking back on the episode, the wives of Hersfeld citizens arrested in the confrontation described a conflict fueled by anger against the immorality of unmarriage."[6]

Worried by this disturbance, the council apologized to the abbot and asked Landgrave Philip what action they should take. Philip ordered the arrest of Fuchs, Rinck, and the leading rioters and, on 29 December, banished them permanently from his territory for inciting violence. However, their supporters in Hersfeld released Fuchs and Rinck from prison, gave them money, and escorted them under armed guard to the border of Hesse.[7]

In 1524 Rinck and Fuchs, through the intervention of Jakob Strauss, pastor at Eisenach in Saxony and a leading Lutheran reformer, obtained new positions. Fuchs was appointed as pastor at Marksuhl. Rinck was appointed as Lutheran preacher in Oberhausen and then pastor in Eckhardshausen, near Eisenach, where he joined a group of reforming clerics and humanist scholars, including Georg Witzel, vicar of Vacha, who was at that point drawn to Luther's teachings but would soon start to express dissatisfaction with them. Strauss, a radical reformer who was popular with the peasants for denouncing usury, seems to have been at least partly responsible for Rinck embarking on a more radical career path. It was likely his influence that resulted in Rinck adopting a believers church ecclesiology, rejecting infant baptism, and advocating generous sharing of possessions.[8]

It was probably also through this group that Rinck first encountered Thomas Müntzer. Both Strauss and Witzel rejected Müntzer's revolutionary agenda, although Strauss seems to have done so only at the last minute, but Rinck was evidently drawn to this, possibly seeing in his expulsion from Hesse a parallel to Müntzer's expulsion from Allstedt. Erich Geldbach concludes: "his departure from the strict Lutheran 'faith only' and his awareness of the need for an inner reformation of the human heart eased this step towards Müntzer."[9] According to Paul Wappler, Rinck castigated the Lutherans for their "idle, foul, and dead faith" and declared: "Thomas Muentzer now, he is a real hero with preaching, through which the word, the power of God, can act enormously; he can do in one year more than one thousand Luthers in their whole lifetime."[10]

Later that year, or possibly in 1525, Rinck married Anna, the daughter of a supporter of Martin Luther, Hans Eckhart. The marriage was not a success and it seems may not have been consummated. Reflecting on the reasons for this, Rinck became convinced that this was a marriage of convenience, not love, arranged by his wife's father in order for her to attain the status of being married to a reformed pastor. As Snyder comments, this surely indicates that Rinck was not yet a follower of Müntzer, even if he was sympathetic to his agenda.[11] Becoming actively involved in revolutionary activities and then embarking on an itinerant Anabaptist ministry were unexpected and unwelcome developments, as far as Anna and her father were concerned.

REVOLUTIONARY

Rinck's first move toward a more radical position was to join Müntzer's cause. He was one of a number of preachers, together with Fuchs, Hans Hut, and Hans Römer, who were instrumental in stirring up discontent in the Eisenach region. A rising of peasants in the Upper Werra valley was soon followed by a much wider rebellion, persuading Müntzer that the time was right to confront the authorities openly in the expectation that God would intervene on behalf of the peasants.[12]

Both Rinck and Fuchs were participants in the disastrous battle at Frankenhausen in May 1525, when the peasants were not saved by divine intervention as Müntzer promised, but were routed and slaughtered by the authorities. Fuchs was killed but Rinck survived. It is unclear how significant Rinck's role was in the peasants' movement, although it seems likely that it was fairly extensive. According to two of his opponents in later years, Justus Menius and Eberhard von der Tann, he was a leading combatant and maybe even a rebel captain at Frankenhausen. Eberhard accused Rinck of never regretting this or abandoning his revolutionary views, and of declaring that God had helped him to escape from Frankenhausen so that he could execute Müntzer's plans. These charges were contained in letters sent by Eberhard to Elector John in 1531 and to Landgrave Philip in 1532. He insisted that Rinck "was present at the recent peasants' uprising as a particular agitator and captain alongside Müntzer and Pfeiffer, and more active than these and others."[13]

Rinck had already refuted these accusations in a letter to Eberhard (sent probably in 1530). He denied ever inciting others to violence, although this is somewhat difficult to believe if he was a captain at Frankenhausen, but perhaps Rinck meant that he had not done so since becoming an Anabaptist. Müntzer's influence on him was significant, at least for a while, and it has been suggested that Rinck was one of the conduits through which Müntzer's views permeated the emerging Anabaptist movement.[14] But after the debacle at Frankenhausen, Rinck seems to have moved decisively away from many of his former mentor's ideas (even if some of his followers still subscribed to them). Whatever his earlier views, by the early 1530s he had rejected armed insurrection as contrary to God's will, even if he was still inspired by the demands for greater social justice that Müntzer had articulated.

Rinck's writings and public statements indicate both the ongoing influence of Müntzer and significant dissent from his perspectives. The mysticism that pervaded Müntzer's spirituality and theology is not entirely absent, especially in relation to Rinck's emphasis on *Gelassenheit* (roughly, yieldedness). But Rinck was much closer to Luther in teaching the need for divine grace, rather than self-reliance, and to other Anabaptists in his call for repentance and his concern to establish believers churches. Müntzer had criticized the baptism of infants, but he continued this practice and had never instituted believers baptism, the practice that became central to Rinck's understanding of discipleship and ecclesiology. Rinck may have been influenced by Müntzer's commitment to community of goods and efforts to develop a disciplined Christian community in Zwickau and Allstedt, but he interpreted this differently, advocating generous and radical sharing of resources, rather than common ownership, and establishing believers churches. And whereas Müntzer drew heavily on the Old Testament and placed reliance on visions and dreams, Rinck adopted the typical Anabaptist emphasis on the New Testament and especially on the Gospels.

Rinck's positive and consistent affirmation of the role of the civil authorities as ordained by God, despite his criticism of them for overstepping their mandate and persecuting true Christians, as Geldbach comments, "stands in stark contradiction to the views of Thomas Müntzer."[15] Whereas Müntzer, the apocalyptic revolutionary, had declared that the time had come to overthrow the "godless" civil authorities, Rinck attempted to persuade the authorities to act within their divine mandate and warned them only of future judgment. He may have regarded them in no better light than Müntzer, but he never suggested they had lost their divine mandate or that they should be overthrown.

Whatever Rinck's personal views, he was surrounded by others who had been inspired by Müntzer and had been involved in the peasants' movement. When he was not on the road or in prison, he most likely lived in Sorga. Almost all the villagers had apparently been involved in the peasants' movement in April 1525, pressurizing the abbot of Hersfeld to accept their demands, although they had offered little resistance when confronted by the landgrave's troops. But they continued to give refuge to both Anabaptists and peasants on the run from the authorities. This community seems to have been a hotbed of radical views, which undoubtedly colored the Anabaptist movement that was centered there.

The leader who first succeeded Rinck, Alexander (surname unknown), was another who had escaped from Frankenhausen. After Alexander's execution, leadership passed to Klaus Scharf and Heinz Kraut. At his trial, Kraut repeated the peasant mantra—"When Adam delved and Eve span, who was then the gentleman?" One of their successors, Jakob Storger, who was described as "being drenched" in Müntzer's writings, was interrogated in 1537 with several others, who all expressed continuing respect for Müntzer. One of them insisted that Anabaptism was a continuation of his teaching. Another said that Müntzer's teaching was correct, but that the violence had not been.[16] It is not surprising that Anabaptists in this area who were arrested and interrogated were regularly asked about their involvement in the peasants' movement and their views on Müntzer's teachings. Rinck may have dissociated himself from at least the more revolutionary aspects of Müntzer's views and activities, but his ministry as an Anabaptist took place in a context where many were still drawn to these, even if they no longer espoused violence.

ANABAPTIST

Having escaped the slaughter at Frankenhausen, Rinck wisely disappeared from view for the next eighteen months. His movements are unknown until the beginning of 1527, when he reappeared in the company of Hans Denck and others who were engaged in extended conversations with the reformer Johannes Bader in Landau. Bader was deeply attracted to Anabaptism, and the group had high hopes that he would join them, but he eventually chose not to do so. Rinck, however, was persuaded and was baptized, very likely by Denck.[17] There is some suggestion that there was an Anabaptist congregation in Landau by this point. It is clear that Rinck held Bader in high esteem, seeking his counsel on the issue of baptism, and then making a confession to him before his baptism, in which Bader participated as his sponsor.[18] He was dismayed when Bader, apparently quite suddenly, decided to defend infant baptism.

On 20 January 1527, Denck and Bader held a public disputation on the issue. Bader published the proceedings in the form of a tract, entitled *Brüderliche warning für dem newen Abgöttischen orden der Widertäuffer*, attacking Denck's views on baptism, and Rinck responded with a short refutation, *Widderlegung eyner Schrifft So Johannes Bader, vermeynter pfarrher zu Landau, newlich than hat, den Kindertauff als Christlich zuerhalten*, in which his bitter disappointment with Bader is evident.[19] He wrote that he "considered him to be my brother in the Lord" and recalled that he had agreed to be godfather to one of Bader's children—affirming infant baptism at that time and later lamenting this decision. Rinck's refutation expressed dismay that one so "adept in debate" as Bader should have "maligned the eternal and immutable truth with such pompous and brazen words" and deliberately misrepresented Anabaptist teachings, claiming that they taught that the baptism of believers "makes people perfect." His disappointment was exacerbated by knowing that during the discussions that had taken place in his home, Bader "often was convinced of the truth but then later certainly came to disdain such matters, maligning to the greatest degree the truth he had recognized, against his own conscience." With sadness, Rinck queried Bader's integrity and referred to him as a "supposed pastor" in Landau, warning him of coming judgment.

It seems that, in February 1527, Denck and Rinck went on, separately or together, to Worms,[20] where Rinck began to spread Anabaptist ideas in the city. He was apparently instrumental in the conversion to Anabaptism of two city preachers, Jakob Kautz and Hilarius, against whom an edict was issued on 31 March 1527. A chronicler names Melchior Hofmann, a "man learned in all languages and the common reformer of all Anabaptists," as the person in conversation with Kautz, but Hofmann was in Dorpat at this time, so it seems a different Melchior was meant. This description fits Rinck better than Hofmann, paying tribute to his learning and to his subsequent widespread influence. Denck, meanwhile, worked with Kautz and Ludwig Haetzer on a German translation of the Old Testament prophets. Kautz credited Denck, Haetzer, and Rinck in a foreword to the "Seven Articles" he posted on a church door, in which he opposed his Reformed colleagues and invited people to a disputation on 13 June.[21] Rinck was probably one of the participants. As a result of this involvement, Rinck was expelled from Worms.

Denck seems to have had a decisive influence on Rinck at the end of 1526 and beginning of 1527.[22] It was probably Denck who weaned him off Müntzer's ideas and apocalyptic expectations. Denck's continuing influence is evident in some of Rinck's statements and writings. The articles Rinck presented at the Marburg debate in 1528 closely paralleled Denck's *Von der wahren Liebe* ("Concerning True Love"), published the year before, with which Rinck was certainly familiar. But there were also significant differences, especially in relation to hermeneutics and spirituality.

Both regarded love as God's most sublime characteristic, but Rinck's articles do not have Denck's emphasis on the "inner word."[23] He did not share Denck's Spiritualism but embraced a biblicist approach and insisted that the preached Word was essential for salvation. Unlike Denck, who rarely drew directly from Scripture, Rinck answered scripture with scripture throughout the debate and was willing to be convinced only by "sufficient and unfalsified Holy Scripture." His focus on following and imitating Christ very likely derived from Denck, as almost certainly did his use of the language of love to explain human rebellion and the result of salvation. However, John Oyer is overstating the case when he suggests that Rinck's dependence on Denck was such that "the gaps in our knowledge of Rink's theology could logically be filled with Denck's ideas."[24]

It is likely that at this time Rinck also wrote another tract, *Vermanung und warnung an alle so in der Obrigkeit sind*, in which he protested vigorously against the authorities' treatment of the Anabaptists and urged them to restrict their activities to those ordained by God—which did not include controlling the religious views of their subjects.[25] It has been suggested that Rinck wrote this tract during a period of imprisonment in 1530 or 1531, but it appears in a document together with the response to Bader, and Geldbach argues persuasively that it must have been written shortly after that response.[26]

Rinck next surfaced in the area around Hersfeld in the summer of 1528, where he worked as an itinerant evangelist and established congregations in western Thuringia, centered on the village of Sorga. It seems that Rinck lived in this village and made it the center of his mission work in both Hesse and Thuringia. Initially, he followed the example of other Anabaptist evangelists by speaking privately with individuals and attempting to avoid public attention. Like them, he preached a gospel of repentance and conversion, and he baptized those who responded. Since many of the villagers in this region had been involved in the peasants' movement, their continuing discontent may have made them especially receptive to Rinck's preaching. The authorities certainly suspected connections between Anabaptist convictions and the concerns of the peasants' movement, frequently interrogating converts to find evidence of insurrectionist tendencies as well as theological heterodoxy.

Rinck, however, was not content to embody the Lutheran characterization of Anabaptists as unauthorized "sneak preachers."[27] Emboldened by the very encouraging response to his preaching, but encountering opposition from the local Lutheran pastor, Balthasar Raidt, he presented a petition to be allowed to preach openly in Hersfeld, which reached Landgrave Philip. The authorities responded by requiring him to put into writing what he was teaching, especially on the issue of the sacraments, and to justify his views on the basis of Scripture alone. Before he could comply with this demand, however, Rinck was summoned to a personal interview at Philip's hunting lodge in Friedewald, to the east of Hersfeld. This surprising development is surely indicative of Rinck's significance as an Anabaptist leader. The landgrave examined him, discussed his teaching, and gave him three options: he could recant his heterodox views, he could be expelled from Hesse, or he could present his ideas at a disputation with theologians at the University of Marburg.

Not surprisingly, Rinck chose to present his teaching at the disputation, which took place on 17–18 August 1528. He was invited to summarize his teaching, which he did in five quite brief theses. He was opposed by Raidt, who first presented twelve charges relating to the topics that had been discussed by Rinck and Landgrave Philip earlier in the month. For most of the first day, the discussion focused on Raidt's charges and Rinck's responses. Then, toward the end of the day and throughout the next day, the theologians examined Rinck's own theses.[28]

The record of the disputation provides important insights into Rinck's teaching, but it also indicates the level of bitterness involved between the primary participants. Raidt accused Rinck of conducting secret meetings, seducing people with false teaching, and "bringing a new turmoil" into the community. He named two of those who had attended these meetings—Claus Schiffman and a barber, Jörge Zedell. Having complained about these clandestine gatherings, he then expressed outrage that Rinck had sought permission to preach openly in the area. Raidt did not acquit himself well in this debate. Obviously offended and threatened by the impact Rinck was making in the area where he assumed that he had pastoral responsibility, Raidt accused him of all manner of things, many of them apparently bearing no relationship to what Rinck had actually taught or willfully exaggerating what he had said. Raidt accused Rinck, for example, of teaching that those who had received the Lutheran sacrament had received the devil

Marburg. From *Cosmographia* (1544) by Sebastian Münster.

and of saying that Luther at first had the Spirit but later became the devil and the true antichrist.

Rinck responded in four ways to these charges. First, he requested evidence from Raidt, asking him to provide witnesses that he could question to ascertain whether he had in fact taught what he was accused of teaching and in the places where he was supposed to have done so. He evidently distrusted Raidt, but it seems that he also wanted to ensure that he had enough detailed information to reply honestly to the accusations. Second, he refuted some of the charges as inaccurate—he had not taught that anyone receiving the sacrament was in fact receiving the devil, nor had he denied predestination. Third, he accepted that he had taught some of what Raidt reported and offered to defend his teaching on the basis of Scripture. And fourth, he responded to Raidt's bitter tone with very critical statements of his own about Luther personally and about what the Lutherans taught.

The record of the debate indicates that no substantive discussion took place on the issues Raidt raised. Rinck's responses and refutations stand unchallenged in the record, despite the huge gap between the positions of the two men. Oyer concludes that this suggests that Raidt was deliberately defaming Rinck.[29] Not surprisingly, once the debate moved on to a consideration of Rinck's own theses, the Marburg theologians took over from Raidt, who was struggling to make any headway.

Rinck's first three theses outlined his understanding of the doctrines of creation, sin, and justification. These followed a classic Pauline approach and were accepted by both sides. His fourth thesis was a critique and rejection of infant baptism. Raidt attempted to present a justification of infant baptism, but this was unconvincing and he was interrupted by the presiding rector, who invited the Marburg theologians to address this issue. Their defense of infant baptism was adjudged to be decisive and, despite his protestations, Rinck was declared to have lost the debate and to be in error. Consequently, his fifth thesis on the Lord's Supper was not discussed.

Three days later, Raidt wrote to the landgrave, reporting on the debate and dismissively rejecting Rinck's position as unsupported by any biblical evidence. Raidt encouraged him to allow those who wanted to remain in the land to do so after "public penitence," but he expressed his fear that other Anabaptists in the area had not yet been discovered by the authorities: "There are without doubt others out there."[30] Unwilling to recant his views or do public penitence, Rinck was duly expelled from Hesse.

This banishment was not, however, very successful. Rinck refused to accept the verdict of the theologians or the sentence of exile. He continued to work in the border area of Hesse and Saxony, taking advantage of the opportunity this afforded to move between jurisdictions in order to avoid arrest. He is known to have baptized Hans Hechtlein, the pastor of Schalkhausen in Franconia. In 1529 he reappeared in Hesse, passing through Fulda, before returning to the Hersfeld region. His influence was prompting increasing concern in Saxony, where the authorities instructed Eberhard von der Tann to curtail his activities and, if possible, arrest him. In March 1529 the governor of Kassel warned the landgrave that "Melchior Rinck is very active in spreading Anabaptism and has been sending the accompanying booklet to his disciples everywhere. It is, therefore, of concern that if he is not opposed and measures are not taken to oppose this unchristian abuse, many subjects in the area will submit to rebaptism."[31] Despite these threats, Rinck continued preaching in the border area between Hesse and Saxony and in the districts of Eisenach and Marksuhl.

Rinck was eventually arrested in Hessian territory and interrogated at Großenbach in April 1529. He was imprisoned for the next two years in the monastery of Haina, where he appears to have lived quite comfortably, as indicated in a letter written from prison, in which he assured his followers that both he and his fellow prisoner, Antonius Jacobs, were alive and well.[32] Several people visited Rinck in prison, attempting to persuade him to recant his erroneous views, but to no effect. The authorities in Saxony sent evidence in writing of Rinck's guilt and tried to persuade Philip to deal less leniently with him, but Philip rejected any interference. In December, Elector John urged Philip, if he insisted on allowing Rinck to live, to "at the very least banish him from our principality, land and people, forever."[33]

During these months in prison, the issue of Rinck's troubled marriage came to a head. It seems his father-in-law tried to get von der Tann to persuade Rinck to grant his wife an annulment or a divorce. Rinck initially responded with outrage in a short letter, quoting Matt

19:6 and expressing amazement that von der Tann should advise him, contrary to biblical teaching, to break the marriage. However, in a longer tract on marriage which soon followed this letter, Rinck defended his actions and set out more fully his views on marriage and divorce. He quoted other Old and New Testament texts, in which he noted different situations in which divorce was apparently justified. Although it has generally been concluded that Rinck continued to refuse to divorce his wife, this document might indicate that he was open to this possibility after all, partly to set Anna free to enter into a real marriage, but mainly because he was unconvinced that his marriage was anything more than a sham.[34]

Rinck complained that Anna had married him under pressure from her parents and for a "quiet life" with a respectable Lutheran pastor, as he then was, not for love. But when he abandoned this role to itinerate as an Anabaptist apostle, their true motives became clear. He acknowledged that he had not visited her for some years, but he blamed this neglect partly on those who pursued him and prevented him from visiting her freely, and partly on Anna herself for not accompanying him. His tract might imply that the marriage had not, in fact, been consummated. It seems that he may also have needed to defend himself against a suspicion of sexual immorality. But he felt he had been deceived and was now being maligned, and he expressed relief that his traveling spared him the pressures of an unhappy marriage.[35] Rinck also exchanged sharp letters with Anna and her father, which are not extant. The record is silent as to whether Rinck eventually agreed to a divorce or an annulment.

At least, this is the picture historians have traditionally painted of Rinck's marriage, and it is probably correct, but two phrases in correspondence from Eberhard von der Tann to Elector John on 25 November 1531 might indicate a different outcome.[36] In his letter, von der Tann claimed that "up till now, he has abandoned his wife here in this province and has traveled around in various lands." Does "up till now" imply that Rinck is continuing to abandon his wife or that this is no longer the case? And, in an attachment to the letter, asking for advice about the treatment of the Anabaptist prisoners, there is a phrase that can be translated as "offenders, both male and female" or as "both offenders, husband and wife." If the latter translation is correct, might this mean that there had been a recent rapprochement and that Anna was now with her husband?

As well as writing these letters and the tract on marriage, Rinck also wrote a brief tract on baptism, in which he castigated Catholics and Lutherans for allowing Satan to enter their flocks through the medium of infant baptism. He expounded and offered a rather different interpretation of a New Testament passage that some used to justify infant baptism: "When Jesus saw this, he was indignant. He said to them, 'Let the little children come to me, and do not hinder them, for the kingdom of God belongs to such as these'" (Mark 10:14 NIV). He urged his readers to join the flock of true believers, which was disciplined and faithful.[37]

The landgrave resisted the demands from Saxony that he should execute Rinck. Instead, he was expelled again on condition he left the region for good. But Rinck simply refused to accept that it was legitimate for any child of God to banish another from a territory or for him to accept banishment. The early Anabaptists frequently quoted Ps 24:1 ("The earth is the LORD's, and everything in it, the world, and all who live in it," NIV) to insist on their freedom to evangelize without geographical restrictions.[38] Rinck cited this verse "insolently"[39] and returned to Hesse, where he continued to operate in the Hersfeld region and also in Amt Hausbreitenbach. On 11 November 1531 he was arrested again with twelve others in the village of Vacha, when the authorities interrupted a gathering of suspected Anabaptists. Some of those arrested had previously recanted their Anabaptist convictions, but they had evidently not actually renounced their beliefs. Others had refused to recant and had been exiled but had secretly returned to the area.

In a brief letter to Landgrave Philip the following day, Martin von der Tann, the mayor of Vacha and Eberhard's brother, reported that the authorities had been on the lookout for returning exiles and were aware that they might slip into the town under cover of visiting the market. Market days, when towns were crowded with people from the wider region, offered opportunities for Anabaptists to gather unobtrusively, as reports from other areas confirm. An account written by Elias Schad, a Lutheran minister who infiltrated a large nighttime meeting in a forest in 1576, noted that Anabaptists from various places had come "under the pretext of attending the Strasbourg Fair."[40] Martin knew that the

Anabaptists gathered secretly in parks and private houses and he told the landgrave that "house searches in the suspicious locations" had enabled him to discover and apprehend this group.[41] Martin also told Eberhard, who instructed Martin "under no circumstances to release Rinck without my advance knowledge."[42]

The names and places of origin of those arrested with Rinck are known from the record of their interrogation.[43] Little else is recorded about some of them, but others had evidently been in trouble before. The meeting had been discovered in the house of Greta and Hans Werner, citizens of Vacha, who had previously recanted their "rebaptism" and had later again denied that they were Anabaptists. Jörg Grusselbach and his wife (name unknown), former citizens of Vacha, had recanted, then reaffirmed their Anabaptist convictions, had been banished as a result and had secretly returned. Others arrested with them were Adam Angersbach, a blacksmith from Nidernhaun, near Hersfeld, Hermann Adam, a farm worker from Springen to the north of Vacha, Cort Mulher from Ausbach to the west of Vacha, Heinz Ot from Kathus, a village to the north of Hersfeld, Bilg Scherer from Motzfeld, a village to the south of Hersfeld, and Anna and Ursel Zoberin, maidservants from Großenbach, currently employed in Treischfeld, also to the south of Hersfeld. None came from far away, but most were visitors to Vacha when they were arrested.

It is likely that this meeting was some kind of discussion group rather than an established congregation. Hermann Adam and Cort Mulher swore that they were not Anabaptists but had been visiting the house for social or business purposes when the authorities arrived. Adam testified that he had attended Rinck's wedding several years earlier, had had no contact with him since then, and simply wanted to see him again. Mulher explained that he had come to purchase cloth in the market and called into Hans Werner's house to listen to Rinck but had no desire to act upon what he had heard. They were released, although it is by no means clear that they were telling the truth. Hermann Adam was arrested again two years later and admitted to being an Anabaptist then.[44] Adam Angersbach, Bilg Scherer, Heinz Ot, and sisters Anna and Ursel Zoberin received instruction, recanted, and were released. Greta and Hans Werner, however, were banished, as were (for the second time) Jörg Grusselbach and his wife, even though he protested that he had been urged by his child to return to the city and abide by the earlier decree so that he would not lose his possessions, and that he was at the meeting to discuss this with Rinck.

Eberhard wrote to Elector John a few days later and subsequently wrote at some length to Landgrave Philip. These letters testify to the importance attached to Rinck, his influence in the region, and the growing concern of the authorities as Anabaptism continued to spread.

Writing to Elector John, Eberhard repeated the accusation that Rinck was a revolutionary as well as a heretic, that he had not renounced his participation at Frankenhausen and that he was pursuing Müntzer's agenda under cover of his Anabaptist activities. He was the "main instigator of the Anabaptists."[45] Eberhard candidly accused Landgrave Philip of mishandling the situation, exercising much greater toleration of Rinck and his colleagues than Eberhard thought appropriate. He knew Elector John was of the same opinion.

Writing to Landgrave Philip, he expressed deep concern that the landgrave's "multiple merciful admonitions and clemency" were only encouraging Rinck and his colleagues. He impressed on him the view, held by himself and others, that the Anabaptists should be "punished to the highest degree."[46] As he had previously advised, this was necessary "to extinguish their flame."[47] While Eberhard understood Philip's reluctance to act harshly against those who held heterodox views but were not an obvious threat to his realm, he argued that this tolerant approach was enabling the spread of the Anabaptist movement. People were assuming that the landgrave's mild policy implied that the movement was acceptable to the authorities.

Furthermore, Eberhard insisted to Philip that Rinck had not renounced his revolutionary intentions but was "secretly slithering about" and "passing around his poison," provoking upheaval through his teachings. He was not just a heretic and blasphemer, Eberhard insisted, and someone who had abandoned his new wife, but a rebel and a threat to social order. Rebaptism was a cover to enable him to "foment another uprising." He insisted that "Rinck's teachings and those of Müntzer's are in complete agreement" and that his sole intention was to "resurrect an insurrection with a view to an overall break-up and destruction of the magistracy and the social estates." Though he knew Rinck denied this accusation, Eberhard insisted that there was evidence of this in Rinck's writings, which he had obtained and some of which he had already passed on to the landgrave.[48]

He concluded that "the Anabaptists' teaching and life—and especially that of Melchior Rinck—prove in this regard that they embody the greatest public blasphemy, are also rebellious, standing in opposition to the magistracy."[49] There was no possibility that Rinck would recant his views or refrain from his preaching. He urged the landgrave to make a public example of him. Accusing Rinck of promoting anarchy in his sermons and writings, thereby endangering the state, he insisted that he should be "punished to the highest degree, first of all, as a blasphemer, and secondly as an inconvincible, stubborn, unrepentant insurrectionist and a despiser of every divine and human order." Eberhard advocated this approach for four reasons: "the honor of God, and to maintain a common peace, the improvement of [Rinck] himself, and as an abominable example to others."

While Eberhard might have been content with life imprisonment for Rinck, the Saxons demanded the death penalty. Writing to Philip in December 1531, despite using formally polite language, Elector John was clearly furious that Rinck was still alive. Describing Rinck as "a leading teacher of the onerous and seductive Anabaptist sect" and an "old insurrectionist and leader,"[50] he argued that, in accordance with imperial mandate issued at Speyer in 1529, Philip was legally obliged to execute him. And, since Rinck had been active in Saxony as well, someone from his territory should be present at his sentencing and execution. The elector sent a copy of his letter to Eberhard, presumably in the hope that he would bring further pressure to bear on the landgrave. The elector also had the support of the leading reformers. Alberto Melloni notes that Luther and Melanchthon "were among the Saxon luminaries who attempted to persuade Philip of Hesse of the need to execute Melchior Rinck."[51]

But Philip refused to execute him, arguing that his conscience would not allow this. On 3 January 1532 he informed Elector John that he had decided on life imprisonment instead "so that he no longer can seduce or make anyone a follower."[52] He assured John that he was serious about rooting out the threat of Anabaptist "seduction" and attached the Ordinance he had issued at the end of December. John was not impressed, as his response on 15 January makes very clear. He regarded Philip's actions and the Ordinance as inadequate and contrary to imperial law. And he insisted that his own conscience required him to execute heretics. Though he could not persuade Philip, he again sent a copy of his letter to Eberhard, urging him to deal more vigorously with any Anabaptists he discovered in his region.

Philip did not agree with the Anabaptists. This is evident from the Ordinance, which refers to them as a "scourge" and sets out an extensive process intended to restrict their activities and lead them, if possible, to repentance. But he had some sympathy with their critique of the state churches and acknowledged that the rampant immorality and hypocrisy found in a supposedly Christian society were provoking the Anabaptists and causing them to reject these churches and separate themselves. Philip did not hesitate to execute those convicted of insurrection, but he evidently regarded Rinck and the other Anabaptists arrested in his domain as heretics, rather than seditious or a threat to public order. Oyer comments wryly that "Rinck was either fortunate or foresighted enough in always being caught by Philip's men."[53]

At his hearing, Rinck argued that the order to leave a territory forever was contrary to the lordship of God over the world. Since he was a child of God, he shared this freedom in all parts of the world. Any government that judged a child of God with expulsion or with the sword was itself judged in that very act, for this was not within its divine mandate. Rinck said that he was not surprised by persecution, but he insisted it could not be justified. He warned of judgment on those who acted in this way. He denounced the magistrates for using torture and said that any oaths (such as promises not to return to a region) obtained under duress were invalid.

Rinck was sentenced to life imprisonment in Katzenelnbogen, well away from the area in which he had been evangelizing. A letter from the landgrave to the governor of Marburg in December 1538 indicated that release was possible, but only if Rinck was prepared to recant and publicly testify to this.[54] Despite many attempts to persuade him to recant, he remained steadfast in his beliefs. One of his visitors, who had already begun to argue with him before his arrest, was Georg Witzel, who was drawn to Anabaptism because of its emphasis on discipleship, but who was passionate about maintaining the unity of the church and so could not accept rebaptism. Another was Peter Tasch, a former

Anabaptist and colleague of Melchior Hofmann whom Martin Bucer had persuaded to rejoin the state church. At Bucer's suggestion, Tasch was released from prison after recanting his Anabaptist views and dispatched to Rinck to try to persuade him to follow suit. The letter from Philip to the governor of Marburg authorized this visit but stipulated that Gerhart Ungefug, a local magistrate, should be present to act as a witness to this conversation.

Bucer himself seems also to have visited Rinck, in a further effort to persuade him to recant. He certainly appealed to Philip in March 1540 to improve the conditions of Rinck's imprisonment. Philip replied that he was not to be tortured but was to be held in "light confinement." Rinck may have spent the previous nine years in a deep dungeon at Braubach.[55] Bucer's intervention succeeded and Rinck was moved to more comfortable confinement at Rheinfels.

The year of Rinck's death remains unknown. It was previously thought that he might have died by the mid-1540s, but Geldbach reports on the discovery of a document indicating that Superintendent Goltwurm and Reinhard Schenck, the magistrate of Katzenelnbogen, visited Rheinfels "to debate with a learned Baptist, Melchior Rinck, who was highly skilled in the Hebrew, Greek, and Latin languages."[56] Ellen Yutzy Glebe suggests an even later date: "Probably Rinck survived until at least 1561. Heinrich Beulshausen has found an entry in accounts in Rheinfels, where Rinck may well have been imprisoned at the end of his life, for expenses to provide paper and clothing for 'the Anabaptist' in 1561. This would have to refer to a (literate) Anabaptist who was well known enough to make it unnecessary to name him."[57] And Rinck was certainly still alive when the Hutterite document "Beginnings of the Congregation of God in German Lands" was composed. The date of this document is uncertain, but Werner Packull argues that it was most likely written during the late 1550s or early 1560s. He suggests Rinck might still have been alive in 1563, his longevity explained by the relatively comfortable conditions of his imprisonment.[58]

RINCK'S CONGREGATIONS

The most influential congregation, and the base for Rinck's mission activities, was in the village of Sorga, near Hersfeld. This was led initially by Rinck and Nicholas [Claus] Schreiber, and after Rinck's expulsion, by a schoolmaster from Einbeck named Alexander who had fought alongside Rinck at Frankenhausen and had operated as an itinerant Anabaptist leader in northern Thuringia and elsewhere. The congregation also had links with Hans Römer, the furrier from Eisenach, who, like Rinck, escaped from Frankenhausen but, unlike Rinck, continued to promote violent resistance and tried to rekindle the peasants' movement. Römer's deep appreciation of the Sorga group is evident from his recommendation that another Anabaptist leader, Ludwig Spon, should go there, reporting that "there is a congregation that leads a good Christian life. Everyone helps everyone else with goods and food when someone is in need. Forty or fifty people get together there."[59]

In 1533 (as noted in the previous chapter), twenty-five members of the Sorga congregation and nineteen members of the congregation in Berka were arrested. They were interrogated about their attitude to the churches and to the state. There were also questions about their attitude to the peasants' movement. This is not surprising, given that most of the villagers had been caught up in the peasants' movement in 1525, pressuring the abbot of Hersfeld to accept the movement's Twelve Articles[60], before submitting to Philip's troops. They had also provided refuge to people fleeing the conflict. It seems that at least nine of those interrogated had been involved in some way, some of them in leadership roles, including Hans Plat and Heinz Hutter, Hans Zisen, Hans Koch, and the man named only as Gilg. Only one of those interrogated, Marx Baumgart, denied any involvement, and only three said that the peasants' movement had been wrong. Most answered evasively and said that they did not know if the movement was godly or not. Heinz Hutter said he would leave the question to God. Gilg said he would not call it right or wrong but commended the rebels to God's mercy. A couple named Groschen and Margarethe were also ambivalent: "The recent rebellion had to do with temporal goods, for which reason it was ungodly. However, as to whether it took place for the sake of the Gospel, this they do not know."[61] But Margret Garköchen named Rinck in her forthright and unrepentant answer: "The revolt in which Müntzer and Melchior Rinck were involved was a divine occurrence."[62]

Philip, however, concluded that they were not seditious at this point but sectarian and so banished them. But Alexander, having been arrested in Frankenhausen, was executed in that year, so leadership passed first to Klaus Scharf and Heinz Kraut and then to Hans Both (or Bott).

Since 1526, Hans Both had operated as an Anabaptist preacher and recruiter in the border region of Hesse and Saxony. Initially a firebrand, preaching apocalyptic sermons that anticipated imminent judgment coming on society, he soon embraced a quieter form of Anabaptism, in which he emphasized sanctification and brotherly love. He appeared in the bishopric of Fulda in 1530, baptizing converts at Stadtlengstfeld, before being expelled and making his way to Sorga, where he assumed leadership of the congregation.

Those members of the Sorga congregation who had been arrested and banished moved to Auspitz in Moravia, as did many others before and after the trial, seeking liberty for their practices. This move was at the invitation of the founder of the Auspitz community, Jörg Zaunring, who had been in Sorga in 1532. Two groups reached Moravia, led by Heinz Hutter and Gilg Schneider. However, they struggled to integrate fully into the Hutterite community there, only reluctantly embracing the common purse approach to community. Hans Both initially refused to surrender all the possessions the Sorga group had brought with them, but eventually yielded to pressure. Then Both was banned from preaching because, according to the Moravian elders, he taught that there were neither angels nor devils. This was one of a number of charges brought against him, some more plausible than others, leading Oyer to conclude that he was being defamed by the Hutterites.[63]

Hans Both responded that they were attempting to block his stream of living water, and that Rinck preached the same doctrine. Eventually, anyone who took Both's side in this dispute was banished from the community. Disputes also arose over issues of dress and food (during which Rinck's views were quoted as offering authoritative guidance) and, toward the end of 1533, most of the emigrants returned to Hesse, although a few chose to remain, joining the Philippite community until being expelled from Moravia in 1535, along with most other Anabaptists there.

One of those banished who definitely returned to Hesse was the articulate and outspoken Margret Garköchen (or Garköchin). There is a record of her appearing before Balthasar Raidt and others between 18 and 22 May 1537 in what was officially described as "a friendly and trusting conversation" and certainly appears to be an unusual example in this era of the testimony of a woman being taken seriously and treated with respect. Accused of heresy, sins, and "harming her soul," she asked for some time to consider this and then gave a "resolute" answer, reaffirming her Anabaptist commitment and repeating the testimony she gave in the Berka hearing. Contrasting the teachings of Rinck with the teachings of the Catholic and Lutheran preachers, she declared that Rinck was the true teacher. It seems she was not banished again or punished in any other way at this time but was allowed to go free as the assembled pastors sadly shook their heads at her recalcitrance.[64]

Both also returned to Hesse, where he continued to operate as an Anabaptist leader until he disappears from the historical record. It seems that Peter Riedemann, the Hutterite leader, pursued him to Hesse and attempted to wean him away from his disagreements with Hutterite teaching and practice.

The Sorga congregation continued to wrestle with various issues. There was uncertainty about how to understand economic discipleship, with advocates of various positions: not holding property at all, holding property as long as it pleased God, abandoning it when God or neighbor required, understanding holding as not holding, holding in the spirit of *Gelassenheit*, or acting as stewards for the needy.[65] The congregation later experienced a schism over whether Anabaptists should divorce non-Anabaptist spouses (an interesting echo of Rinck's marital situation). And there was also ambivalence on issues of violence and participation in government. According to the record of interrogations, almost all of those questioned rejected military service and various members asserted that a Christian prince could not go to war, that a ruler could hang a thief, and that vengeance belonged to God. One of those accused confessed that he did not know if a Christian could be a ruler or not. The interrogators concluded that most of them believed that a Christian could not be a ruler.[66]

The interrogation of members of the Berka congregation revealed that they were more sympathetic to the notion of community of goods, apparently advocating not only the renunciation of property holding but seizing the goods of others in the congregation in cases of need. According to Margret Schneider, "Christians are to have all possessions in common, where one may partake of the other's possessions to meet one's own needs." And Margret Kessel testified that "all possessions among Christians are to be held in common."[67] Both congregations reflected Rinck's views that economic discipleship meant more than simply giving alms.

RINCK HIMSELF

From his own writings, from the testimonies of his followers and colleagues, and from the assessments of his opponents, it is possible to gain some, albeit limited and partial, insight into Melchior Rinck's character and personality. As one might expect with a first-generation Anabaptist leader, Rinck was passionate, determined, courageous, and quite irrepressible. Despite various attempts to curtail his activities and to persuade him to recant his views, he persisted and refused to give way throughout his relatively brief years of ministry and lengthy period of imprisonment.

Oyer notes that Rinck was an evangelist, rather than a pastor or congregation-builder, a wanderer rather than someone with a settled ministry. He concludes that "Rinck was an intensely dedicated proclaimer of the Word, a man ready and willing to suffer without developing a martyr complex."[68] Georg Witzel admired Rinck's courage despite disagreeing with his position on baptism. And in their letter to Matthias Hansenhan, the Hutterites wrote about Rinck, whom they had not met personally: "We only hear about his integrity and constancy in affliction."[69]

Witzel also recognized that Rinck was an erudite man, a description affirmed by George Williams in his assessment of Rinck's life.[70] He was the most educated and articulate leader of the Hessian Anabaptists, winning the grudging respect of his opponents. Walter Koehler concluded that Rinck was "a man of strong, charming personality."[71] Despite provocations and attempts at character assassination, Rinck generally used measured language in his debates and on trial. Oyer records one of these occasions: "Rink was the victim of a major attempt at defamation in his trial by Balthasar Raidt in 1528, unless he was completely dishonest in his rejection of Raidt's charges against him. In view of the various character depositions on Rink, and because the Marburg theologians did not protest or contest Rink's rejection of the charges, such purported dishonesty is difficult to accept."[72]

However, in his writings, Rinck often displayed anger against the secular and ecclesial authorities. Williams describes him as not only erudite and passionate but irascible. And Oyer, who rather surprisingly opines that Rinck was "rarely angry," then provides several examples of Rinck raging against the Lutheran princes and theologians, accusing them of being bloodthirsty false prophets, serving their bellies rather than God, and castigating those who brought false accusations against him or wanted to arrest his followers. Oyer detects in Rinck's intemperate language echoes of the hostility toward the authorities that had energized the peasants' movement,[73] although Rinck seems to have reserved his fiercest criticism for the theologians and clerics rather than the secular authorities. In his tract on the subject of marriage, defending himself against accusations of desertion and maybe also of immorality, he expressed himself with a degree of anger and bitterness, at times appearing rather self-righteous, but he concluded with a humble confession of his own sinfulness.

Reflecting on the legacy of Melchior Rinck offers an opportunity to explore the ecclesial, theological, and political perspectives of an Anabaptist leader who did not fit neatly into any of the major branches of the movement but developed his own approach. Examining his life and ministry offers important insights into the flourishing and demise of Hessian Anabaptism in one of the only sixteenth-century contexts in which substantial numbers returned to the state churches. And exploring fresh translations of writings by and about him and his followers enables us to assess the conviction of some of his contemporaries that he was one of the foremost leaders of the early Anabaptist movement.

THREE

Tracts, Interrogations, Letters, and Testimonies

THOROUGH EVALUATION OF Melchior Rinck's theological and ecclesial convictions is hindered by the very limited amount of evidence on which to draw. We know that he wrote letters and tracts that are no longer extant (or at least are lying undiscovered in an archive). Eberhard von der Tann mentioned various books, some printed and some handwritten, to which we do not have access. Some of Rinck's followers spoke (although no doubt exaggerating) of "hundreds" of writings by Rinck. What evidence we do have comes from the few extant writings, from records of a disputation and trials, and from the testimonies of those who quoted him as an authority on various subjects or opposed his teachings. As the records and some of the testimonies are from hostile sources and the testimonies of his followers and colleagues may not be entirely reliable (either because they had not fully understood his teaching or because they were giving evasive answers to their interrogators), we need to be cautious in assessing Rinck's views from these sources.

This chapter gives an overview of the extant writings by or about Rinck, including those translations presented in the Primary Sources. Some of these writings appear in other sources, as indicated in notes throughout the chapter.

WRITINGS

1. Widderlegung eyner Schrifft So Johannes Bader, vermeynter pfarrher zu Landau, newlich than hat, den Kindertauff als Christlich zuerhalten

Except for a book of Latin poetry, published in 1516 before Rinck encountered Anabaptism, his earliest known writing is a tract written (probably in 1527) on the subject of baptism. The long title translates as "Refutation of a text which Johannes Bader, supposed pastor at Landau, recently wrote, holding to infant baptism as being Christian." This was a response to Rinck's erstwhile friend Johannes Bader, Reformed pastor in Landau. Deeply disappointed by Bader's refusal to embrace believers baptism, Rinck wrote a passionate refutation of Bader's arguments. It was discovered as a handwritten manuscript and was probably never printed. The tract is unsystematic, probably not all written at the same time (the tidiness of the handwriting varies considerably), and in some places is rather confusing. In it, Rinck grappled with the Zwinglian argument that baptism is to the new covenant what circumcision was to the old and that infants should therefore receive baptism. It contains sharp rebukes to Bader and others who hold this view.[1]

2. Vermanung und warnung an alle so in der Obrigkeit sind

In 1527 or shortly afterward, Rinck wrote another tract from prison, protesting the persecution of the Anabaptists by the magistrates, arguing that they had no right to govern in religious matters. The title of this tract can be translated as "Admonition and warning to all who are part of the magistracy."[2]

3. Letter to Eberhard von der Tann and a tract on marriage

Probably in 1530, while in prison in Haina, Rinck responded to a letter from Eberhard von der Tann, apparently rejecting his suggestion that he divorce his wife. The contents of this letter and others to Anna and her father were noted in the previous chapter. Rinck also wrote a tract on the subject of marriage at this time, which von der Tann forwarded to the landgrave.[3]

4. Letter and a tract on baptism

Rinck and a fellow prisoner also wrote a brief letter, *Eenen Sendthbrief van Melchior Rinck gene Antonius Jacobs* (*A Communiqué from Melchior Rinck and Antonius Jacobs*), which they sent to friends in the Netherlands. Rinck also, probably at this time, wrote a short tract on baptism. The tract appears anonymously in an undated collection of manuscripts, immediately after the letter written by Rinck and Jacobs.[4] John Oyer argues that the phraseology in this tract points to Rinck as the likely author and suggests that the editor of the collection placed it after the letter to indicate its authorship.[5] However, he acknowledges that this tract might have been written earlier and might be the "booklet" referred to in a letter to Landgrave Philip in 1529 warning about Rinck's influence.

5. Zue widerlegung des vermainten Euongelisten Glauben

This is the title of a lost tract on the subject of communion. This tract was mentioned by the Hutterites as evidence that Rinck supported the practice of communion of goods. But nothing further is known of its contents.[6]

LETTERS ABOUT RINCK

There are several extant letters written by various people about Rinck. The governor of Kassel wrote to Landgrave Philip on 10 March 1529. Elector John wrote to Philip on 4 December 1529. Martin von der Tann, mayor of Vacha, wrote to Philip on 12 November 1531.[7] Eberhard von der Tann wrote to John on 25 November 1531, again on 1 March 1532, and once more after this (this letter is undated).[8] John wrote to both Eberhard and Philip on 21 December 1531. Philip replied on 3 January 1532. John wrote again on 15 January 1532 to both Philip and Eberhard. In 1537 the Hutterites wrote to Matthias Hansenhan, expressing their concerns about the behavior of Hans Both and challenging his assertion that Both derived his position from Rinck's teaching. On 17 March 1540, Martin Bucer wrote to Philip about the conditions of Rinck's imprisonment, and Philip replied on 22 March, eliciting a brief acknowledgment from Bucer three days later.

INTERROGATIONS INVOLVING RINCK

1. Marburg Disputation (17–18 August 1528)

At the Marburg disputation, arranged to investigate Rinck's teaching, Balthasar Raidt set out his objections to Rinck in twelve articles, identifying the many errors he discerned in Rinck's teaching. As noted earlier, Raidt was not a persuasive or effective debater, and in due course others took over from him. Nor should we assume that Raidt intended to be fair to Rinck in these articles. Nevertheless, they give some insight into the accusations he faced and the subjects on which he was known to have taught.

Rinck was invited to respond to these charges, and the record of the disputation provides a summary of his answers. He presented his own five articles, entitled "Account of My Faith in God through Jesus Christ." The debate moved on to consider these articles, after which Rinck briefly summarized his presentation with an appeal for a careful debate informed by the Scriptures. Raidt and Rinck then debated further before the theologians decided that no progress was being made, since Rinck would not recant his views, and brought the debate to a close.

2. Interrogation of Rinck and other Anabaptists in Vacha (1531)

The arrest of Rinck and twelve other Anabaptists, apprehended while meeting in a house in Vacha, sparked the aforementioned correspondence between the mayor of Vacha, Martin von der Tann; his brother, Eberhard von der Tann; Landgrave Philip of Hesse; and Elector John of Saxony. It subsequently resulted in Rinck's sentence of life imprisonment. Before this, however, the prisoners were interrogated about their beliefs.

TESTIMONIES OF HIS OPPONENTS

Justus Menius, the Lutheran reformer and superintendent at Eisenach, has been described as "one of the bitterest literary and personal enemies of Anabaptism on the Lutheran side during the period of the Reformation. With strong prejudice, frequently against his better knowledge, he interpreted as the work of the devil the fruit he could not fail to see. By his books Menius for a long time determined the character of writing about the Anabaptist movement in Middle Germany."[9] Given that Menius was so unremittingly hostile—Oyer suggests that he "considered the terms Anabaptist and devil to be synonymous"[10]—his testimony in relation to Rinck's teaching should be treated with considerable caution.

Menius had some personal dealings with Rinck, although the extent of these is unclear. But he did refer to Rinck several times. In 1528, he joined Eberhard von der Tann in writing a report to the Elector of Saxony, warning him about Rinck's activity. In his treatise, which can be translated as "The doctrine and secret of the Anabaptists refuted from Holy Scripture" (1530), Rinck is mentioned five times.[11] Three of these references are to Rinck's teaching or activities before he became an Anabaptist in about 1525.

Menius reported that Rinck had told him five years earlier that "Christ did not say 'theirs is the kingdom of heaven' (i.e., the children), but 'theirs is the kingdom who are like children.'"[12] According to Menius, Rinck also taught that in the communion service the words "for the forgiveness of sins" had been "thrown in by the devil himself."

Menius also accused him of doubting the accuracy of biblical translations, reporting that Rinck had said that "all the books of the New Testament are written in all kinds of languages—Greek, Latin, German etc. And they are all together wrong and not right upon the earth anymore."[13] Menius regarded Rinck at that point as a disciple of Müntzer, whom he identified as the chief source of the Anabaptist heresy.

lich frey sein/ was aber frey ist/ das kan jhe warlich
kein sunde sein/ man thu es gleich/ odder lass es.
Vnd mag sie nicht helffen/ das sie sagen/ wie
denn der Melchior Rinck jnn seinen buchlin (dere er
etliche von der kinder/ vnd seiner Rotten tauffe zusa-

derumb zu ruck vmbgetrieben/ich will geschweigen/
das jhr etliche/ als der Rinck vnd Hans Römer bie
von Eissenach/ vber das funffte jar von jhren ehe-
weibern jm buben leben vmbgelauffen vnd noch

kein sunde sein/man thu es gleich/odder lass es.
Vnd mag sie nicht helffen/ das sie sagen/
wie denn der Melchior Rinck jnn seinen buchlin (dere er etliche von der kinder/ vnd seiner

da jr Rotten / wie da / Ich wolt hie gerne ei-
nen klugen geist hören/ Er müste aber klüger
sein/denn des Melchior Rincken geist für funff
jaren war/ welcher mir also fur gabe/ Christus

kunst/Gottes rat/Gottes stercke/ vnd Gottes
Gottseligkeit.
Aber des Melchior Rincken/welchen man
hiebey vns den Greken zunennen pflegt/sampt

References to Rinck in Justus Menius's *Der Widdertauffer lere und geheimnis, aus heiliger schrifft widderlegt* (1530).

cipasse. Von seinen Schriften heißt es in JOH. WIGANDI *dogmat. & argumentis Anabaptistarum:* (Lipſ. MDLXXXII. 4.) p. 456. MELCH. RINCK *libellos contra baptismum puerorum scripsit & sparsit. Item* BALTHAS. HVBMEIER, ROTTMANNVS *Monasteriensis*, MENNO

Hofmannianer, Ubbo Philipps, der in ſ. Attestatie u. ſ. ſ. p. 44. (vergl. mit Jehrings Uebers. §. 7. S. 192.) schreibt, Onder desen (D. BALTH. HVBMOR, MELCH. RINCK u. ſ. w.) is opgestaen MELCH. HOFFMAN, ende is uyt *Hoegduytslant tot Embden gekomen, te doopen in't open-*

References to Rinck in Justus Menius's *Von dem Geist der Widerteuffer* (1544).

But fourteen years later, when Rinck had been in prison for several years and was clearly no longer any kind of threat, in "Concerning the spirit of the Anabaptists" (1544), Menius mentioned Rinck only twice and very briefly, associating him much more accurately with Balthasar Hubmaier and Melchior Hofmann as fellow Anabaptists.[14]

Balthasar Raidt, Lutheran pastor in Hersfeld, and Rinck's opponent in the disputation in Marburg, complained: "Melchior Rinck met in secret near Hersfeld with a few people, taking it upon himself to teach them concerning the Holy Gospel differently than what has until now been preached here. And he has introduced a new insurgency into our gracious prince's holy land by reportedly rebaptizing some of his followers, as if infant baptism should not be considered [a proper] baptism, and has gathered people around him and won a number of followers."[15]

TESTIMONIES OF HIS FOLLOWERS AND COLLEAGUES

Additional insights into Rinck's teaching can be found in the testimonies of those he had baptized and integrated into Anabaptist congregations. Rinck's periods of banishment and imprisonment, and eventual life imprisonment, did not curtail his influence. Not only did he correspond from jail and continue to disseminate his writings, but the communities he founded persisted and their members paid tribute to his teachings and influence.

Ellen Yutzy Glebe warns that Rinck "had little direct contact with the communities he had founded" during the long years of his imprisonment and concludes that "he had only so much control over the movement and its interpretations of his message."[16] She rightly alerts us to the danger of assuming that his followers all accurately reflected his teaching when questioned about their beliefs and practices. Erich Geldbach issues similar warnings, noting the lack of education among Rinck's followers, the consequent inadequacy of their responses under interrogation, the tendency of the interrogators to ask loaded questions, and the ease with which uncongenial answers could be expunged from the court record, so that we may have access to only a distorted version of their statements.[17]

Furthermore, several other influential Anabaptist teachers in the region had differing views and emphases. It is not always clear from court records which stream influenced those on trial, many of whom may have been instructed by teachers from different streams and entirely unaware of the differences between them. Of the nineteen interrogated at Berka, for instance, a number were baptized by Moravian missionaries and only one named Rinck as the person who baptized her —although Anabaptists often refused to reveal who had baptized them in order to protect them, so Rinck may have baptized others. But the testimonies of those who were interrogated at Sorga indicate influences from more literalist, Spiritualist, and communitarian sources. Even if we can reliably identify individuals whom Rinck baptized or connect them with the congregations he founded, their testimonies may reflect the influence of others beside Rinck.

Of course, it may also be true that Anabaptists who were associated primarily with other groupings, such as Jörg Schnabel from the Hofmannite stream, had learned from Rinck. Within a relatively small territory like Hesse (Rinck and Schnabel might have grown up in the same small village and might even have been related[18]), cross-fertilization was highly likely. Although Schnabel (and others influenced by Melchior Hofmann) espoused an unorthodox Christology, on many other issues his teaching agreed with Rinck's. Some of his statements will, therefore, be included in the analysis of Rinck's theology and legacy in the following chapters. Furthermore, many of those involved in the Anabaptist movement, including its leaders, had also been involved in the peasants' movement and probably knew each other as former comrades. And if there is diversity among the different Anabaptist streams in Hesse, the records of interrogations also reveal no small variety in the beliefs even of members of the same congregation.[19]

Nevertheless, some testimonies include explicit references to Rinck's teaching. This is especially true in the record of the interrogation of the twelve arrested with Rinck at Vacha. Unsurprisingly, since they had been arrested at a meeting with Rinck and were being questioned alongside him, they frequently referred to his teachings and writings. Those questioned at the Sorga hearings also expressed their dependence on what they had heard Rinck teach. And when they were subsequently exiled to Moravia, they defended their views on the basis of the teaching they had received from Rinck. It seems that they were deeply offended when the Moravians were not persuaded by this appeal to Rinck's authority. The Hutterites wrote to Matthias Hansenhan in 1537: "Our answer was that even if Melchior Rink did say and teach this, it still was not right. We did not believe Melchior took this position, however, and thought Hans Both and his followers might have misunderstood him. They then said we were calling Rink a false prophet and were furious."[20]

By comparison with the educated Rinck, most of his followers were poorly equipped to answer their interrogators or to nuance their responses. His removal was undoubtedly a serious blow to them. But across Europe, inquisitors were frequently impressed, irritated, and bemused by the ability of illiterate Anabaptists to offer biblical arguments for their beliefs, suggesting that they had imbibed much from the more educated members of their communities. And as we will see, the limited and unsophisticated responses of Rinck's followers cohere strongly with what we know of Rinck's teaching from his own writings and the record of the Marburg debate.

Furthermore, the permeability of incarceration in this era means that, while imprisoned, Rinck may have continued to have greater influence than Glebe allows. Gustav Hammann describes the imprisonment of the group captured at Lindenborn: "The Anabaptist leaders experienced a very easy imprisonment, for the entire bulwark could not be locked . . . . The Anabaptists could easily be visited by their families, and without trouble or risk go to their homes for a time to look after their work."[21] Indeed, Christian Hege records that one of the prisoners, Jörg Schnabel, baptized nearly thirty people in this period![22] James Stayer agrees that the incarcerated Rinck continued to exercise considerable influence: "Although almost continuously imprisoned by Landgraf Philip . . . Rink continued to have great authority in Central German Anabaptism."[23] And Oyer concludes: "His followers and others carried on the clandestine work after his enforced withdrawal. But his theological influence remained."[24] Without dismissing the cautions expressed by Glebe and by Geldbach (who argues that any presentation of Rinck's teaching needs to be based solely on his verified statements), in the following chapters we will also examine the testimonies of Hessian Anabaptists to gain additional insights into Rinck's teachings and their impact on his followers.

FOUR

Rinck's Theology

MELCHIOR RINCK, IN common with most other Anabaptist leaders, had no opportunity to produce a systematic statement of his theological convictions. Not all Anabaptist leaders, however, would have welcomed such an opportunity, their emphasis being more on living out the faith than systematizing it. Furthermore, the loss of many of Rinck's tracts and letters on various subjects means that any attempt to summarize his theology must remain tentative and incomplete. What evidence we have from his own writings, the testimonies of his followers, the debate in Marburg, and the comments of his opponents, indicates that his theology was influenced by Luther, Müntzer, Denck, and the humanist tradition, but that he wove these influences together with his own understanding of the Bible to develop his own perspectives and emphases. Hans-Jürgen Goertz writes: "The fact that his thought included quite distinct Lutheran, humanist, Müntzerian and Denckian elements has been responsible for the uneven verdict of scholarship. It is, however, undisputed that Rinck endeavored to support his arguments from Scripture, that he stressed readiness for repentance and that he inclined towards Christian pacifism."[1]

Rinck seems not to have shared the mystical views of Denck or, once he had embraced Anabaptism, the apocalyptic and revolutionary tendencies of Müntzer. His main concerns were coming to faith from hearing the Word, repenting, being baptized, and living a new life. His tracts and teachings display similarity to, but no dependence on, the views of the Swiss Brethren. The only evidence of a personal connection with Swiss Brethren leaders is the inclusion of a short letter and tract by Rinck in a Swiss Brethren anthology in 1560.

Two others, whom Rinck knew and from whom he no doubt learned, even if he did not subscribe to all their ideas, were Hans Hut and Jakob Strauss. Hut should probably be regarded as the founder of Thuringian Anabaptism, and as such, he exercised wide influence through his travels, preaching, and writing. The continuing influence of Müntzer on Hut is clear from many phrases in Hut's writings,[2] but this is not the case with Rinck, who did not embrace the apocalyptic vision that Müntzer and Hut shared. Rinck seems to have moved much further away from Müntzer than Hut. Strauss may have influenced Rinck's perspectives on believers baptism, a believers church, and community of goods, as well as helped him identify concerns about Luther's teaching. But Rinck was very much his own man in theology and practice.

Rinck was not a trained theologian, and on occasion he seems to have misunderstood what others had said or written. At times, his frustration with his opponents and outrage at practices in the state churches seems to have led him to make intemperate statements. And, as he moved from being a reformer to a revolutionary to an Anabaptist, his thinking developed and his emphases changed. His primary passion appears to have been to assert the need for believers baptism and a disciplined church community in contrast to what he regarded as the undisciplined behavior in the state churches that was the inevitable consequence, in his view, of the practice of infant baptism. On whatever subject he wrote or spoke, Rinck usually included comments on this issue.

LOVE

When he was invited to present a summary of his teachings at the Marburg disputation in 1528, it is highly significant that Rinck's first article opened with the words "Since God is love . . ." However much he was indebted to Denck for this insight, Rinck undoubtedly believed that love was the primary characteristic of God and the highest calling of human beings. With reference to familiar biblical texts, he explained that the love of God "is not self-seeking," that humanity, having been created in God's image, was therefore also "created in the image of love" and shared God's mind on this, and that Jesus Christ, as the perfect image of God, was "the firstborn of love." His opponent Balthasar Raidt added a footnote to the court record that this meant for Rinck that humanity "was created to love God with one's whole heart, whole soul, etc., and the neighbor as oneself." Raidt would later attempt to nuance this emphasis on the love of God, inviting Rinck to confess that God "is wise, devout, just, and holy," as well as loving. Rinck did not demur from this, but it is clear that he was primarily captivated by the love of God.

Rinck continued in his second article to use love as his controlling theological and ethical reference point. Expounding his understanding of the fall, he declared that humanity, "on account of unfaith and contempt of the divine word, became an image of false love," and that this resulted in "love of conflict." In his summary of Rinck's responses, Raidt noted that Rinck, quoting from 1 Tim 1:5, had asserted that the Holy Spirit produces in the believers "love that comes from a pure heart, a good conscience, and sincere faith."[3]

In his reply to Reformed pastor Johannes Bader, Rinck quoted two well-known texts from John's Gospel to define true discipleship as loving obedience: "Christ also says (John 14[:21]), 'They who have my commandments and keep them are those who love me.' Also, (15[:10]), 'If you keep my commandments, you will abide in my love.'"[4] In his subsequent tract on baptism, he accused those who defended this practice out of purported love for children of failing to show love toward either natural children, since infant baptism offers them to Belial (the devil), or "the children of the spirit" (his congregations), whom they labeled "fanatics." He regarded this practice as a ploy of Satan lest "a church should arise manifesting obedience to Christ not only with the mouth and heart, but also with deeds and love."[5]

Although Denck has long been regarded as the first-generation Anabaptist who spoke and wrote most often about love, and has been designated the Anabaptist "apostle of Christian love,"[6] this theme appears to be just as much Rinck's primary motif and concern. In the tone he adopted in his writings and debates, he may not have always demonstrated what he advocated, but there is no doubt that he aspired to a life of loving obedience and urged his followers to embrace this.

CHRISTOLOGY

The unorthodox doctrine of the "celestial flesh" of Christ (the claim that he did not derive his human flesh from Mary but brought it with him from heaven, so that the "celestial flesh" was human flesh as it was before the fall) was held and taught by some Hessian Anabaptists, such as Jörg Schnabel and Peter Tasch, and perhaps also by some of Rinck's associates, such as Hans Both. But there is no indication that Rinck himself was drawn to this teaching. What limited evidence we have from what he wrote and taught suggests that he was orthodox in his Christology and uninterested in speculative theology.

In the Marburg disputation, Balthasar Raidt's eighth charge against Rinck was that he had taught that "Christ was not obedient to the Father according to the flesh, but rather, flesh strove against Spirit and was disobedient, yet without sin." The source of this accusation, according to the court record, was the conversation Rinck had had with Landgrave Philip, in which he had "spoken to my gracious prince and lord at Friedewald that in the garden Christ strove against the flesh with the spirit, causing him to sweat bloody sweat." Raidt claimed that this statement implied that Christ was disobedient to his Father, but Rinck denied this.

Later in the debate Raidt accused Rinck of denying the divinity of Christ and teaching that he was a created being: "You . . . say, humans were created in the likeness of God and that one is to see the same in Jesus Christ, who for this reason also is to be named an image of God." Again, Rinck denied this as a perversion of what he actually taught. He insisted that he taught the full divinity of Christ. Raidt appears to have accepted this, as the record states that "they had reached agreement" on this and other doctrinal issues.[7]

Raidt's accusations seem to be attempts to malign Rinck by placing upon some of his statements a heterodox interpretation that is not required by them. In fact, what Rinck's statements seem to imply (if Raidt's gloss is set aside) is the typical Anabaptist emphasis on the true humanity of Christ and his exemplary role for those who would follow him. For Rinck, as for other Anabaptists, this did not mean any denial of Christ's divinity.

SOTERIOLOGY

Rinck's approach to soteriology was influenced by his involvement in the peasants' movement and his relationship with Müntzer. George Williams writes: "Rinck tried to continue Müntzer's work by means of strong polemics against Luther's doctrine of justification, the proper fruit of which, he thought, were scarcer the more closely one approached Wittenberg."[8] According to Justus Menius, in 1525 the pre-Anabaptist Rinck castigated the "dead faith" of Luther and contrasted this with the living, heroic faith of Müntzer.[9] John Oyer, however, concludes that Rinck's developed soteriology "is a mixture of Luther and Denck with very little of Müntzer remaining."[10]

It was undoubtedly the soteriological teachings of the Anabaptists that most alarmed the reformers, who feared that they were undermining the doctrine of justification by faith. It seemed undeniable to them, despite disclaimers, that the Anabaptists were teaching that good works were essential for salvation. And this teaching was made more dangerous by the Anabaptists' frequent criticism of the low moral standards in the state churches. Oyer reports that Menius, for example, "was stung by their accusations that the Lutheran faith was dead because it did not issue in good fruit. . . . Menius interpreted Rink to mean that the Lutherans believed salvation to be a forensic act unrelated to man's experience of Christ."[11] Ironically, Menius was himself later criticized by fellow reformers for placing too much emphasis on good works. Oyer suggests that "in view of Menius' frequent encounters with them, it is logical to assume that he derived some of his convictions on the importance of good works from his running battle with the Anabaptists."[12]

Rinck and his colleagues consistently criticized Luther's teaching for the lack of fruit this produced in the state churches. Adam Angersbach, for example, arrested with Rinck at Vacha, said that he had "seen little good coming from the Lutheran preachers, just decadence, freedom, licentiousness—far worse and more evil than under the Papacy." He declared that "where God's word, the truth, and the Holy Spirit are taught, it yields fruit; people cease sinning and mend their ways." But this was not the case in the Lutheran churches (any more than it had been "under the Papacy")—and the fault lay with the preachers. Quoting Matt 7:16, where Jesus says false teachers will be recognized by their fruit, he complained that the preachers were inconsistent, greedy, and leading sinful and decadent lives.[13] This chapter was frequently quoted by Anabaptists. In the 1538 debate, Jörg Schnabel criticized "the church of the new pope" (by which he meant Luther) and, with reference to Matt 7:12, concluded: "The results are the evidence by which one may and ought to test the tree, as Christ himself says."[14]

Rinck himself expressed surprise and dismay that "the most learned and widely famous evangelists of Wittenberg, together with their following, would have been so far from the true gospel," suggesting that they had been like wolves in sheep's clothing but that their true nature had now been revealed.[15]

Rinck's lack of respect for Luther and his teaching on justification by faith constituted the first charge at Marburg. According to Raidt, Rinck "blasphemes and maligns the holy gospel of Jesus Christ, which God has revealed to us at this time." Apparently, Rinck had claimed that "such is a false pharisaical, hypocritical gospel, and all who follow Martin Luther, and who teach as he does, are leading the people to the devil." Rinck denied he was blaspheming the gospel of Christ but insisted that Luther's teaching was in error and promised to demonstrate this if given the opportunity. He was pressed hard on this point but he did not withdraw the charge of hypocrisy or the suggestion that Lutheran teaching led toward the devil rather than Christ. Later in the disputation, Raidt objected to Rinck's referring to him and other Lutheran theologians as phonies, hypocrites, and seducers. No doubt Raidt also had in mind Rinck's identification of the Lutherans as the antichrist, an accusation Rinck made repeatedly in his *Admonition*, in which he designated Rome as the beast of the book of Revelation but designated the Lutherans as "the rabble of the scribes" and as "the total Antichrist."[16] To Raidt's objection Rinck made no reply, choosing to focus instead on more substantive theological issues.

Oyer gives a concise summary of the soteriological points raised in the disputation.[17] He concludes that Rinck did not provide a fully integrated account of his soteriology, not least because he referred variously to the writings of Paul and John and to Old Testament passages without explaining these at any length. According to Oyer, Rinck never defined what he meant by "faith" or explained his understanding of the atonement. Nevertheless, the Marburg theologians failed to detect any soteriological heresy in his statements.

In his closing statement after the discussion of Rinck's first three articles, Raidt attempted to summarize what Rinck claimed he had taught:

> You have avowed that in order to come to faith and the Spirit, no work of the law helps, nor does relinquishment of possessions, of works, of sensual desires, or of one's self, for through the law comes the knowledge of sin, bringing a person to repent and sorrow for his or her sins. Therefore, the law also precedes the Gospel, but this in accordance with the image of God, namely, in order to become devout, just, and holy before God, the only thing which helps is a genuine and true faith—which alone trusts and depends on God's grace and mercy—offered to us in Christ as a gift. The same faith receives the Holy Spirit, which works and brings 'love that comes from a pure heart, a good conscience, and sincere faith' (1 Tim 1:[5])."

Raidt checked that he had understood this correctly, and Rinck agreed: "Yes, this I have stated and avowed." Indeed, he had said in his response to Raidt's twelfth article that "man cannot prepare himself and come to the Spirit, to faith, and to the Father." Lest there be any doubt, he denied categorically that he had taught that "humans, through their own capacity, can do this, and not through God's strength." Raidt concluded (in relation to soteriological issues): "Since we are one in understanding with one another, it is not necessary for us here to quarrel." But Rinck's teachings undoubtedly included distinctive emphases, some of which can be found in the writings and testimonies of many Anabaptists in other regions, and some of which indicate the impact of medieval German mysticism on Rinck and other German Anabaptists.

Undoubtedly influenced by Denck, Rinck (as noted above) insisted that love was the pre-eminent quality in the divine nature and that human beings, created in the image of God, had the capacity to love God wholeheartedly. The fallen human condition consisted in turning away from this true expression of love and setting up a false love that disfigured humanity. This led to pride, self-sufficiency, and unwillingness to accept God's mercy, relying on one's own righteousness to stand before God. Salvation meant, therefore, under the tutelage of the Law that revealed sin, judgment, and condemnation, returning to the original image of love and standing before God as those who are truly righteous.

Raidt argued that the divine nature was constituted by qualities such as wisdom, holiness, and righteousness as well as love. He also probed Rinck's teaching in search of evidence that he was advocating salvation through works, rather than by faith. Was Rinck teaching that "relinquishment of possessions, of works, of sensual desires, or of one's self" was of assistance in salvation? Or did he believe that salvation depended on "a genuine and true faith—which alone trusts and depends on God's grace and mercy—offered to us in Christ as a gift"? As noted, Rinck insisted: "Yes, this I have stated and avowed"; and Raidt pronounced himself satisfied on this point.[18]

Raidt and his colleagues may have exonerated Rinck from soteriological heresy, but their probing questions and Rinck's own statements indicate that his emphases were different from theirs. Although Rinck may not have fully understood Luther's teaching, there is no reason to doubt that he truly affirmed the doctrine of justification by faith. Indeed, in his teaching on baptism, he insisted in many places that it was faith that was the prerequisite. But he seems to have regarded both faith and good works as gifts from God. Indeed, in the *Admonition*, he stated that God had sent his Son into the world "as a sacrifice, for reconciliation, the sole basis of atonement" and, later in the same sentence, described "obedience to God" also as "the sole basis of atonement."[19] His critique of the "dead faith" of the Lutherans suggests that in his teaching Rinck insisted on a stronger link between justification and sanctification and that he agreed with Anabaptists elsewhere that authentic faith must produce fruit.

Perhaps Rinck's emphasis depended, at least in part, on whom he was addressing. He often chastised the Lutherans for their failure to encourage discipleship, which may have sounded to them suspiciously like a return to "salvation by works," but he utterly rejected what he regarded as this Catholic teaching.[20] In his writings for his followers he strongly emphasized their dependence on God's grace for salvation. Defending Rinck against the charge of Pelagianism, Oyer argues that

Rinck was concerned to challenge what he saw as Luther's illegitimate and damaging disconnection of justification and sanctification but concludes: "Rinck always insisted that each stage in this process toward God was itself the product of God's work."[21] In his tract on baptism, Rinck described the Catholics and the Lutherans as hypocrites and scribes, rejecting their common commitment to infant baptism as a false gospel responsible for producing disorderly churches. As noted above, he celebrated the emergence among his own followers of a community "manifesting obedience to Christ not only with the mouth and heart, but also with deeds and love."

This was certainly the emphasis that Rinck had communicated to his followers and their understanding of salvation. Oyer notes the testimonies of two Anabaptists, Köhler and Scheffer (surnames unknown), interrogated after their arrest in 1537. Although lacking Rinck's theological sophistication, they strongly linked salvation and discipleship. They claimed that only those who imitated Christ could receive any benefit from his death.[22] Similarly, Heinz Kraut, responding to Melanchthon's questioning, rejected forensic notions of salvation and conjoined justification and sanctification as a single process.[23]

Köhler and Scheffer also criticized the sinful lives of some of the state church preachers and concluded that they should not listen to them or expect to receive truthful teaching from them. This was a common theme in Anabaptist writings in Germany and other regions. Hans Hut, in *On the Mystery of Baptism*, did not mince his words: "No worldly, pleasure-seeking scribe can know the judgments of the Lord."[24] Similarly, Menno Simons wrote in his *Brief Confession on the Incarnation*: "The pure Word of God and the teaching of the Holy Spirit cannot be pointed out and taught by servants who are themselves unclean and carnal."[25] And Menno's colleague Dirk Philips insisted on assessing preachers by their lifestyles, arguing that "the fruit which a true teacher brings forth is a blameless life, walking in accordance with the gospel."[26] Rinck's teaching appears to be in line with other Anabaptist leaders.

The Marburg disputation contains a very brief exchange on the subject of predestination. In his seventh article, Raidt accused Rinck of having denied this doctrine in his meeting with Landgrave Philip before the debate. Rinck's reply was that he taught what Rom 9 taught on this subject. This is a classic biblical passage on predestination, but it is unclear whether Rinck interpreted this in the same way as the Lutherans. Anabaptists in general have not been enamored of this doctrine. From Rinck's writings it seems clear that he rejected the Lutheran understanding of original sin and emphasized the freedom of the human will to respond to or reject the grace of God.

Rinck wrote little, as far as we know from his extant writings, about the work of the Holy Spirit. However, his jibe about the Lutherans' dead faith implies that the Spirit was not at work in their churches. In his first article in the Marburg disputation, Raidt accused Rinck of saying that "Luther had God's Spirit at the beginning" but had now become a devil and "the true Antichrist." By contrast, in his tract on baptism, Rinck called his own churches "the children of the Spirit," albeit their enemies regarded them as fanatics.[27] Then, in his twelfth article, Raidt accused Rinck of teaching that the Spirit was received "through forgiveness, repudiation, and rejection of [a person's] endeavors. . . . In this way, God's grace through Christ is completely disavowed"—another attempt to convict Rinck of teaching salvation by works. According to the court record, Rinck acknowledged that he had taught along these lines but denied that he had preached that "humans, through their own capacity, can do this, and not through God's strength." Raidt seems to have accepted Rinck's assurance on this issue.

But Rinck was not impressed by Bader's claim that outer baptism was not bound to the inner and his rejection of believers baptism because it was not possible, even for the apostles, to look into human hearts and determine who was fit for believers baptism since the Lord alone was the discerner of hearts. Rinck was confident that, because all power belongs to Christ (Matt 28:18), true believers could rely on the Spirit's help to discern who belonged to Christ and who did not.

His followers were also convinced that the Holy Spirit was largely absent from the state churches but was powerfully at work in their own communities. In his trenchant critique of the Lutheran churches, Adam Angersbach pointed to the decadent behavior of the preachers as evidence of this. The court record states that "he does not believe that they have the Holy Spirit, for the Holy Spirit does not waver as they do." Consequently, the teaching in these churches could not be trusted: "Where the Holy Spirit does not reside and is not taught, there the truth also cannot be taught and acknowledged." But, Angersbach asserted, "where God's word, the truth, and the Holy Spirit are taught, it yields fruit; people cease sinning and mend their ways." And, speaking of those who had been executed for submitting to believers baptism, he insisted that if they had not had the Holy Spirit, "it would not have been possible for them to remain so steadfast."[28]

HERMENEUTICS

Rinck's approach to biblical exegesis and interpretation, as is the case with many other early Anabaptists, can be discerned mainly through examples in his writings, rather than through any attempt by him to set out his hermeneutical assumptions or principles. But it is clear that he was deeply critical of the hermeneutics of his opponents. In his tract on marriage, he complained about their "shameful" approach, quoting biblical texts to justify "persecution, tyranny, betrayal, and the shedding of so much innocent blood and other greater outrages."[29] His own approach might fairly be described as eclectic. It has been suggested that "the basic lines of his system of theology were mysticism and a thoroughly Spiritualistic view of the Scriptures."[30] But this is not supportable from his extant works or his use of Scripture in the Marburg debate. Erich Geldbach rightly insists that for Rinck, "the Bible is the highest measurement for decision-making" on ethical issues.[31] But Oyer's conclusion that his interpretations "ran the range from Spiritualism to literalism" can be demonstrated from Rinck's writings and the testimonies of his followers.[32]

At the literalist end are his writings and statements on baptism, in which he insisted that infant baptism lacked biblical warrant and contravened the order found in Scripture. Faith must precede baptism, faith was a response to having heard the Word preached and so, as infants were unable to make this response, infant baptism was wrong. Rinck quoted Mark 16:16 as his primary text on this subject, along with many other biblical references. His interpretation of biblical teaching on marriage was also literalistic, despite the difficulties caused by this to himself and to his estranged wife. Quoting Gen 2:24, Matt 5:32, Matt 19:4–6, and several other Old and New Testament texts in his tract on marriage, Rinck expounded their meaning and declared himself bound by their teaching. Rinck, it seems, embraced the familiar Anabaptist confidence that much of Scripture was not very difficult to understand and should be applied literally without the need to wrangle over its interpretation.[33] In his response to Bader, he insisted that what Paul wrote "needs no additional commentary," and in his *Admonition* we find the phrases "Paul describes the situation so clearly" and "in these passages one clearly sees."[34]

In common with most Anabaptists, he drew primarily on texts from the New Testament, although he also quoted Old Testament texts if they were helpful to his argument. Raidt reported Rinck's paraphrase of Ezek 18 as an additional argument against infant baptism: "The person who sins shall die. A child shall not suffer for the iniquity of a parent, nor a parent suffer for the iniquity of a child."[35]

His challenge to his opponents in the Marburg disputation was whether they could prove with "sufficient and unfalsified Holy Scripture" that his teachings were erroneous.[36] This reference to "unfalsified" scripture might indicate his concern that translations were not always true to the original text and might thereby offer unwarranted support to current church practices. As noted above, Menius accused Rinck of teaching that "all the books of the New Testament are written in all kinds of languages—Greek, Latin, German, etc. And they are all together wrong and not right upon the earth anymore."[37] In light of Rinck's frequent reliance on New Testament texts to defend his teachings, this is a hostile and inaccurate interpretation of what Rinck must have actually said, but it probably reflects his concern that accurate translations be used in debates.

Having peppered his articles with biblical references, he required his opponents to answer him, if they could, with biblically based arguments. Raidt recognized this insistence in Rinck and his followers, acknowledging in his fifth Marburg article that their position in relation to the rite of baptism had been adopted on the basis of Scripture and that he would need to challenge them on this basis. Earlier, in a letter to Eberhard von der Tann, Rinck had insisted that he could tolerate the charge brought against him of having been rebaptized if his accusers "could prove this from even one iota out of Holy Scripture."[38] His followers also reported that Rinck used "hundreds of scriptures" to undergird his teaching.[39]

On other occasions, however, Rinck appears to have adopted a less literalistic approach to biblical texts—which was the way most German Anabaptists interpreted Scripture. An early example of this, according to Menius, was that in 1525 (before Rinck identified himself with the Anabaptists) he argued that Jesus did not mean literal children when he said "theirs is the kingdom of heaven" but those who are "like children."[40] According to Heinz Ot in the Vacha hearing, Rinck argued against the Lutheran doctrine of the "real presence" in the Lord's Supper by offering a more Spiritualistic exegesis of the relevant passages in the New Testament. Claiming that Christ was truly present in the preaching of the gospel, rather than in the bread and the wine, Rinck drew on John 6 to present this more Spiritualistic view of the subject.[41] Ot also testified that Rinck demurred from the typically literalist Anabaptist exegesis of the Sermon on the Mount and offered an unusual allegorical interpretation of Matt 5:40, in which the coat and the cloak meant temporal goods and life itself, both of which the followers of Christ must be ready to surrender. However, Ot also insisted that Rinck refused to accept anything that he could not prove with Scripture.

We should note, however, that these examples of less literalistic interpretations all come from the testimonies of others, be they followers or an opponent, whereas the examples of more literalistic interpretations come from Rinck's own writings or statements. The one possible exception to this is the exchange between Raidt and Rinck in the Marburg disputation. In his third article Raidt said that Rinck interpreted Gen 2:17 as referring to spiritual death and not that of the body.[42] According to the court record, Rinck did not dispute this. However, this is not really a spiritualizing interpretation of the text. This is not to suggest that spiritualizing interpretations were absent from Rinck and his followers—highly unlikely in the milieu of German Anabaptism—but that some degree of caution is needed. Oyer's summary, quoted above, may overstate the case. Rinck's hermeneutics seems more in line with the Swiss Brethren than with most other German Anabaptists.

The same might be said for Rinck's use and interpretation of the book of Revelation. The feverish speculation among German Anabaptists about the timing and details of Christ's second coming is not apparent in any of Rinck's extant writings, nor is any indication that he regarded the Anabaptists as preparing the way for this or likely to be involved in the meting out of judgment. Apart from his attribution of the term *antichrist* to those with whom he disagreed and his insistence that the practitioners of infant baptism owed allegiance to the great whore of Babylon, he showed no interest in such topics. Despite his suspected involvement in the revolutionary peasants' movement, which was imbued with millennial speculation, and the inflammatory rhetoric of Hans Hut, Hans Römer, and others, Rinck was not interrogated about his eschatological views. Some of his followers (including Hans Both and Margret Garköchen) seemed rather more interested in the subject, with predictions of imminent judgment, especially on those who had crushed the peasants.[43] And Doll Frank testified during an interrogation in Großenbach (in the Fulda area) between December 1529 and June 1530 that he had been taught by Rinck and two others that "God will punish the world with seven plagues through water, blood, fire and stone," but confessed that he did not remember the other three plagues![44] But Rinck himself was mainly interested in faithful discipleship in the present age.

BAPTISM

Baptism was the subject on which Rinck felt most strongly and wrote most often and, at times, intemperately. He was convinced that baptism following believing was a command given by Jesus and insisted that this was "the very minimum in outward obedience" that Christ could expect from his followers.[45]

Infant baptism

If his extant writings are indicative, Rinck focused most of his attention on a critique of infant baptism, rather than expounding his understanding of believers baptism. He was convinced that this practice was contrary to Scripture, deeply damaging to the spiritual health of those who had received it, and responsible for appallingly low moral standards in the state churches. He pulled no punches in utterly condemning it and commented on it in relation to any subject on which he was writing.

As mentioned above, Menius reported that, as early as 1525, Rinck had insisted that the kingdom of heaven belonged not to literal children but to those who had become like children, undercutting an argument for infant baptism. Oyer writes, "Insofar as Christ's words applied to children directly, they meant that children were included in the Kingdom despite the absence of infant baptism."[46] Before becoming an Anabaptist himself, Rinck evidently shared Müntzer's conviction that there was no biblical basis for infant baptism. Müntzer may not have proceeded to affirm or practice believers baptism, but Rinck did.

As noted, his first tract was a response to Johannes Bader's unwelcome defense of infant baptism. In this he addressed Bader's arguments in turn, refuting them and explaining why infant baptism was so problematic.[47] The themes in this tract would reappear both in his later writings and in the testimonies of his followers and colleagues.

Bader, according to Rinck, "acknowledges the innocence of children" yet still argued for infant baptism. Rinck regarded this as "astounding," given that baptism was "for those who are guilty of sinning" and who confessed their guilt and received forgiveness. Since infants were unable to seek forgiveness, and were in any case innocent of sin, infant baptism made no sense. He challenged Bader to demonstrate that infants could be held accountable and could possess faith, urging him to discuss their spiritual state with their parents. If he was unwilling to do this and could not show that they had faith, baptizing them was wrong and promising salvation for infants on the basis of their being baptized was contrary to biblical teaching. Rinck was evidently amazed that his opponent could hold such views in the face of biblical teaching and common sense.

Bader had asserted that outer baptism was not bound to the inner, because only God was a discerner of hearts. Since human beings could not know the state of each other's hearts or be sure that repentance was genuine, linking outer baptism with inner baptism (being in a right relationship with God) was presumptuous. The practice of infant baptism required no such presumed discernment. Rinck dismissed this argument with reference to the classic baptismal texts (Matt 28 and Mark 16), quoted frequently by the Anabaptists, which provided authority from Christ to baptize on the basis of confession of faith. The practice of believers baptism linked knowledge, faith, and commitment, whereas Bader's position meant baptizing "innocent infants against their knowledge and will"—forced baptism—as well as being "outside the commandment of Christ."

Rinck was deeply unimpressed by Bader's attempt (shared with many of the reformers) to compare baptism to circumcision, and he advanced two arguments against this. First, circumcision was an old covenant rite, whereas the baptism of believers was established by Christ as a sign of the new covenant. Christians were to be disciples of Christ, not of Moses. Second, the rite of circumcision was a "sign of the yoke of servitude" and "a work of law that is devoid of faith," whereas baptism "is a sign and confession of the childlike covenant, under which no one is to be either coerced or pressured through the force of compulsion." Circumcision symbolized the yoking of people to the law, whereas baptism symbolized a free relationship between human beings and God. Voluntarism was an essential aspect of the Anabaptists' understanding of baptism. The phrase "childlike covenant" is significant. In his later writings, Rinck would contrast natural children with spiritual children. Although he did not elaborate further on the phrase here, it seems to imply that baptism is for those who receive Christ with childlike faith, rather than for literal infants.

Bader had demanded "an explicit proscription" from Scripture against infant baptism, but Rinck gave this short shrift. Referring again to Matt 28, he argued that the command of Christ in relation to baptizing believers was clear and permitted no deviation. Bader needed nothing further except to listen to Christ. Infant baptism was a purely human invention with no biblical warrant. Actually, Rinck continued, it was worse than this—it was sinful, because it did not "proceed from faith," and it was the mark of the beast to which Rev 13 referred. Rinck would expand on this in his later writings.

Bader's final argument was that the Anabaptists were distorting the Evangelical gospel by claiming that "baptism makes people perfect." Rinck told Bader he should be ashamed of making such a false claim. He insisted that the crucial issue was not baptism (hundreds of baptisms will not save people), but faith in Christ, and that baptism was for those who had faith and "desire to follow" Christ. He concluded by warning Bader that he risked eternal consequences if he continued to defend infant baptism and to promise salvation to those baptized as infants. Those who did this, he wrote with reference to Paul's criticism of the Galatians that they were preaching another gospel, were "under the curse and malediction, and have no part in Christ." Rinck's perspective on this subject could not be more serious.

In his letter to Eberhard von der Tann in 1530, defending himself against accusations that he was still committed to the revolutionary agenda of the peasants' movement, Rinck listed the oppressive ways in which he and his followers were being treated by the authorities: "They strive to coerce me and all who share my faith into accepting their lies—through murder, theft, prison, fire, water, the sword, and other such arguments." He concluded that these false accusations and threats of persecution demonstrated that "it is *their* baptism which is anti-baptist, and it is *they* who are actually the Antichrist about whom all prophets, Christ, and the apostles have previously spoken."[48] Rinck seems to mean that their behavior showed that what they regarded as baptism, namely infant baptism, was illegitimate and produced evil consequences. Calling the practice of infant baptism "anti-baptism" ingeniously turned the accusation of re-baptizing back on his opponents.

Shortly after this, Rinck composed a short tract on the subject of baptism, in which he said nothing about believers baptism but argued passionately against infant baptism. He had evidently been challenged by his opponents on the basis of Christ's command to "let the little children come to me, and do not hinder them" (Mark 10:14 NIV), because this verse heads the tract. Rinck immediately countered their argument that this implied baptizing infants with arguments of his own.[49]

First, he insisted that children who were too young to respond to the gospel could not exercise faith and so should not be baptized: "One cannot preach to them, nor can they listen." Second, as young children had no knowledge of good and evil, they could not be condemned for unbelief any more than they could be saved by faith. Third, as those who received infant baptism were given false confidence that they had received the blessing of salvation, those who practiced infant baptism were not demonstrating love for children but hatred, presenting them "not to Christ but to Belial." Fourth, the practice of infant baptism served to "retain and perpetuate . . . their false Christendom." Satan knew that if infant baptism were to be abolished, "it would become obvious that his gospel and Christendom are a groveling abomination." Fifth, infant baptism meant that the state churches were full of people who were actually enemies of Christ, who had learned from a young age how these churches operated and so were ideally positioned to damage them.

Using the images of a city with enemies within and a sheepfold with wolves, lions, and bears among the sheep, Rinck acknowledged that state church leaders were taking action to deal with this issue by attempting to reform the church, but castigated them for asking the civic authorities to help them with "that which they cannot do themselves" and for failing to recognize that this was a problem that "infant baptism has brought into being."

In his *Admonition*, Rinck used even more inflammatory language,[50] arguing that those who practiced and defended infant baptism were behaving idolatrously, since they "have paid homage not to Christ, who is God, but rather to the pope and Antichrist, albeit under the name of Christ." He and his colleagues were messengers from God, calling people back to proper baptismal practice and true worship. If the magistrates opposed this, they were placing themselves in danger of judgment. Actually, if they paid attention only to the clear teaching of Scripture, the magistrates should have approved of believers baptism, as those being baptized in this way were demonstrating their obedience to the One from whom they themselves derived legitimacy as magistrates. As Geldbach writes, making explicit what Rinck's argument implies, "Baptism, therefore, should be viewed positively by Caesar since the baptizand, through baptism, renders obedience to the Lord of the worldly magistracy."[51]

Rinck characterized believers baptism as a wedding ceremony in which "the church now weds itself only to its true bridegroom, Christ." But infant baptism, which was not authorized by the Scriptures, was "a banquet with the great whore, the Antichrist." This was not a legitimate marriage but fornication or prostitution. Anyone baptized as an infant, who wanted to be truly married to Christ, the bridegroom, should be baptized as a believer in order to regularize their sinful relationship through a proper ceremony.

Changing the imagery, he further described believers baptism as "a ceremony in which the person, upon the requirement and power of faith, yields self to God as a sacrifice." In the case of infant baptism, however, the child was offered "to the devil, even if it took place under the name of God," just as in times gone by "the Jews offered their children to demons." Rinck was outraged by this, referring to those who advocated infant baptism as "murderers, whores and Baal—that is, the whole jumble of muck and horror," charging the reformers with setting themselves up against God and charging the magistrates with supporting this stance.

These tracts gave Rinck an opportunity to state again his views on infant baptism, which he had rehearsed in other settings. The subject of baptism had been one of the main topics in the debate at Marburg in 1528.[52] In his opening remarks, Raidt complained that Rinck had baptized some of his followers, "as if infant baptism should not be considered [a proper] baptism." After this, seven of Raidt's twelve articles (the second, third, fourth, fifth, sixth, ninth, and tenth) all dealt with infant baptism in one form or other. The second, third, and fourth articles explored what Rinck was accused of teaching about original sin and the status of infants. According to Raidt, Rinck had taught that "original sin from Adam damns no one until a person reaches accountability and willingly sins." Therefore, infants "before the age of accountability, and before they consciously enter into sin, are neither just nor unjust, neither redeemed nor unredeemed, but rather carry within themselves from the time of birth, good and evil seed." The sixth article returned to this issue, broadening the focus, reporting that Rinck taught that all the biblical verses about sin and judgment did not apply to infants. Rinck accepted these articles as stating accurately what he taught.

The fifth article charged Rinck with teaching that those who were baptized as infants did not receive Christ but rather received the devil. Rinck denied he had said this but said that he wanted an opportunity to dispute Luther's teaching on this subject. However, there is evidence in his writings that Rinck did use this kind of inflammatory language, which no doubt appeared in his preaching as well. The ninth article repeated this accusation in other words: Rinck taught, Raidt charged, that "in baptism all children are offered to the devil, and all those who take communion are receiving a devil." Rinck denied the second part of this charge but confessed his belief that "children who are baptized are being offered to the devil."

Finally, the tenth article again set out Rinck's primary objections to infant baptism: that infants were unaware of good and evil, could not respond to the preaching of the gospel, and so could not repent. Since repentance was essential for true baptism, infant baptism was wrong—in fact, blasphemous. Raidt went on, though, to explain that from Rinck's perspective it was not enough to refrain from baptizing infants: those who had been baptized as infants needed to renounce this and receive true baptism as believers. Rinck was charged with teaching that "it is necessary that a person submit to [adult] baptism, thereby forsaking the first baptism, and then confess anew as if it [the baptism] had just now occurred." Rinck accepted that this was what he taught.

When Rinck was invited to present his own articles, the fourth set out his understanding of baptism. This was the article that formed the crux of the disputation. His first three articles were accepted as orthodox after some discussion and his fifth on the subject of the Lord's Supper was not discussed in light of the theologians' decision that his fourth article must be rejected. That article referred to a mix of Old and New Testament verses and argued that the baptism of infants was wrong for three reasons: "children are without guilt of sin, even though they were born in original sin"; "they are also without faith"; and "infant baptism is truly against John the Baptist's baptism." In this article Rinck repeated his criticisms of infant baptism and urged his opponents to be guided by the teaching of Jesus and the example of John the Baptist, both of whom had called for repentance and changed lives as a prerequisite for baptism.

Testimonies from Rinck's followers in the Vacha hearing contain similar arguments and provide evidence of other aspects of Rinck's teaching on this issue.[53] Adam Angersbach recalled taking a child to be baptized when the state church was still Catholic and hearing the priest insist that godparents were needed if he were to baptize the child, since baptism depended on the faith of the godparents. Angersbach regarded this as unsatisfactory, placing too much emphasis on the godparents. But he also criticized the unsatisfactory halfway house that Lutheranism occupied, with its emphasis on saving faith that sat uncomfortably with infant baptism. He complained that "[even] if they knew children did not have their own faith, they still wanted to baptize them." Several times, according to the official record, he referred specifically to what Rinck had taught as the authority for his views. "Melchior Rinck taught them that infant baptism was a human statute, arranged by the pope, at the time when clergy were forbidden to marry." As a human institution introduced at a time when the church was enforcing other unbiblical practices, this had no authority and was deeply suspect.

Angersbach also repeated arguments against infant baptism that Rinck had presented on many occasions. Quoting the familiar baptismal texts from the end of Mark's Gospel, he recalled Rinck's insistence that instruction and faith must precede baptism. "Melchior Rinck taught him that he needs to be instructed ahead of time by God, for faith comes from hearing." His response to Rinck's teaching was to reject the legitimacy of his own baptism as an infant: "since baptism without faith is nothing, therefore he had no report or knowledge of his having faith or having a clear conscience before God." He "had experienced no abstaining from sin" as a result of his infant baptism—and the same was true of others. Angersbach also echoed Rinck's argument that infants have not willfully committed any sins and so "they have no need of baptism." And he offered another argument not found in Rinck's extant writings, asking, perhaps mischievously, why communion was denied to infants if sacramental acts were efficacious in themselves. And should baptized infants also be expected to pay their tithes?

Hans Werner also recalled Rinck saying that "infant baptism was conceived by Satan and mankind in the era when clergy were forbidden to marry." Like Angersbach, Werner insisted that "children have no sin until the time when they will to sin" and that "children have no faith, therefore they are not to be baptized." Infant baptism is both unnecessary if children have no sin and inappropriate if they have no faith. He continued that children are not Christians but needed to be taught the Scriptures so that faith can grow and then they can be baptized. His wife, Greta, insisted that Scripture taught believers baptism and that young children were not contaminated by original sin because they did not consciously sin. After persistent interrogation, she finally declared that she accepted the validity of child baptism as long as it was understood that the godparents were exercising their own faith, since they could not believe for the children. But Kat Hill comments: "Greta had also clearly adopted many of the Anabaptist views on human nature: original sin did not damage anyone and children knew nothing of sin.

Whether she really did value infant baptism or sought to appease her interrogators remains obscure."[54]

Heinz Ot followed Rinck's teaching that an infant was neither damned nor saved until the child reached the age of accountability. He argued that Christ had "blotted out" original sin on the cross and taken it away, so that infant baptism was not needed for this purpose. He also seems to have espoused a form of dualism, stating that any person who "comes to knowledge has two spirits: one which is good, the other evil. The good spirit stirs one to do good, the evil, to do evil." Although Anabaptists acknowledged that temptation was an ever-present reality and the struggle against sin was life-long, unlike the Lutherans they rejected the notion that children had "damning sin."[55]

Some of those questioned in the Berka hearing expressed strong opposition to infant baptism.[56] Gela and Hans Zwingen were so averse to allowing their young child to be baptized that they had arranged for him to stay elsewhere. Heinz Cleue presented three familiar arguments against infant baptism: "First of all, he held infant baptism to be wrong for the reason that nowhere did God command that infants be baptized; second, that infants are not able to believe; third, that infants are blessed and saved without [infant baptism]." Hans Kessel repeated the last two points and described infant baptism as "an abomination and atrocity in the eyes of God, out of which nothing good has ever come, but rather all forms of sin." Peter Leinweber simply asserted that infant baptism was wrong because Christ had not commanded it. This was the main argument of Hans Heylman, although he added that only those who had been brought to faith should be baptized—and that infants could not believe. Lentz Rüdiger and Margret Kessel agreed that infants could not believe but assured their interrogators that the innocence of infants meant their salvation was assured. Elsa Erben argued that infant baptism was wrong because Jesus was not baptized until he was thirty-three years old. Others repeated these familiar arguments or simply stated that infant baptism was wrong, without offering reasons. Only Hermann Adam was less dogmatic, saying that he respected those who were satisfied with infant baptism but that he himself was not at peace with this.

Others took the fight to their interrogators. Heinz Kraut and Hans Peissker told Melanchthon: "No infant, whether heathen, Turk or

Christian would be damned. God would never damn an infant because of the absence of what they contemptuously called a little water."[57]

Mark 16:16—"Whoever believes and is baptized will be saved" (NIV)—seems to have been Rinck's favorite baptismal text (rather than the Matthean passage). It appears frequently in the testimonies of Rinck's followers and colleagues, including Angersbach, Werner, von Ostheim, and Schnabel (and of many other Anabaptists), offered as conclusive New Testament evidence against infant baptism. The ordering was regarded as all-important: belief precedes baptism. As this was impossible for infants, they should not be baptized. Schnabel insisted in the 1538 debate with Bucer: "The teaching of the gospel is that men are first to be convicted of their sin, afterwards they are incorporated in the fellowship of the holy church; which [ordinance] you let fall when you baptize infants." He added provocatively, "Since then the ordinance of the apostles isn't to be kept, baptize the children and let it stay that way, teach no repentance and improvement."[58] Schnabel rejected the attempt of Bucer to persuade him that infant baptism was analogous to circumcision or that little children were baptized in the time of the apostles. He declared, "I prefer to stand by what I am sure about, namely, that the apostles baptized those who repented. I prefer to let go points on which I am uncertain."[59]

It is clear from Rinck's use of this text in the Marburg disputation and elsewhere that his followers had picked this up from Rinck himself. Hill concludes: "A pragmatic sense of small children's limited capabilities underpinned Anabaptist theology."[60]

Believers baptism

Although Rinck wrote less about believers baptism than against infant baptism, there is no doubt that what he regarded as true baptism was fundamentally important to him. This was what created a community of faithful followers of Jesus—a community comprised only of those who had repented of their sins, received God's forgiveness, committed themselves to Christ for the future, and received baptism as a mark of this commitment. A community made up of such people would be markedly different from the state churches. Furthermore, Rinck insisted, the baptism of believers was biblically mandated, whereas infant baptism was not.

Rinck's most basic rationale for believers baptism was obedience to the commandment of Christ in the frequently quoted Mark 16:16—"believe and be baptized" (in that order) or less often Matt 28:19–20. He regarded this as the minimum obedience that Christ required of any who would be his followers. Baptism was the crucial point in the process of becoming his disciples. Rinck insisted in the Marburg debate that only those should be baptized who showed convincing evidence of repentance and changed behavior. He declared that baptism was for those who "mend their ways, quit sinning, desire to repent, believe in the forgiveness of sins," and demonstrate this openly by the way they live.[61] Although it is understandable that his opponents might have interpreted his teaching as a return to salvation by works or even (as Bader charged) an expectation of post-baptismal perfection, this does not seem to have been Rinck's intention. Just as John the Baptist urged his hearers to "produce fruit in keeping with repentance" (Luke 3:8 NIV), so Rinck looked for evidence that people were serious about being disciples before baptizing them.

His followers frequently followed Rinck's lead in stating that they had received baptism in response to Christ's command or following his example.[62] Heinz Ot testified in the Vacha hearing that he had been "taught by Brother Melchior" with hundreds of writings and had been persuaded by comparing Rinck's teaching with the Scriptures and finding that these were aligned. Greta Werner said that, like her husband, Hans, she wanted to follow Christ's example. Referring to the pleasure expressed by God the Father at the baptism of Jesus, she explained that she "could not understand otherwise" than that her baptism as a believer was similarly pleasing to God. She added that in the book of Acts, only adults were baptized. Adam Angersbach testified that "his conscience did not have any instruction other than the command of Christ, and the correct, veracious teaching, and he submitted to baptism." Bilg Scherer also testified that "his conscience had not taught him otherwise" and recalled that Brother Melchior had taught that baptism should be undertaken as "a command of Christ" but "not for the sake of salvation or for the forgiveness of sins" (for it did not guarantee salvation of the soul) and "out of love and obedience to the command of God, upon the goodness of Christ."

However, baptism was not simply a matter of obedience to the biblical command. Adam Angersbach referred to baptism as "a covenant of a good conscience with Christ, among people who begin a good life and desire to abstain from sin." And Hans Werner used a similar phrase (as did his wife), no doubt derived from Rinck's teaching, that, although "baptism does not save," it was "a covenant of a good conscience with Christ, out of which good and blessedness follow those who have faith and who abstain from sin."

Rinck seems to have experienced the power of baptism himself, writing from prison in 1530 that he and his fellow prisoner "hope to remain [true] to the end to both teachings—baptism and the Supper of Christ—and to remain true to Him in all other things, through the support and help of God."[63]

Oyer summarizes the significance Rinck saw in believers baptism. "It had both a two-fold ceremonial character and a two-fold meaning. Ceremonially it represented man's death with Christ and also his marriage with Christ, the Bridegroom. Rink believed that baptism both sealed one's confession of faith and also was a promise on the part of the candidate to follow Christ in holiness of life and also in death if necessary."[64] In relation to this twofold meaning, Rinck seems (if Menius is to be trusted) to have differentiated John's baptism, which was about repentance, from Christ's baptism, which was about being buried with Christ and about surrender and loving obedience. As noted above, he wrote in the *Admonition*: "Baptism is a ceremony in which the person . . . yields self to God as a sacrifice." Not all his followers made this connection between baptism and suffering, according to Cornelius Dyck: "In Thuringia, baptism also signified the acceptance of future suffering. By contrast, some Anabaptist statements notably did not emphasize suffering." He gives as an example "those made by . . . Rinck's disciples in the environs of Vacha in 1531."[65] But Adam Angersbach had clearly picked up this teaching from Rinck, writing that "true baptism follows the cross" and noting that many brothers and sisters had gone to their death as a result, "witnessing, on account of such baptism, with their blood."[66]

In relation to the twofold ceremony, it seems that Rinck regarded the congregation, not just the person being baptized, as the bride, introducing a corporate dimension to the ceremony. Believers baptism created a community that was committed to purity and faithfulness; not a perfect community but a disciplined community, and a community on which the Holy Spirit had been poured out. A persistent criticism of Anabaptism in the sixteenth century and since has been the way in which this tradition is perceived to be advocating an unattainable pure church. Rinck and his followers undoubtedly held to a high view of the church and discipleship, but they were not perfectionists or unrealistic about the flaws and failings of individuals and communities, as evidenced by the role of church discipline in their teaching and congregations.

In his summary of Anabaptist beliefs in 1538, Jörg Schnabel wrote that baptism was

> a bath of rebirth (Titus 3:5), which keeps us and makes us holy, and a covenant of a good conscience with God through the resurrection of Jesus Christ. (1. Pet 3:21), a washing away and forgiveness of sins (Acts 2:38, 22:16). Item, it is a burial with Christ (Rom 6:4; Col 2:12) in his death, so that the dead person [i.e., a person dead to sin] allows himself to be buried and separated from the company of the living in the world. Item, it is the incorporation of the body of Jesus Christ, that is, in the community of the saints [i.e., those of a righteous life], so that the baptized person becomes one body with them.[67]

As for the mode of baptism, nothing is known about Rinck's practice, but it may well have been in line with what is known of the baptismal practices of other Anabaptists in the region. This involved an interview with the person coming for baptism, in which he or she would share their testimony and commit themselves to Christ and the community, after which the candidate would kneel and the person performing the baptism would dip a finger in water and make a sign of the cross on the candidate's forehead, baptizing in the name of the Father, the Son and the Holy Spirit. This was followed by encouragement to be faithful and to submit to the discipline of the community.[68]

THE LORD'S SUPPER

Although Rinck was particularly outraged by the practice of infant baptism and its malign implications for discipleship and ecclesiology, he also objected strongly, if not as often in his extant writings, to the way in which the Lord's Supper was understood and practiced in the Catholic and Lutheran churches.

As noted above in relation to his hermeneutics, Rinck rejected the Catholic doctrine of the "real presence" of Christ in the bread and wine and the way in which the Lutherans interpreted this in their churches. He insisted that the presence of Christ could not be restricted to sanctified bread in a communion service, for God was omnipresent, and he taught that attempting to make an image of God from material things was idolatry. In his tract on marriage, he complained about the priests' "idol of bread."[69]

Rinck's teaching on this subject was one of the main concerns of his opponents. Eberhard von der Tann, writing to Elector John in 1531, noted that, as well as opposing infant baptism, Rinck adhered to a "seductive, onerous error against the holy sacrament of the body of Christ."[70] This had been one of the topics in the Marburg disputation,[71] when Rinck was interrogated in relation to his doctrinal teachings, especially concerning his position on "the sacraments of baptism and the altar." Raidt's eleventh article stated that Rinck had "persuaded several people at Hersfeld that Christ's body and blood are not present in the sacrament of the altar, who then spewed blasphemous words against it to the dismay of many people." However, we should note that this was the only article in which this topic was addressed, after several that explored Rinck's teaching on baptism, and that the article does not report Rinck using the extreme language he used in relation to baptism.

In response, Rinck said that he did not remember teaching that "the body and blood of Christ are not present in the sacrament of the altar," but he was open to challenge on this if anyone had evidence to the contrary. However, he acknowledged this was his view and that he might have spoken about it somewhere! He wanted an opportunity to demonstrate to the theologians in Marburg that "Luther in this case is teaching erroneously" and that his own position was correct. He continued in his own fifth article: "Whoever says that Christ declared his natural and adopted body and blood to be in bread and wine as food and drink is truly against Christ, John 6, and cannot maintain such an interpretation with divine and unfalsified scripture."

Rinck wrote a tract on the subject of the Lord's Supper,[72] but this is not extant, so it is unclear what he taught positively on the subject. From the testimonies of his followers, it seems that, expounding the teaching of Jesus in John 6 about "the true bread," he argued that apostolic preaching and the outpouring of the Spirit constituted the "real presence" of Christ among humanity. He may have taught that Christ was present whenever believers shared bread together in everyday meals. And there is some, although limited, evidence that he regarded the practice of the Lord's Supper as of secondary importance or perhaps a mystery that should be taught mainly to those who were more mature in faith. This is the impression given by his brief contribution on this subject in the Marburg disputation. His fifth article sets out his position but deals only briefly with the subject, and when he was given an opportunity to expand on this the court records say that "he did not want to dispute or clarify his position concerning the fifth article." This seems surprising given his earlier request to explain his view, but by that point the debate had moved on. Having been found at fault in relation to his teaching on baptism in his fourth article, the Marburg theologians were not interested in further debating the fifth article.

His followers, however, were often questioned on this issue. Not all of the accused in the Berka hearing gave reasons for their beliefs.[73] Anna Leinweber, Hans Heylman, Barbara Adam, Hans Zwingen, Katharina Young, Könne Wilhelm, and Hans Cleue simply said that they did not accept the "real presence" in communion. Hans Kessel offered a reason: he "does not believe that Christ's flesh and blood are in the Lord's Supper, saying that one can see what body and blood are; since, however, one cannot see [body and blood in the sacrament], so [body and blood] can [not] be therein." Margret Schneider argued similarly, as did Peter Leinweber: "As for the Lord's Supper he says that bread is bread, wine is wine, and Christ did not place his body and blood in the elements, since one can neither see nor taste these." Margret Kessel insisted that if Christ is in heaven, no human being can bring him into the bread and wine. Lenz Rüdiger expressed agreement with this position but added (perhaps in line with Rinck's teaching) that he understood Christ's command to "do this in remembrance of me" to apply to "any eating and drinking."

These brief statements are rather more definite than the responses of those questioned in the earlier hearing of the twelve arrested with Rinck at Vacha.[74] The record of that hearing states, in relation to questions on the Lord's Supper, that his followers "all answered that they have not yet been well taught" and that they regarded this as "a great mystery of God." Nevertheless, two of them offered comments, representing their views as having been learned from Rinck's teaching or writings. They did not, however, speak with one voice, which may indicate that this had not been a subject on which Rinck had yet taught much. Indeed, Hans Werner testified to this effect—that "Brother Melchior has not wanted to teach anything concerning the Lord's Supper." It seems what united them—that this was "a great mystery"—reflected Rinck's own perspective. Werner reported that "Brother Melchior holds it to be a high mystery and work."

Werner considered the Lord's Supper to be a sacrament (as did Adam Angersbach in a passing reference) and said that "whoever is worthy in his heart may receive it," adding that he believed himself to be unworthy to do so (or possibly Rinck or others had made this assessment). Heinz Ot, on the other hand, who spoke at greater length on the subject and insisted on referring to the Lord's Supper as "the breaking of bread," was clear that this was not a sacrament and did not convey forgiveness of sins. This statement seems to have provoked the interrogators to question him further. Ot rejected the notion that God could be bound to a particular loaf as if this were an image and declared that "God is in one loaf of bread just as he is also in another loaf—just as he is otherwise also in other creatures." God is the one who breaks the bread, not the bread itself. Referring to John 6 and to the writings of Rinck on the subject, Ot emphasized that the life of God is received by believers through preaching and the work of the Spirit, rather than the act of eating bread. He concluded that what was celebrated in the state churches of his day was not truly the Lord's Supper and pointed back to the practice of the apostles, who broke bread in each other's homes and accompanied this with preaching.

Reviewing the evidence, Ellen Yutzy Glebe comments: "An insistence on a symbolic presence of Christ in the elements of communion was one of the most consistent claims of Hessian Anabaptists in interrogations."[75] They also complained that the sacrament was misused by the state churches because of the lack of church discipline. Schnabel told Bucer: "That they misuse it, and that in disorderly manner, has been exposed to the light of day; for they use it with drunkards, usurers, and harlots."[76]

It seems that at least some of the Hessian Anabaptists abandoned the Lord's Supper. Two comments from the Berka hearing may point in this direction. Hans Cleue stated that he was unaware that the Anabaptists were observing the Lord's Supper and Hans Kessel insisted that "whoever is living out God's righteousness is eating his body and drinking his blood."[77] This may well sum up their reticence about participating in the state church practice, but it could equally mean that they imbued many domestic meals with spiritual significance, especially if these meals were accompanied by biblical teaching. As Dyck concludes, their approach may have been that "one might as well recite the words of the institution whenever one had food and drink."[78]

ECCLESIOLOGY

Apart from his teaching on baptism and the Lord's Supper, Rinck seems not to have said much about the nature of the church. This may have been because he was an evangelist rather than a congregation-builder. Oyer comments: "His doctrine called for the creation of a highly disciplined brotherhood; but he was not the man to develop such a body."[79]

However, in his critique of the secular authorities claiming jurisdiction over spiritual matters, he presented an understanding of leadership in the congregations that involved election by the community, accountability to this community, and an absence of clerical control. He was deeply critical of any attempt by priests to introduce or oversee practices that were not, in his view, biblically authorized. He charged those who did this, whether in relation to infant baptism, the mass or wedding ceremonies, with "setting themselves above God and Christ."[80] He spelled out a more egalitarian approach to congregational leadership: "If anyone among you desires to be a bishop or teacher, such a person shall not govern the church with his own teachings. He shall neither introduce nor maintain his own teachings with coercion. But he is solely a servant of the church, whose teachings the church may judge, rejecting or accepting [the same]."[81] It seems that, as in other branches of the Anabaptist movement, Rinck's churches operated as hermeneutical communities, in which teachings were discussed and other perspectives than that of a single authoritative teacher were welcomed.

Rinck's ecclesiology was integrally connected to his understanding of baptism. He was passionately committed to a church that was free from state control and made up of those who took discipleship seriously. He argued so strongly against infant baptism on the grounds that this practice undermined both of these ecclesial goals. Only the baptism of believers could provide a secure basis for a free church of would-be disciples.

DISCIPLESHIP

Discipleship was of fundamental importance to Rinck, as to other Anabaptists. Oyer writes: "In Rinck's surviving works, or the testimonies of his followers, one encounters much more emphasis on ethics than on soteriology."[82] Following and imitating Christ were at the heart of their faith. Sanctification could not be separated from justification. Faith must bear fruit. This was the basis of their persistent critique of the Lutheran churches and the teaching of their theologians and preachers: their doctrine could not be true if it produced so little fruit. Rinck concluded in his tract on marriage that their works "everywhere give evidence that the masters are neither God nor Christ but Satan and the Antichrist."[83] Indeed, their emphasis on justification and their rejection of anything that might imply salvation by works seemed to have resulted, according to Rinck and others, in the lifestyle of many Lutherans being more corrupt than that of the Catholics.

It was the commitment of the Anabaptists to serious discipleship that attracted others to their communities. An Anabaptist called Adrian testified that God had mercifully led him to the Anabaptists when he despaired of the sinfulness of those around him.[84] And Adam Angersbach testified that he had found such purity of life and earnest efforts to abstain from sin among the Anabaptists that he had become a follower of Rinck. Quoting the teaching of Jesus that false teachers and false prophets will be known by the fruit they produce, Angersbach told the hearing at Vacha that the Lutheran preachers had clearly demonstrated by their licentious lives that their teaching was false, whereas

Rinck had lived in such a way that he "could not help but recognize—that [Rinck] has been teaching the truth." Angersbach had committed himself to "living out the divine good, abstaining from cursing, gluttony, boozing, and other sins."[85]

Rinck and his followers embraced the notion of *Gelassenheit,* understanding this as the readiness to suffer the loss of all things, resignation to the will of God, renunciation not only of sin but of attachment to material goods and selfish desires. This is the meaning of Rinck's acknowledgment in the Marburg disputation that "repudiation and rejection of his endeavors" were nonnegotiable accompaniments of true faith in Christ. He insisted that "there is no creature who is of service and useful unto Christ, leading to salvation, unless there follows in the heart a willing unmindfulness and yieldedness [*Gelassenheit*] in all things."[86] This yieldedness was a gift of God, not a human accomplishment. Some of the testimonies of his followers also made reference to *Gelassenheit*—unsurprisingly, since this term was widespread among German Anabaptists. Angersbach testified that Rinck had been "teaching them about *Gelassenheit,* that is, that one must yield oneself completely before God, not connecting one's own life and heart to the temporal; that a person who loves something more than Christ is not worthy of him; and that one must avoid sinning and resist the devil and evil."[87]

One aspect of *Gelassenheit* was open-handedness with possessions and readiness to share one's resources with those in need. To the Hutterites this meant community of goods and the abolition of private property, but that was not how Rinck and his followers interpreted this. That became clear when exiled members of the Sorga congregation in Moravia were unwilling to accept community of goods, even though the Hutterites claimed that Rinck had advocated this practice. But it is also clear from the interrogations of members of the congregations in both Berka and Sorga that they rejected any notion of an absolute right over their own property and that they shared their resources very extensively. It seems that they could echo the testimony of the early church in Jerusalem that "no one claimed private ownership of any possessions" (Acts 4:32), even if they did not actually pool all their possessions and resources.

Not all of those interrogated at Berka expressed opinions on this issue. According to the report of the proceedings, Hermann Adam refused to be drawn on what he believed about this matter. Others did not address it at all. Those who did respond espoused divergent convictions. Heinz Cleue asserted that a Christian could own a house and farm. Margret Schneider also assumed that individual possession of property was allowed, but said that "Christians are to have all possessions in common, where one may partake of the other's possessions to meet one's own needs." Könne Wilhelm, on the other hand, said that a Christian "is not to own possessions on earth." Hans Heylman agreed: "A Christian is not to own anything, but those who desire to be true Christians need to hold all possessions in common, and if a prince enters their order [i.e., their community of faith], he also needs to hold all possessions in common." Others presenting this more radical position were Margret Kessel, who stated that "all possessions among Christians are to be held in common," and Hans Kessel, who declared: "No Christian dare own property." Anna Leinweber, similarly, testified that she had been taught that "Christians are to have and utilize all possessions in common." This was also the belief of Katharina Young. Others, it seems, held simply that Christians were expected to help other members of their community in times of need. Lentz Rüdiger insisted that "a Christian is obligated to help another person with his own [possessions]," but Peter Leinweber limited this to other members of his congregation: "All who hold to his views and faith have as much right to his possessions as he does. He did not share [in this manner] with others."[88] Glebe concludes that "there is little evidence of a consensus on the issue of community of goods"[89] in the Berka community, although it seems that most of those who answered this question presented views that were radical enough to worry the authorities.

At the Sorga hearings, the interrogators asked whether a Christian could own property and whether it was lawful to seize the property of another person in cases of need. The responses varied, although the majority said they should not seize goods from others.[90] The minority view was that "if someone is a proper Christian, he will take nothing more than he needs."[91] On the owning of property, Greta and Hans Plat represented the most common reply—that a Christian might "own property but yet should act as if he had none, and that no one should own possessions." Similarly, Else and Hen Lutz and Cunz and Gele Hutter all testified that Christians could have possessions but that "they should not place too much importance on them" (or that "they should remain *gelassen*"). And the group's leader, Gilg, and his wife Anna, said: "[As for] having, or not having possessions, they hold nothing as their own as long as this is pleasing to God. But when God or a neighbor requests, then they give it over." Elsa and Hans Koch, Heinz and Konne Hutter, Groschen and Margarethe (surname unknown), and Catharina and Heinrich Lutz all endorsed mutual aid rather than community of goods. But Elsa and Hans Zisen rejected private property, since in their view "a Christian should not own anything, for he needs simply to be like Christ." On whether it was legitimate to seize the property of others in case of need, Hans said it was not, but Elsa said it was. Endres Lober was also willing to accept that in cases of need it was right to take another's possessions. He accepted that one could own possessions, but said these must be available to those in need. Hen Schmidt disagreed, insisting that consent was needed if another's possessions were to be taken.[92]

James Stayer writes: "Having as not having, having with *Gelassenheit*, acting as stewards for the needy, is the common denominator of the apparent contradictions in the statements of these Sorga Anabaptists."[93] As very little on this subject appears in his extant writings, Rinck's teaching on possessions can mainly be discerned from the testimonies of his followers and the practices of his congregations. However, Stayer identifies comments that offer at least indirect evidence of Rinck's views. He notes Rinck's insistence that "anyone who has authority in the congregation of Christ must be the servant of all, unlike worldly rulers who 'own their subject as slave and property, to dispose of like their inheritance according to their pleasure or arbitrary will' . . . Christian princes should not behave in such a way with the Christian congregation and its possessions."[94]

And in his brief tract on baptism, Rinck also criticized the Lutheran "hypocrites and scribes" for professing love for the infants they wanted to baptize, whereas, in fact, they were "precisely the ones who devour and fatten themselves with the bread that rightly belongs to the children and to the poor orphans."[95] Heinz Ot was equally trenchant in his critique of those who had land and possessions, warning that their economic practices "could be dangerous and onerous in damaging the neighbor," accusing them of looting the poor.[96] There was evidently concern for social justice in Rinck's communities, and it seems clear that this derived from Rinck's teaching.

There is also a comment in a letter from Eberhard von der Tann, sent immediately after the interrogation of Rinck and others at Vacha. We cannot be sure whether this is a fair representation of Rinck's teaching or exactly what this implies, but von der Tann claimed that Rinck desired "to introduce here on earth a fictive equality and fellowship of all people and possessions." Interestingly, he felt obliged to acknowledge that equality was something "which we hold and anticipate to be Christian," but he insisted that this was to be experienced only in "the future life."[97]

Although usury is not mentioned in the Berka or Sorga hearings, the attention given to the issue by Schnabel in the 1538 Marburg debate with Bucer may indicate that this was another common Anabaptist critique of the practice of the state churches. In his summary of Anabaptist beliefs in 1538, Schnabel also explained that "the community of goods among believers is constituted in this way: each one willingly assists his poor brother with what is superfluous in food as is needed."[98] He denied that this meant goods were taken without consent or that wives were shared in common.

Menius ignored the variation in Anabaptist teaching and practice. In his 1530 treatise he wrote that the Anabaptists "rejected private property and insisted on holding all material things in common. Indeed, they went so far as to deny themselves the right to 'own' a wife. Some even took the next step . . . and held wives in common." Oyer comments: "He had more direct evidence for the charge of abandoning wives. Rink had done this."[99]

Another implication of *Gelassenheit* was nonresistance and willingness to suffer for their faith. Understandably, in light of the recent peasants' movement and the suspected involvement of some Anabaptists in this, the authorities frequently interrogated members of Anabaptist communities, sometimes under torture, on this point and on their attitude to civil authorities. This will be considered further below. But it seems that Rinck and his followers had renounced the violence associated with the final stages of the peasants' movement, even if some were reluctant to disavow its aims and their involvement in it. And, for many of them, suffering and martyrdom were expectations that they regarded as consequences of faithful discipleship. As in other branches of the Anabaptist movement, the experience of suffering was interpreted as evidence that their teaching was true and that they belonged to the true church. Quoting Matt 10:17–18 in his tract on marriage, Rinck identified himself and his followers with those who were persecuted for the sake of Christ. And, in his accompanying letter to Eberhard von der Tann, as already noted, he complained that he and his colleagues were being threatened with prison, fire, water, and the sword. This, he concluded, was evidence that they were "the Antichrist about whom all prophets, Christ and the apostles have previously spoken."[100] Those who persecuted the Anabaptists could not claim to be the true church.

There is no indication that Rinck was surprised by the suffering he experienced. Writing from prison in Haina, he assured his followers that he and his fellow prisoner, Antonius Jacobs, who were "imprisoned for the sake of the truth" hoped "to remain true to Him in all other things through the support and help of God."[101] This sounds as though he anticipated being executed, although on this occasion he was released. It was not that Rinck accepted treatment of this kind without demur. His *Admonition* was a protest to the authorities for wrongly persecuting the Anabaptists. But he accepted in the Marburg disputation (incorrectly, as it turned out) that he was likely to be executed at some point and expressed his readiness to "testify with his body that his is a true gospel."[102] Angersbach also reported that "Brother Melchior offered many times, before all the brothers and sisters, to prove this with his blood, and to prove this vis-à-vis the whole world, with hundreds of writings."[103]

Not all his followers were as resigned to suffering as Rinck. There are several reports of Anabaptists recanting in order to escape suffering, some perhaps in order to continue to spread their teaching rather than remaining confined in prison. But Hans Both opposed this practice and reprimanded those who had recanted. And Rinck himself, according to Heinz Ot, urging his followers to submit to the authorities only insofar as they did not require obedience that contravened biblical commands, instructed them that they should be prepared to suffer injustice and endure persecution.

The theme of injustice permeates Rinck's tract on marriage, as he complained about how he had been treated and unfairly blamed for his behavior. Although this tract sets out his teaching on the subject of marriage, albeit with his own very painful experience of marriage in view, it is not entirely clear what conclusion he reaches. Commentators have generally held that he strongly affirmed Jesus' teaching on the illegitimacy of divorce for any other reason than adultery (thus preventing him from divorcing his wife), and he certainly refers to this. However, he also quoted a number of other passages and implied that these justified divorce in other situations. In one of these (Deut 24:1), Moses allows divorce if a man finds something objectionable in his wife. Elsewhere, Paul (in 1 Cor 7:15) considers the situation in which a marriage involves a believer and an unbeliever (which Rinck seems to apply to his marriage to Anna).

Although his argument in this tract is rather tortuous, Rinck seems to be saying that his marriage was not actually a marriage at all—either because it was never consummated (he refers to his "supposedly espoused wife") or because his wife never loved him but was forced into it or colluded with her parents' wrong motives, or because her behavior since their wedding demonstrated that there was no real marriage relationship. He wrote bitterly about his "unmarried marriage" and accused his father-in-law of "selling" Anna to him, rather than giving her to him. Perhaps her father had also encouraged her to remain with him rather than join her husband—in which case it was she who had abandoned him, not he who had abandoned her, as his opponents charged. In light of this, he did not feel bound and expressed relief that his itinerant ministry and Anna's refusal to join him had resulted in a de facto, if not de jure, separation.[104]

Rinck's teaching on marriage and divorce is rather more nuanced than first appears—and less dogmatic than that of many other Anabaptists. In very striking language he suggested that it could not be assumed that God had joined together all those who were officially married. The marriage ceremony had been corrupted by the state church just as surely as baptism and the Lord's Supper. Some had, in effect, been joined together by Satan, in which case it was entirely legitimate for them to separate. Otherwise, he argued, those who had slept with prostitutes must also be prohibited from separating from them. Forced marriages or marriages entered into with impure motives were no better than prostitution, and divorce was an appropriate remedy. Rinck concluded his tract by insisting that Christ required loyalty to him to come before loyalty to family ties. In some situations, Rinck seems to have taught that separation or divorce was an appropriate expression of discipleship.

CIVIL AUTHORITY

The final element in our examination of Rinck's theology is that of civil authority. Although Rinck did not attempt to offer a comprehensive account of the role of the civil authorities, we have more material on this subject in the sources than on any other subject apart from his views on baptism.[105] Rinck set out his own views in the *Admonition* and in a letter he wrote to Eberhard van der Tann in 1530; and the authorities' perspective on his views is evident in letters from Eberhard to Elector John in 1531 and Landgrave Philip in 1532.

Eberhard attempted to persuade the authorities in Hesse and Saxony that Rinck was not only a heretic but a revolutionary and represented a threat to civil order. His arguments need to be treated with considerable caution as polemical exaggerations, but his letters do reveal how hostile the civil authorities were, while memories of the peasants' movement were still fresh, toward any hint of dissent. In his letter to Elector John, Eberhard described Rinck as a "major and leading participant" at the Battle of Frankenhausen and reported that Rinck had shown no sign of repenting of his involvement in the peasants' movement. He expressed regret that Rinck had previously been exiled rather than punished more severely and had been able to come back and was "spreading his poison."[106]

In a brief letter to Philip, Eberhard depicted Rinck as fomenting an "unchristian rebellion" and expressed concern that his lenient treatment by the authorities was tempting him and his followers to conclude that "his cause must be a good and just one."[107] In the longer letter that followed, he described Rinck as "an arouser and instigator of the recent peasants' insurrection" and "an inconvincible, stubborn, unrepentant, insurrectionist." He claimed, as noted earlier, that Rinck's intention was to "again resurrect an insurrection," choosing the term *insurrection* to indicate the threat to public order. Eberhard wrote, somewhat disingenuously, that he offered no opinion as to whether Rinck should be executed, but then immediately warned that he was not only heretical in his teachings but also intent on causing an uproar, once again raising the specter of public disorder.[108]

In the remainder of this letter Eberhard offered a summary of what he claimed Rinck had taught on the subject of the civil authorities. Rinck not only "denigrated the magistracy in the hearts of the people," but had taught that "there should be no magistracy." John Stalnaker notes that Eberhard "is referring specifically to the belief he attributes to Rinck that a true Christian needs no earthly authority over him."[109] Interpreting this as advocating anarchy, Eberhard spelled out the frightening consequences—no peace, no food, no protection from crime, arousing "a Müntzer-like horde, devoid of government." He reported that many people had abandoned their workplaces, families, and pastoral responsibilities, and he envisaged the region plagued by "a desolate, disorderly mob of unreasonable and preposterous people," who "desire to act and do what they want according to their own fancy, completely free and without boundaries."[110]

It is clear from Rinck's own writings that he did not advocate anarchy or the overthrow of the authorities. Eberhard either misinterpreted Rinck's teaching or, more likely, was willfully misrepresenting it, summoning the ghost of Müntzer and playing on the fears of the authorities. More accurately, he reported that Rinck taught that "a Christian shall not be an overlord"—this undoubtedly represented denigration of the office, but it did not equate to calling for the abolition of the civil authorities. Eberhard, however, was clearly offended (and assumed the landgrave would also be offended) by the disdain with which Rinck treated official pronouncements. He described him as a "despiser of every divine and human order."

Eberhard also reported that Rinck advocated that the congregation should "have the power to appoint and dismiss the magistracy" and dismissed this as unrealistic and sure to result in the destruction of both spiritual and civil authority. Far from ushering in a godly and peaceful society, this would result in chaos, in which "there would be far less possibility of teaching God's word and raising children unto God's fear and discipline" (an outcome he assumed that Rinck should want to avoid). If this is what Rinck was actually teaching, this goes beyond what other Anabaptists were proposing. It is similar, however, to what Müntzer had advocated—which could indicate either that Rinck had not entirely given up on some of his former colleague's aims or that Eberhard was once more attempting to tar Rinck with that brush. More likely, Rinck was suggesting that the congregation should exercise authority in spiritual matters and that the magistracy should not interfere in this, not that the congregation should replace the civil authorities.

Rinck's teaching also had an economic dimension, according to Eberhard. As noted above, he wrote that Rinck "desires to introduce here on earth a fictive equality and fellowship of all people and possessions."[111] That Rinck and his followers advocated the sharing of resources is clear from their writings and statements, but there is no evidence that Rinck urged the practice of community of goods.

Eberhard concluded that Rinck's teaching and Müntzer's were "in complete agreement." Rinck might emphasize believers baptism as a shield for his true intentions and Müntzer might espouse "Christian brotherhood," but both were "intent on instigating a common insurrection." Rinck was not just a misguided heretic but a revolutionary and a threat to public order, of whom an example should be made.

It is clear from Philip's response and future actions that while Elector John was persuaded that Rinck should be executed, the landgrave did not accept Eberhard's judgment and continued to regard Rinck and his followers as misguided heretics rather than dangerous revolutionaries. But if we sift through Eberhard's charges and discount the exaggerations and calumnies, it is likely that he had correctly identified certain elements of Rinck's teaching on appropriate relations with the civil authorities. For example, he noted that Rinck relied on Ps 24:1—"The earth is the LORD's"—to reject the absolute authority of any human power. This was very frequently quoted by Anabaptists, so it is unsurprising to learn that Rinck did so too. And as indicated earlier, Rinck no doubt did teach that the congregation, and not the civil authorities, should exercise authority in matters of faith and discipleship, using the ban rather than the sword to maintain discipline; but this did not imply anarchy or that the Anabaptists rejected the right of the civil authorities to maintain public order or punish wrongdoing.

Rinck's teaching and writing

Rinck's own teaching on the role of the civil authorities can be discerned from his *Admonition*.[112] The classic New Testament passages on this subject are Rom 13 and the book of Revelation, with the former commending obedience to the authorities as God's servants and the latter offering a trenchant critique of tyrannical authorities. The tract begins with explicit references to both texts. Rinck quoted the dramatic declaration of Rev 18:2: "It has fallen, it has fallen, Babylon the Great." After addressing his purported readers, the civic authorities, with a courteous and traditional greeting, Rinck immediately asserted: "Every magistracy and power is from God, and a servant of God and of Christians, to punish those who are evil and protect those who are good." He returned to the Rom 13 text again and again, quoting it at length and exegeting its meaning. This was the biblical basis for his admonition to the civic authorities. But it is clear that he also regarded them as rebellious powers that were in danger of suffering the fate of Babylon the Great in Rev 18. The result is a nuanced and passionate critique of the magistracy.

Rinck's main concern was to establish appropriate limitations on governmental authority in relation to matters of faith and conscience. For once, he agreed with Luther (or at least with the early Luther), who had taught that faith as a gift from God could not be coerced, although Rinck was less impressed with the application of this principle by most Lutheran princes and theologians. Goertz writes (translating part of this tract): "His attacks on the reformers were passionate: 'who would have ever dared to imagine that the most learned and renowned evangelists of Wittenberg and their followers would depart so far from the true Gospel and good government? For do they not prove themselves so to the whole world, with their shameful deeds, persecutions, tyrannies, betrayals and the shedding of so much innocent blood?'"[113] Rinck insisted that the authorities were exceeding their God-given mandate if they tried to impose religious conformity in their territories, and that the reformers were wrong to encourage this.

Rinck acknowledged throughout the tract that the civic authorities were ordained by God, although he regarded this as relativizing their status rather than glorifying their position, insisting that "the Emperor, along with his underlings, is nothing other than a servant of God." His purpose in writing to the authorities was to encourage those who "desire to act rightly" and to instruct them as to their legitimate tasks—"what they are to hold to." His expressed pastoral concern was to help them avoid falling under the judgment of God. It was possible that some of them had, not realizing that they had exceeded their sphere of authority. Rinck wanted to warn them so that they could repent now and would "need to apologize less before God" when required in the future to give account of their actions. As he continued, detailing the failures of the authorities and the malign influence of the reformers who advised them, his warnings became sharper: "Woe to the servant who . . . does not carry out the known will of his Lord." He accused them of "rising up against God their Lord" and warned them to ponder "what kind of punishment awaits them from the Lord and Father of Jesus Christ." Only at the end of the tract does a pastoral concern reappear, as he urged the magistrates to reconsider and prayed, "May God protect from sacrilege all those who so desire it."

Rinck further relativized the status of the supposedly Christian authorities by insisting at the beginning of the tract that they were no more or less God's servants than "Assur, the Turk, Nebuchadnezzar . . . along with all godless tyrants." Later, protesting against the way the magistrates were overstepping their authority, he argued provocatively that the pagan governors mentioned in the New Testament, Pilate, Festus, and Gallio, refused to do this and offered good examples of how the civic authorities ought to act. He challenged his readers: "Who would not need to call the pagan Pilate holy, if compared to the current [magistrates] who call themselves Christian and Evangelical princes?" And, comparing the Lutheran princes with pagan rulers, he insisted, "if the Turk . . . is indeed a persecutor of Christ (as it is claimed), it is certainly by measure a minor evil deed in comparison to those who now call themselves Evangelical princes."

Rinck recognized that the authorities had a legitimate role in maintaining civil order and punishing evildoers. He acknowledged that "God has children who have need of the rod" and regarded the authorities as those who are competent to wield this rod. This is the role of "the sword" (referred to in Rom 13). He also agreed that the authorities had the right to receive revenues and taxes, in return for which they had responsibilities to upright citizens: "those however who do what is good are to be protected and sheltered." But his complaint was that rather than protecting the innocent and being a terror to those who behaved badly, the authorities were protecting and rewarding evildoers and instead pursuing those who were doing good. He appealed to God, "a Lord of all magistracies," about the travesty of this behavior—"all this has been reversed to the greatest degree, where those who commit all sorts of evil receive the greatest praise and protection under the magistracy, whereas those, however, who live exemplary lives—or desire to do so—have neither place nor space." Furthermore, these evildoers were the ones who "want to give neither taxes nor revenue to the magistracy" and who instead "take in much more of these." The magistrates were losing out financially by favoring such people. And these evildoers were also the ones who were bringing accusations against Rinck and his followers, defaming them as "insurrectionists against the power of the magistracy" and inciting the authorities to take action against them.

There is no doubt to whom Rinck was referring. They were the Lutheran reformers, who were advising the civic authorities and relying on their power to suppress the Anabaptists. Not only was this an illegitimate partnership, an example of the "false Christendom" that Rinck had castigated elsewhere, but the reformers were attempting to persuade the magistrates to overstep their God-given authority by adjudicating on matters of faith. And they were not speaking truthfully, "cursing the children of God as heretics and fanatics, contrary to all honesty and to their own consciences." Rinck described them as "antichristian scribes" and "pharisaical hypocrites." Whereas he expressed a measure of pastoral concern for the magistrates who might have been misled, he warned only of judgment on those who were responsible for misleading them and causing such distress to Rinck and his followers—"innocent blood" is "coming upon them."

Although he was critical of various aspects of the magistrates' exercise of their authority, Rinck's main contention was that the authorities had no jurisdiction over the beliefs and practices of the members of the congregations that he served. All spiritual matters and decisions about church property and activities were for members of the congregation, not the civic authorities. This was the point he made repeatedly in this tract. "What has the emperor and his staff to do with such matters of faith?" he asked. After quoting at length from Rom 13 and briefly from 1 Pet 2, he answered his own question: "Matters of faith have nothing whatsoever to do with the emperor." He expressed outrage that the authorities and their ecclesiastical advisors were acting "as if faith is not a gift of God but rather that of the magistracy or of human power." He found it extraordinary that anyone should be uncertain "how broadly the office of the emperor's commands extended." Even the pagan ruler Gallio knew that his authority concerned matters of "crime or serious villainy," not matters of faith or religious practice.

Rinck based his argument on the example of Jesus, who spoke and acted freely, needing no mandate from either the Roman or Jewish authorities. He asked rhetorically: "Was not Jesus outside the emperor's command, riding to Jerusalem without the permission of Pilate and all the magistrates, allowing himself to be greeted as a hereditary king of the Jews after having traversed for a long time the land with such a great multitude of people—yes, entering the Temple and ousting the merchants and vendors, upsetting the tables of the money exchangers, scattering the money?" If Jesus did not need permission from the authorities for his actions, neither should his sixteenth-century followers.

On two specific issues Rinck accused the magistrates of overstepping their authority. The first was their attempt to regulate property owned by the churches. He insisted that "whoever desires to be a Christian prince in this land shall consider neither the church nor what it possesses as his own, but rather as owned by the church. He shall not relish as his own the properties of the church." The second was their attempt to enforce the practice of infant baptism. According to Rinck, in doing this, contrary to the teaching of Scripture, the magistrates were "not only rising up against God their Lord, but also coercing with force all subjects of God into apostasy and perjury."

Indeed, Rinck insisted, in a rather complicated passage, that by persecuting and killing true Christians, the emperor was in effect murdering the Son of God, the one from whom he had received his delegated authority, thereby undermining his own legitimacy. Since Christ was present in the members of his body, the true church, by killing them the emperor became "the murderer of the Child, of the very one who made him into a powerful servant." Rinck repeated this accusation later in the tract—that "they, the magistracy, trample the Son of God, their Lord, with their feet." Geldbach comments: "This sets, consequentially, the limits of governmental power; since the magistracy is the servant of God, the church, however, a child of God, the church stands, unequally, higher."[114]

Stayer concludes: "His main point . . . is the intolerable presumption of rulers who think that their worldly power gives them the right to dictate to their subjects in matters of religious faith."[115] Rinck demurred from this view, arguing that "truly" Christian rulers should behave quite differently. They should, in fact, operate on the same principles as those with authority in the congregations, adopting the stance of a servant. He rejected the Lutheran teaching that different ethical standards applied in different contexts.

Despite his outrage at the authorities' overstepping the mark, Rinck did not fully embrace the perspective of those Anabaptists who taught that magistrates could not be Christians or at least act in a Christian manner. Early in the tract he addressed the magistrates as "dearly beloved servants of Christ," and throughout the tract he appealed to them on the basis of Scripture to act in ways that would befit those who claimed to be Christians. On the other hand, on several occasions, he questioned the legitimacy of this claim. He referred to "the general magistracy, which calls itself Christian" and compared Pilate to the current magistrates "who call themselves Christian and evangelical princes." He complained that the magistrates and their clerical advisors were "confessing themselves to be either Christians or Evangelicals with their mouths, yet taking pleasure in either the pope's or Luther's command without works." They might regard themselves as Christian princes, but their actions belied this designation: the prince might indeed repress Christians and even kill them for reasons of state, but he had no right to claim that he was thus discharging a Christian duty. Rinck did not pronounce on whether a "true" Christian (such as one of his followers) could become a magistrate. Some of his followers evidently thought this was impossible, though others were prepared to consider this.

In other writings, as noted above, Rinck accepted that persecution was the lot of faithful disciples and encouraged his followers not to resist. But in this tract, he demurred from the common understanding that suffering under a tyrannical government implied that the church was being punished by God for its sins. Rather, such suffering was the result of the authorities' overstepping their God-ordained limits.

Rinck rejected the use of the term *Schwärmer* (rabble-rousers or fanatics) to describe his followers, protesting that this was not an accurate designation.

In his letter to Eberhard von der Tann, Rinck expressed himself equally vigorously and made clear his low opinion of the authorities with whom he had come into contact.[116] He continued to affirm their God-ordained status, unhesitatingly equating "the order of God" with the magistracy, but he asked: "Where can one prove that God's mandate concerning the sword has jurisdiction over matters of faith?" He expressed incredulity that anyone should think that God had established this mandate "in order to exterminate his children" and accused the authorities of "frightful wantonness and sacrilege of Christ to the highest dishonor." As in his longer tract, Rinck regarded the behavior of the magistrates toward true Christians as not only unjust and outside their mandate but also sacrilegious. He offered little by way of pastoral admonition in this letter, suggesting of anyone who persecuted his followers that "it would be far better if one had a millstone hanging around his neck."

Testimonies from Rinck's followers

On two specific issues relating to participation in civil society—the swearing of oaths and the legitimacy of lawsuits—there is nothing in Rinck's extant writings. On the first issue, his followers Köhler and Scheffer (surnames unknown) stated that oaths were unnecessary if one obeyed Jesus and simply told the truth,[117] and Heinz Kraut and Hans Peissker rejected the swearing of oaths.[118] It is possible that others may have accepted the legitimacy of civil oaths (Anabaptists in other regions did not all agree on this issue). Both Jörg Schnabel and Peter Tasch in their 1538 writings rejected the outright refusal to swear oaths that the authorities suggested the Anabaptists taught.[119] Schnabel acknowledged that the teaching of Jesus in Matt 5 appeared to preclude the swearing of oaths, but (unusually for an Anabaptist teacher) he chose to set this passage aside and be guided by other biblical texts. Köhler and Scheffer also rejected the legitimacy of lawsuits for true Christians, as did Heinz Ot at the Vacha hearing.[120]

Rinck's followers expressed similar concerns about civil authority, although they gave various answers to questions on this subject.

Stayer notes that Hutterite missionaries were also active in this area and that their teaching may have influenced Rinck's followers, so that it is not clear to what extent their views represent his. In relation to the Berka and Sorga hearings, he comments: "The non-resistant tendency of these congregations . . . did not amount to a broadly accepted and clearly defined teaching, and it is not certain that Rink was responsible for it, in any case."[121]

Stalnaker insists that "virtually all Hessian Anabaptists admitted, often under the pressure of interrogation, the necessity of the civil authority, and most affirmed its divine institution."[122] Some of them protested strongly against accusations that they denied this. However, this recognition did not imply unqualified obedience or any great respect for an institution they regarded as primarily concerned to restrict evildoers. Heinz Ot is reported to have accorded only conditional obedience to the authorities, saying that "one is to obey the magistracy, as long as it does not act in opposition to God's commandments."[123] Rinck's followers shared his conviction that true Christians did not need to be compelled by threat of punishment to behave well. It is understandable that the authorities were irritated by this limited respect for their role.

At the Berka hearings,[124] Peter Leinweber rebuked those who insisted on honorific titles because "God has said that they are not to name themselves 'lords' here on earth, for there is one [Lord] in heaven, whom one is to acknowledge." Hermann Adam said he would obey the authorities but would not agree to attend the local church. Hans Heylman testified that "a Christian cannot occupy the office of magistrate with good conscience, although he is committed to suffer the magistrate's use of force and remain subservient." Hans Cleue acknowledged the divine order of civil government and the need to be obedient, but he also indicated that such obedience had limitations, reserving the right to resist exile. Hans Kessel insisted that obedience to God was more important than obeying the magistrates and that he would refuse if commanded to kill another or attend the state church. Margret Kessel also agreed that obeying the magistrates was right but not if they insisted on attendance at the parish church. Glebe notes: "Others rejected the possibility of reconciling a life led by Christian values (primarily the rejection of violence) with a position of secular authority: a commitment to the former necessitated the abandonment of the latter."[125] This was the position of Margret Schneider. Lentz Rüdiger expressed uncertainty as to whether a prince wishing to be baptized would need to leave his office, but he could not see how a true Christian could be a magistrate. Some were reluctant to answer questions on this subject. Anna Leinweber simply refused to respond. Könne Wilhelm said that she had heard many different views on the subject and did not know what to think, but she regarded the civic authorities as bloodthirsty. But Katharina Young offered a different perspective—that no Christian should exercise dominion over others or impose physical punishment; rather, a Christian should offer forgiveness. Reviewing these various responses, Stayer concludes: "Many . . . were uninstructed in attitude toward government and repeated either the Lutheran catchword that the temporal authority was a godly ordinance or the Müntzerite slogan that God alone was their ruler."[126]

At the Sorga hearings,[127] Hans Koch said he would not do military service; he would pay taxes and tithes but was unsure about paying war taxes. Hans Plat accepted the legitimacy of the secular authorities but declared that a Christian prince should not kill or require his subjects to go to war. He claimed not to understand some of the questions about tax and property but stated that, although he had been involved in the peasants' movement, he would not serve in the military. He insisted that the authorities should use the taxes they raised to help people in need. Heinz and Konne Hutter also accepted that the magistrates should be obeyed but were unsure whether a true Christian could be a magistrate. Heinz would not pay war taxes or take up arms, but he would pay other taxes. But Endres Lober offered only conditional obedience to the authorities: "As for matters wherein he has an obligation, he will do what he considers to be acceptable, but not do things he considers harmful." He would rather be killed than take up arms.

Elsa and Hans Zisen also recognized the secular authorities and went further than Plat, accepting their right to execute thieves and other criminals, as did Catharina and Heinrich Lutz. Hans Zisen declared that "they are taught daily that they should [have] a Christian magistracy, that they are to be subject to the magistracy." He was unsure whether the authorities had the right to demand interest and taxes, but if he was required to pay these he would do so. Schmidt Hen accepted the legitimacy of the magistracy and would pay taxes but not take up arms. Marx Baumgart rejected taking up arms and paying war taxes. He also insisted that no Christian should pronounce the death penalty. Hermann Stalpf and Heinz and Osana Bill said they did not know if it was possible for a Christian to have authority, for "the Ten Commandments do not give instruction on this point."

Anna and Gilg stated that the secular authority is "a servant of God"—a more affirming statement than found elsewhere in the record of these interrogations. Although he had participated in the peasants' movement, Gilg now rejected military service, though he was willing to pay war taxes for "the sword has been given to the magistracy." According to the very brief record of their testimonies, Else and Hen Lutz and Cunz and Gele Hutter said that they respected the secular authorities, but Gele insisted that "one must pull out the weeds." Cunz also stated that he would be willing to do military service. But these couples appear not to have understood most of the questions the authorities asked them. Glebe draws attention to the opinion of Johann Feige, who regarded pacifism as a tenet central to the group's identity, suggesting to Landgrave Philip that the one person who had declared himself willing to go to war could likely be persuaded to renounce his association with the Anabaptists.[128]

Heinz Kraut told Melanchthon that Anabaptists could not be obedient to an authority that imprisoned them because of their consciences and denied them the exercise of their faith. In that case he owed obedience only to God. A true Christian could not be a magistrate but could approve of one who exercised proper and just judgment. Like Peter Leinweber at the Berka hearing, Kraut was strongly egalitarian, rejecting the doffing of hats to those in authority and the use of *Herr* as a term of address—he insisted on calling the theologians the informal *du*.[129]

Schnabel quoted Rom 13:1 in his 1538 defense and accepted that "the power that exists is ordered by God." He insisted that "we will not refuse the government any proper obedience. Nor have we done so, as far as it does not (as they report) command what is against God." Somewhat surprisingly, he included in this obedience to government the responsibility of Christians to support justifiable military action. If the motivation of the authorities were to defend the innocent and vulnerable, rather than seeking glory, they would have his support. He would "yield his limbs to be weapons of righteousness." He also saw no biblical justification for withholding taxes or tithes. However, he proceeded to give biblical examples (from Acts and Daniel) of instances where civil disobedience was the faithful response to governments if they required believers to go against God's commands, so his submission to the civil authorities was conditional, albeit rather more generous than Rinck's.[130] Glebe notes: "Although briefly mentioned in Jörg Schnabel's outline of the Anabaptist position in 1538, the question of military service does not play a very significant role after that and primarily appears as a result of Moravian influence."[131]

Interestingly, and offering further evidence of shared convictions and teaching between different Anabaptist groups in Hesse, Schnabel also made the unusual and provocative point that had been made earlier by Rinck in his treatise on civil authority, namely, that "the heathen authority acted more correctly than the supposed evangelical one does now," and giving two of the same biblical examples (Festus and Gallio) as Rinck had used.[132]

Striking at the root of Christendom

In his tract on baptism, as noted above, Rinck described the corrupt society of his day as the outcome of Satan's "gospel" and designated this and Christendom as "a groveling abomination." In fact, what purported to be a Christian society was in fact "a false Christendom," upheld by Catholics and Protestants alike through the illegitimate practice of infant baptism. This critique of a so-called Christendom appears in the writings of other Anabaptists—they initially criticized its corruption but in due course questioned the legitimacy of the whole system. This was evidently a perspective shared by Rinck. He may have imbibed this from Müntzer, who "was committed to the total destruction of the medieval *corpus Christianum*."[133] Like Müntzer, Rinck rejected the partnership between church and state that was at the heart of the medieval notion of a sacral society, insisting that faith could not be coerced and the church must be free from the control of the magistracy. This perspective struck at the root of the "false Christendom."

FIVE

Rinck's Legacy

MELCHIOR RINCK—reformer, revolutionary, Anabaptist—was not alone in the first third of the sixteenth century in moving from one camp to another, motivated by a passion to see both church and society reformed. How to achieve such reform was at the heart of many debates, protests, and movements. Was a gradualist or a revolutionary approach more likely to be effective? Was violence necessary, or could reform be achieved peacefully? Were existing church and state structures amenable to the necessary changes, or was something new needed? There is no doubt that Rinck was motivated by this longing for reform. He had witnessed the failure of the peasants' movement to achieve reform through violent revolution. He had no confidence that the Lutherans were able to deliver the reforms he regarded as crucial. So Rinck turned to Anabaptism. In this, his trajectory was similar to that of Anabaptists in many other regions.

Rinck's thinking and practice were influenced by many of those he encountered, worked with, or opposed. He owed more than he might have acknowledged to Luther, despite his profound disagreement with him on some issues and his inflammatory language toward him. Jakob Strauss played a significant role in Rinck's career and in his turn away from Luther. Thomas Müntzer's revolutionary agenda not only captured Rinck's imagination in the short period in which he was deeply involved in the peasants' movement but also continued to undergird his social ethics. Despite frequent accusations that he and other Anabaptists in Hesse were still followers of Müntzer and set on insurrection, it seems clear that Rinck renounced Müntzer's methods and expectations, even if he still yearned for the social transformation Müntzer had advocated.

Hans Denck probably baptized Rinck, and his influence can be detected in the language Rinck used, not least in his insistence that love was the primary feature of the divine nature. Rinck also knew Hans Hut, perhaps the most effective first-generation Anabaptist evangelist. Rinck did not embrace Hut's apocalyptic teaching, but he may well have been inspired by his evangelistic activism. And it seems from his correspondence that he had some links with Anabaptists in both Switzerland and the Netherlands, but the extent of their influence on him is unknown. His biblicism is similar to that of the Swiss Brethren, while his teaching on civil authority is closer to views that would later be expressed by Menno Simons.

But Rinck was his own man, dissenting from all those who influenced him and charting his own course in the maelstrom of sixteenth-century religion and politics. On some of the subjects on which he wrote or was questioned, such as Christology and ecclesiology, he seems to have had little distinctive to contribute. On soteriology, although he insisted that his teaching did not amount to reversion to salvation by works, it seems that he did not fully appreciate the danger of this in his concern to emphasize discipleship. His approach to biblical interpretation may offer a middle way between the biblicism of the Swiss Brethren and the Spiritualism of many German Anabaptists. But as far as we can tell from his extant writings, the record of the Marburg debate, and the interrogations of his followers, his most significant legacy consists in the following: his warnings about the pastoral and ethical consequences of infant baptism; his demystifying of communion; his nuanced views on the role and limits of civil authority; and his emphasis on the love of God.

Rinck was convinced of a direct link between the practice of infant baptism and the scandalously low level of discipleship he detected in the state churches. This was exacerbated by the almost total failure of Christian education and by the inadequacies and moral deficiencies of many state church leaders, but infant baptism itself was the root of the problem. Using powerful metaphors to describe the plight of the state churches—a city with enemies within and a sheepfold with wolves, lions, and bears among the sheep—he urged their leaders and the theologians with whom he debated to admit the damage that was being caused and to confront this issue. The Hessian church's decision to adopt the practice of confirmation (more on this below) addressed some of Rinck's concerns, introducing an opportunity for a personal profession of faith and the Christian education of adolescents. We have no record of the imprisoned Rinck's response to this, but it is highly unlikely that he would have regarded this as adequate. Ameliorating the symptoms was not dealing with the root cause of the problem. Many Anabaptists presented biblical arguments against infant baptism, but no other early Anabaptist offered such a trenchant critique of the practice as Rinck or was so explicit about the damage this practice caused to the churches.

Because Rinck's writing on communion is not extant, we cannot be sure what he taught on the subject, but from references in his other writings and comments from his followers it seems that he was reluctant to delve too deeply into its mystical significance. He denied the doctrine of transubstantiation and the Lutheran interpretation of this, regarding this as a form of idolatry. It seems that he may have taught that every meal was an opportunity to give thanks to God and to remember the work of Christ. He certainly drew on John 6 to offer a spiritual understanding of feeding on Christ's body. Rinck's teaching may have discouraged his followers both from receiving bread and wine in the state churches and from practicing communion themselves. Several comments from his followers indicate (if they are not merely evasive) that they regarded this subject as a deep mystery. But Rinck may also have liberated them to experience a eucharistic dimension in their daily meals. If so, this reconnection of communion with real meals was restoring the practice of the early churches and anticipating a further recovery in many contemporary church circles.

In his teaching on the role of the civil authorities, Rinck did not endorse the absolutism of the Swiss Brethren, who denied that a Christian could be a magistrate. His critique of the authorities betrays something of his revolutionary past and continuing concern for social justice as he castigated them for their personal arrogance and wealth, and denounced the system they operated as unjust. And he categorically denied that they had any jurisdiction over spiritual or ecclesial matters. But he acknowledged not only that civil government was ordained by God (as most Anabaptists did) but also that a ruler acting within the God-ordained bounds of this governmental role could be regarded as a "Christian" leader. This did not necessarily mean that he knew of any such leaders, or that he thought members of his congregations should aspire to such a role, but his position appears to be closer to the more nuanced views of Pilgram Marpeck and Menno Simons. In quoting both Rom 13 and Rev 18 at the start of his main writing on this subject, Rinck indicated that he was wrestling with a tension found within the New Testament—a tension that Christians suffering governmental persecution feel much more acutely than others. His contributions on this subject may not resolve the tension or provide a definite way forward, but they do represent a more nuanced perspective than that of many other early Anabaptists as well as a willingness to speak truth to power, rather than simply consigning the authorities' behavior to the sphere of "outside the perfection of Christ."[1]

What impact did Rinck's ministry and writings have on the wider Anabaptist movement? It is evident from comments made by some of his followers that his teaching continued to be regarded as authoritative among Hessian Anabaptists after his confinement to prison. It seems that his teachings were also influential and his writings read much further afield. The Hutterites were certainly familiar with Rinck's views, as those who had emigrated from Hesse to Moravia drew on his teaching to challenge their hosts' views on issues of property and ownership. Their *Chronicle of the Hutterian Brethren* also refers to a lost tract by Rinck on the subject of communion. We have a letter from Rinck and a colleague sent to friends in the Netherlands. And this letter and Rinck's tract on baptism have been found in an undated (but probably sixteenth-century) collection of mainly Swiss Brethren writings.[2] This indicates that Rinck was probably quite well known in Swiss Brethren circles. Leonard Gross notes that some Swiss Brethren leaders in the 1550s and 1560s possessed Rinck's writings.[3] Robert Friedmann concludes, although without offering much evidence, that through Rinck's writings his influence can be traced within and beyond his own region until the late sixteenth century.[4] Perhaps the discovery of additional manuscripts in European archives will provide support for this claim.

Until then, we should probably conclude that we simply do not know how far his influence spread or how long it lasted.

ANABAPTISM IN HESSE

The Anabaptist movement in Hesse, as elsewhere, did not succeed in dismantling or even seriously troubling the partnership between church and state that was perpetuated by both Catholic and Protestant authorities, despite their mutual antagonism. But in many other regions, continuing networks of dissenting congregations survived despite persecution, to which present-day congregations in Germany, Switzerland, and the Netherlands can trace their roots. In Hesse, such a network seems always to have been more tenuous, and by the 1540s it was already losing coherence. Until recently, historians have paid relatively little attention to Anabaptism in Hesse, perhaps questioning whether there is much to learn from this story. However, both Kat Hill and Ellen Yutzy Glebe have challenged this conclusion, arguing that the unusual character of Anabaptism in Hesse makes this a very interesting study, which might also, by comparison, help us gain a better understanding of Anabaptism elsewhere.

Hill writes: "People here, it has been argued, were not part of a meaningful Anabaptist tradition in the sense that they did not show much theological sophistication and the movement was not numerically strong. However, the picture . . . can just as easily be read as one of survival in difficult circumstances."[5] Glebe suggests that the study of Hessian Anabaptism is significant because its development there "was arguably more natural than in other areas precisely because the persecution was less intense."[6]

The lack of interest in Hessian Anabaptism is one of the reasons why Melchior Rinck has not been accorded as much attention as several other first-generation Anabaptist leaders in Germany and elsewhere. It might be pointed out that Pilgram Marpeck, who engaged in debate with Martin Bucer as Rinck did, but also failed to establish an enduring network of congregations, has not been disregarded in the way Rinck has been. However, until quite recently, Marpeck too was a relatively unknown figure, and his popularity among Anabaptist scholars now is largely attributable to the discovery of a very much larger body of writings than Rinck produced.

The relatively rapid demise of Anabaptism in Hesse can be explained by reference to several factors that were not present in such a combination in other regions where Anabaptism flourished for longer.

First, the unusual leniency of Landgrave Philip toward Anabaptists in his territory, as long as they were not perceived to be seditious as well as heretical, had a marked impact on the nature of the Anabaptist movement in Hesse. Not only did he maintain this policy throughout his long reign, despite external pressure from surrounding jurisdictions and internal pressure from his own theological advisors, but his successors persisted with this approach. His sons acceded to the request in Philip's will: "To kill people for the reason that they believed an error we have never done, and wish to admonish our sons not to do so, for we consider that it is contrary to God, as is clearly shown in the Gospel."[7] Philip, it seems, agreed with the Anabaptists, if not with his own theologians, that state power was not to be used to coerce orthodoxy.

It might be thought that such leniency would stimulate the Anabaptist movement and aid its growth in Hesse. That was certainly the danger about which others warned Philip. This might have been the result of his tolerant policy in the early years, as people interested in Anabaptist ideas could investigate these ideas and attend meetings without fear of severe persecution even if they were arrested and interrogated. They also realized that they could recant their views when required to do so and then return to their Anabaptist convictions quite easily. This was not a context where radical and courageous dissent was necessary.

But perhaps the landgrave's policy, although it seems to have been motivated by honest theological convictions as well as pragmatism, was ultimately more successful than the much harsher policies of his contemporaries in disarming the Anabaptist threat. Did it result in the proliferation of lukewarm Anabaptists who were insufficiently motivated or instructed to be able to form lasting communities? Did the landgrave's leniency enable some who were interested, but not highly committed, to associate with the movement in this less risky environment, knowing they could pull back if pressure increased?

Second, other factors in the emergence of Anabaptism in Hesse may have militated against the development of an enduring network of congregations. Even taking into account their more tolerant context than in most other territories, those identified as Anabaptists there often seem less certain of their beliefs, more diverse in their views, and more open to persuasion than usual. Recanting, rather than resisting, seems to have been quite common, regardless of whether this was sincere, indicating a degree of flexibility not associated with Anabaptists in many other places. Most of those arrested at Vacha, for example, submitted to instruction, recanted, and were released. Some of the others in this group had recanted on previous occasions, only to return to their Anabaptist convictions and gatherings.

The testimonies in the various interrogations are often at odds with each other and are punctuated by claims by those being questioned that they did not understand what they were being asked. This may be thanks in part to the mixed messages given by different Anabaptist teachers. It may also indicate lack of instruction, inadequate discipline, or limited community cohesion among the Anabaptists. Or it might suggest that those who were identified with the Anabaptist movement were inarticulate or uninterested in the finer points of theology and church ritual that so concerned those who arrested them.

A number of interrogated Anabaptists expressed dissatisfaction with the state churches—either with specific local leaders or with the institution itself—rather than enthusiasm for Anabaptist convictions and practices. Criticisms of the ethical shortcomings of the state church were a staple of Anabaptist testimonies, but it is notable that in many cases this was the primary concern of those being questioned. Some, it seems, were not especially interested in being identified as Anabaptists or particularly clear what Anabaptism stood for. They were simply yearning for something authentically Christian. The clergy were widely regarded as corrupt, preaching simply for wages, living lives of ease, and leading the people and the authorities astray. An example of this is provided by Christopher Ocker: "In Hesse, a certain smith named Hen, who had been baptized as an adult in 1530 (he technically *was* an Anabaptist) and who had also participated in the Peasants' War, considered himself in August 1533 neither Lutheran nor Anabaptist nor Catholic, but merely someone who wanted to hear true sermons."[8]

Heinz Cleue from Herda was questioned in the Berka hearing. He had been baptized by a Moravian missionary and gave standard Anabaptist responses to questions about baptism and communion. However, in reply to a question about why he had stopped attending the state church, the record states: "He says, he will not go to [the local] church as long as the current preacher and vicar remain at Herda."[9] Glebe comments: "This statement implies that, were the pastor to be replaced, he would consider attending services, despite his declared doctrinal disagreements."[10] Perhaps these disagreements were the result of his dissatisfaction with this particular pastor, rather than deep-rooted convictions that would preclude a return to the state church.

As noted above, Johann Feige reported that those interrogated in the Sorga hearing despised the state church preachers, complaining that "they do not practice what they preach," and that "the fruits do not appear among the listeners." Rather than presenting a clear and agreed statement of Anabaptist convictions, members of the congregation held "to many an opinion, with each judging according to his own discretion." However, he acknowledged that "they all agreed that our preaching is not from God, and that theirs is true, and if they were to come into our congregation they would be sinning against God."[11] It appears from the answers given in this hearing that there was less discontent with the local preacher than was evident at Berka. Elsa and Hans Koch stated that they had no objection to the preacher or his sermons, but they would still not attend the state church. They declared that they had heard nothing to which they objected but they would not attend because "God said, beware of the scribes." Greta and Hans Plat also testified that they detected no flaws in the preaching of the local pastor and were willing to attend his services, but, perhaps reluctantly, they would not take communion because the preachers "preach according to their self-interest." Groschen and Margarethe objected to what was missing from the sermons, insisting that they wanted to attend preaching services where Christ was preached authentically, criticizing the state churches for avoiding the cost of following Jesus. Marx Baumgart and his wife Herda were more critical of the preacher and said they would not attend the services, because the preacher's behavior was inconsistent with what he preached. Others gave no reason but simply stated that they would not attend the state churches.[12]

Hill takes issue with the assertion that dissatisfaction with the state churches was the only or primary motivation of those who became Anabaptists. She argues that many were not only concerned about issues of morality and the lack of discipline in the state churches; "theological convictions, ritual symbolism, and emotional responses" were also involved. Nevertheless, she concludes: "The concerns of Anabaptists in this region reveal a set of hopes and anxieties which developed out of individual reactions to Lutheran theology and to ideas they heard from preachers like Hans Hut and Melchior Rinck, in conversation with Catholic tradition."[13] If this is the case, many of these Anabaptists are likely to have been less rigid in their views, less theologically articulate, less determinedly separatist, and more open to the possibility of returning to the state churches once their concerns were addressed.

A third factor in the decline of Anabaptism in the region is that in Martin Bucer, the Hessian Anabaptists encountered a reformer who listened carefully and sympathetically to their concerns, took these seriously, and introduced the kinds of reforms in the state churches that addressed their concerns and diminished the gap between these and the Anabaptist congregations. In place of the outright hostility of Justus Menius or the implacable resistance of Philip Melanchthon, neither of whom was willing to respond positively to any of their criticisms of the state churches, Anabaptists recognized in Bucer someone who disagreed with their separatist stance but was willing to acknowledge the truth in at least some of what they said. Like them, he believed that church members should adhere to high ethical standards, and he longed for a pure church. He also came to believe that church discipline was an essential mark of the church and vital in pursuit of this goal. But his pastoral concern for weaker members and passionate commitment to maintain the unity of the church precluded any sympathy with separation. As James Payton writes, "For Bucer, nothing worse could be said of anyone than to be known as indifferent to or an opponent of the unity of the Church."[14]

Bucer empathized with the Anabaptists more than any other major Reformer. Indeed, as David Wright notes, "The fact that shortly before he was banished from Strasbourg he was himself charged with being an enthusiast, tainted with the spirit and doctrine of the Anabaptists, is clear indication that he was far from insensitive to their protests."[15] Among the reformers, only Bucer's colleague Wolfgang Capito demonstrated a similar willingness to engage creatively with the Anabaptists and seek common ground.

This is not to imply that Bucer was uncritical of Anabaptist perspectives or unconcerned about their growing influence. His early biblical commentaries—on Ephesians in 1527 and on the gospel of John in 1528—make several references to the Anabaptists and their errors.[16] But unlike some of his colleagues, he had taken the time to get to know Anabaptists personally and to listen carefully to them. In particular, Bucer had engaged in an extended debate with the Anabaptist leader Pilgram Marpeck in Strasbourg.

Marpeck arrived in 1528 and soon got to know Bucer and other reformers there. Bucer's initial impression was favorable, writing that Pilgram and his wife Anna had blameless characters. Although Bucer became increasingly concerned about the influence of the Anabaptists, he was sensitive to their critique of the state church and tried unsuccessfully for several years to introduce measures to bring greater discipline into the Strasbourg churches. This was not far removed from an Anabaptist approach, but it avoided what Bucer disliked most about the Anabaptists—their willingness to separate from the state churches. He regarded Marpeck as a heretic for breaking the unity of the church. Bucer remained committed to the centuries-old notion of Christendom and to a single divine covenant. Marpeck and Bucer agreed on many issues and clearly respected each other, but their disputes became increasingly acrimonious, not least as Bucer struggled with opposition to his reform agenda on several fronts. Marpeck would have been a valuable ally, but Bucer could not persuade him to abandon his Anabaptist convictions. Nor could Marpeck win Bucer to the Anabaptist cause.

Although the disputes between Bucer and Marpeck grew tense, the generally respectful dialogue between the two gives a tantalizing glimpse into how Reformed-Anabaptist relationships might have been conducted in the sixteenth century. Walter Klaassen and William Klassen conclude: "The Bucer-Marpeck exchange shows that opponents could be respectful of each other even in the midst of controversy during the Reformation, when disagreement so easily developed into legal coercion and even bloodshed."[17] Bucer's discussions with Rinck and with other Anabaptists after Rinck's imprisonment breathe the same spirit: neither side could persuade the other to renounce their views, but both sides listened respectfully and recognized that their concerns had been heard and understood. John Oyer comments: "This dispute was a genuine exchange of religious views, one of few involving sixteenth-century Anabaptists."[18] As noted above, despite failing to persuade him to renounce his Anabaptist views, Bucer persuaded the Hessian authorities to improve the conditions of Rinck's imprisonment, an indication of respect and care for someone with whom he disagreed.

Bucer was by far the most successful reformer in persuading Anabaptists to return to the state churches. No other reformer could point to such an achievement. His conciliatory approach and careful attention to their perspectives was much more effective than the belligerence of other reformers. He seems also to have accepted and not been unduly worried that Anabaptists who recanted and returned to the state churches might continue to oppose infant baptism. The various measures he persuaded the Hessian churches to adopt in 1538 addressed some of the main concerns of the Anabaptists and thus limited their protests and the perceived need to separate. It was primarily Bucer's influence that persuaded state church leaders to engage sympathetically with those they had formerly regarded as heretics from whom they could learn nothing.

Indeed, it is clear that Bucer regarded the Anabaptists not only as sectarians who posed a threat to the established order but as a potential gift to the Hessian churches, if the Anabaptists could only be persuaded to commit themselves afresh to these churches. Bucer wrote to Philip in 1538: "For the encounter with the Anabaptists can in no way be more useful to us and the common man than if they stimulate us to better Christian management of our lives and to a more earnest exercise of Christian discipline."[19] This is a remarkable tribute to those with whom he disagreed on many issues. Bucer recognized that incorporating the Anabaptists into the state churches would not only preclude the separatism that he so strongly opposed but also inject new energy into those churches and encourage higher ethical standards.

In addition, Bucer deployed returning Anabaptists to persuade others to recant and return. Many Anabaptists who had not been involved in the Marburg debate were not persuaded by the assurances which had been given to their leaders, suspicious of the motives of those who had recently been persecuting them. Bucer recognized that the testimony of those who had decided to return to the state churches would be much more effective than anything he could say. Peter Tasch was one of these. Bucer persuaded the landgrave to release him from jail for this purpose.[20] It seems that he was successful in persuading others to return to the state churches, although he failed to persuade Rinck to recant.

Fourth, the efforts of Moravian missionaries to shore up support for the Anabaptist cause in Hesse and to discourage Anabaptists from responding to the overtures of Bucer, Tasch, and others, may actually have further accelerated the decline of Hessian Anabaptism. It is clear that they were very concerned about the outcome of the Marburg debate in 1538. Many, possibly even most, of the Anabaptists were returning to the state churches. The Moravian missionaries campaigned against the agreement that had persuaded them to do this. They advocated a strongly separatist stance and a disciplined community life and encouraged emigration to Moravia by those who shared these perspectives and yearned for freedom to experience these. This deprived Anabaptists in Hesse of some of their educated leaders and more determined members. It also made the movement rather less attractive to those who might previously have joined it but were now put off by the rigorous demands.

Finally, some responsibility for the demise of Hessian Anabaptism must be shouldered by Melchior Rinck himself. It was hardly his fault that his imprisonment before, during, and after the critical Marburg debate in 1538 deprived the community of one of its founding leaders. But questions can be asked about the nature of his leadership when still at large. Rinck appears to have been an itinerant evangelist, rather than a community builder. His energies seem to have been devoted to spreading the movement, rather than establishing it more firmly. Oyer characterizes the activities of Rinck and his colleagues in this way: "The wandering preacher visited a village one evening, preached on repentance and the need for commitment to Christ, baptized those who requested it, and then moved on to another village."[21] It is noteworthy in the above discussion of Rinck's theological views that there is very little about ecclesiology.

Consequently, Anabaptism in Hesse was less organized, less congregational, less well instructed, and less disciplined than in many other areas. We might think in terms of a loose-knit network, rather than an emerging denomination or even a movement. Even the notion of a network in which members were conscious of being part of something wider than in their own locality may be unrealistic. Hill writes: "The immediate impression which emerges from the sources seems to be one of isolated and often incoherent groups of radicals who failed to form stable communities."[22]

Might Rinck, if he had remained at liberty, have given greater attention to community formation? Evaluating the ministry of many first-generation Anabaptists is difficult in light of their very short and prematurely truncated ministries. Some pioneers are unable or unwilling to transition from proclamation and enthusing individuals to the demanding task of building sustainable communities. But others recognize the importance of this and either attend to it themselves or find others to work alongside them. We do not know enough about Rinck's followers and colleagues to discern whether such people were available; nor do we know whether Rinck would have recognized the need for this.

The above five factors comprise an unusual, perhaps unique, combination in the history of early Anabaptism. In other regions, evangelism took precedence over congregational development, at least in the early stages. In other regions, too, those who identified as Anabaptists were at least partly motivated by criticisms of the state churches, but these concerns often led to their embracing distinctive Anabaptist convictions. And emigration to Moravia weakened the movement in other places. But nowhere else were Anabaptists wooed so effectively by a sympathetic reformer or treated so gently by a secular ruler.

If Rinck's legacy is to be assessed by how long a coherent and united Hessian Anabaptist movement survived, the outcome will be disappointing. That the network of communities he helped to develop was suffocated by tolerance rather than decimated by persecution, as in some other areas, does not significantly affect any evaluation. But there are other ways of assessing his legacy.

WIDER IMPACT

Because of the receptivity of Bucer and Landgrave Philip to Anabaptist perspectives and criticisms of the state churches, the short-lived Anabaptist movement had a lasting effect on the Hessian state church and, in due course, in other Protestant regions. Although the Anabaptists' views on infant baptism and separation were never endorsed, reforms were introduced in the state churches that addressed at least some of their concerns.

The *Ziegenhainer Zuchtordnung*, which resulted from Bucer's debate with the Anabaptist representatives in Marburg in November 1538, introduced four significant measures into the state church. Some of the contents of this ordinance seem to have derived from ideas set out in Bucer's *Concerning the True Care of Souls*, published in the same year.[23]

First, the rite of confirmation was instituted. Bucer first mentioned this in 1533 and may well have received this idea from Caspar Schwenckfeld at the Strasbourg synod earlier that year. But it was in Hesse that Bucer had an opportunity to introduce this practice. While this did not address the Anabaptists' conviction that baptism was for believers rather than infants, it provided an opportunity for those being confirmed after being catechized to make a public profession of their faith and to commit themselves to a life of discipleship. This was not believers baptism, nor did it do away with the practice of infant baptism, but it did to some extent reconnect personal faith, discipleship, and baptism, going at least some way toward the Anabaptist position. Amy Nelson Burnett writes: "In Bucer's words, each child was 'to commit himself to the fellowship and obedience of the church.' The concept of committing or surrendering oneself (*sich begeben/sich ergeben*) was frequently used by Anabaptists in conjunction with adult baptism."[24]

Second, the state churches began to give greater attention to the matter of the education of their members, responding to the Anabaptist critique that those baptized as infants did not receive proper instruction at any stage in their lives. In the Marburg debate in 1538 Bucer assured Schnabel: "the children should be catechized diligently when they came to an age of accountability and should be taught to observe everything that the Lord had commanded."[25]

Third, the Order introduced into the state churches the office of elder, a leadership role that ensured laypersons had greater responsibility within the church and opportunities to influence decisions. They could hold the clergy to account. Jean Rott writes that Bucer "had secured that, according to the new church ordinances in Hesse, young people should be confirmed after finishing their catechism, and, most important of all, elders should be appointed to strengthen church discipline."[26]

Fourth, the Order set out the process by which church discipline should be practiced in the churches, including the exercise of the ban in appropriate cases. This had been one of the main topics of conversation in the Marburg debate. Bucer was already convinced that church discipline was required in the state churches, and his conversation with Schnabel and his colleagues reinforced his determination to implement this. Burnett writes: "By 1534 the related concepts of self-surrender and commitment had become a standard part of Bucer's theological vocabulary, and from then on they occurred in almost all of his writings."[27] Bucer had a deep and longstanding commitment to high standards in the church, and in 1538 he declared that discipline was the third mark of the true church, to which the reformers had not yet given adequate attention.

It is clear that Bucer's debates with the Anabaptists, coupled with Philip's lenient policy toward them, had a significant impact on the Hessian church and wider society. Glebe concludes: "the encounter with Anabaptism changed the character of the early Hessian church by forcing it to reorient its attention on discipline and practical morality."[28] Even Paul Wappler, who did not hesitate to designate Anabaptism as a heresy, paid tribute to its positive impact, made possible especially by Philip's policy: "It was due to this lenience toward the Anabaptists, to a great extent, that new life and wholesome recollection of nearly forgotten truths of salvation were brought to the church."[29]

Nor should we ignore, even if we cannot quantify, the influence of returning Anabaptists in the state churches. Congregations in towns and villages across Hesse were joined by committed Christians, who were serious enough about their faith to risk discovery, arrest, interrogation, and various forms of punishment (albeit not the prospect of execution). Not only did those widely known as Anabaptists return to the state churches, but likely many others who shared or at least sympathized with their views but had not identified publicly with the movement (or had not been discovered by the authorities) were encouraged by these developments to play a more active role in the congregations.

Glebe concludes: "It is impossible to know how many Anabaptists who had never been suspected or interrogated by officials 'snuck' back into the Hessian church."[30] It is also impossible to know how many continued to meet together in private homes as well as attending the state churches. But it is just as likely that many more had remained in the state churches while quietly embracing Anabaptist perspectives, and that they were now able to participate more wholeheartedly in churches that were being reformed because of the Anabaptists' influence.

But there is some dispute as to how deep-rooted were the changes in the character of the state churches, how effectively the reforms were introduced, and how long these lasted.

Several scholars, writing in the nineteenth and early twentieth centuries, suggested that Anabaptism had a significant influence on the state churches in Hesse, an influence that persisted long after the movement itself had largely disappeared.[31] They pointed, among other legacies, to the reinvigoration of church life, increased autonomy and responsibility for the congregation, more attention to pastoral care and Christian education, and the practice of church discipline. And Eduard Becker identified to a less institutional but perhaps even more significant legacy: "A considerable number of villages which were known to have been centers of Anabaptism later became centers of pietism and in our day are now centers of the *Gemeinschaften*."[32] Other historians have noted this phenomenon in various contexts—there may not be identifiable historical links or any conscious dependence on earlier movements, but some locations seem to be unusually prone to renewal and expressions of radical discipleship.

Other scholars are less convinced that the Hessian churches really experienced deep and lasting changes. Stalnaker, in an article examining the influence of Anabaptism and Martin Bucer on the evolution of the church in Hesse, writes: "The rise and decline of Hessian Anabaptism does indeed have important implications for the shaping of the Hessian Protestant church, but not because the measures taken to eliminate Anabaptism brought about any decisive constitutional changes in the church."[33] Cataloging the limited impact of the reforms, he notes the many accusations and recriminations that characterized the following decades and concludes that the results were disappointing. He concludes: "The innovations of the Ziegenhain ordinance of 1539 were stillborn, or nearly so. . . . From the perspective of the mid-1540s it can be seen that the successful conversion of the Anabaptists was not a portent of generally more orderly and obedient Hessian parishes."[34]

Bucer returned frequently to Hesse over the next few years and constantly complained about the lack of progress. Evidence of moral improvement in the churches was very limited. The introduction of elders was patchy and largely ineffective. And despite his best efforts to encourage this, church discipline within the state churches rarely extended beyond an experimental period. Only the introduction of the rite of confirmation and the attempt to provide good Christian education in the churches seem to have been of lasting significance. Much harder to document or measure, though, is the continuing yearning for spiritual and moral authenticity that, if Becker is right, persisted in less formal settings and burst into life again in a subsequent generation.

But the struggle between the Hessian Anabaptists and the state church, even if the depth of its impact on the Hessian churches was limited, did have a much wider geographical impact as the rite of confirmation was commended to and gradually adopted by Protestant churches in many other territories. Furthermore, Bucer's influence on his younger colleague Jean Calvin should not be underestimated. Calvin joined Bucer in Strasbourg in 1538 (the same year of the debate between Bucer and the Anabaptists in Hesse) after his expulsion from Geneva, accompanied him to several inter-Protestant dialogues in the early 1540s, and introduced a comprehensive approach to church discipline when he returned to Geneva. This form of church discipline, which involved the civic authorities, would not have commended itself to the Anabaptists, but it was a serious attempt at developing a more disciplined church—and it is not fanciful to trace this policy back to Bucer's influence on Calvin and, beyond this, to Bucer's discussions with both Marpeck and Rinck.

DISSENT AND REFORMATION

A perennial question confronting those throughout church history who have yearned for the reformation of the church is whether separating in order to embody their convictions in new ecclesial communities is more effective than remaining within and working for the changes they espouse. A further question is whether such separation is justifiable in any circumstances in light of the biblical emphasis on the unity of the church. Of course, in some contexts those who press for reform do not voluntarily separate from the church but are excluded, especially if their language is intemperate, their influence is growing, or they put their beliefs into practice without permission.

Bucer, along with other reformers, placed great emphasis on the unity of the church and reacted strongly to the separatism he found among Anabaptists. Whatever the defects of the church, which Bucer acknowledged more freely than many of his colleagues, he was convinced that separation was illegitimate. There is considerable irony in this stance, given the ongoing separation of the Protestant churches from Catholic churches throughout the sixteenth century. But for the reformers, the church was still understood in territorial terms, so that there should be only one church in a parish and each region should consist of only Protestant or Catholic churches. Dissent within a region and the establishing of alternative ecclesial communities was not to be tolerated.

Some Anabaptists were sensitive to this critique, concerned that their actions were not in line with biblical teaching on the unity of the church. But they became convinced that the church was beyond reformation and that restitution, or a fresh start, was required. If the church had become corrupt in its doctrine, practices, and morality, maybe it was no longer truly the church, and so separation was legitimate and necessary. Most did not deny that there were true Christians within the state churches, but many regarded the institution of the state church as beyond redemption.

In light of this frequent and passionate debate between reformers and Anabaptists across Europe, what happened in Hesse is interesting. Because of the various factors noted above, it seems that separation from the state churches was less sharp than in many areas and that allegiance to the Anabaptist communities was less fervent. And once evidence emerged that genuine, albeit limited, reformation was taking place in the state churches, numbers of Anabaptists no longer concluded that separation was required. However, without the separation that had occurred, and without the courageous insistence of Rinck and his colleagues on calling the state churches to account, the longed-for reformation would not have transpired. Perhaps periods of separation and a series of dissenting movements are necessary for the reformation and renewal of the church.

As has been evident in the earlier chapters, Anabaptism was worrying to the authorities not only because of the resulting separation from the state church but also because Rinck and many others shared the concerns of the recently crushed peasants' movement for social and economic reform. Rinck was known to have been an ally of Müntzer and to have been at Frankenhausen. However strongly he denied that he was using Anabaptism as a cover for further insurrection, his opponents remained suspicious. His insistence that God would judge the authorities for their refusal to act justly and for persecuting true Christians no doubt reinforced their concerns. But Rinck insisted that he had renounced violent means and that the authorities, despite their shortcomings, should be accorded respect as servants of God. This nuanced perspective of "subversive respect" is not easy to maintain, especially in contexts of gross injustice and corrupt authorities, but it remains essential for faithful Christian discipleship.

Primary Sources

Translators

Leonard Gross and Ellen Yutzy Glebe

THIS SECTION CONTAINS translations of all the extant writings by or about Melchior Rinck. They are organized into three sets. In the first set are six tracts or letters of varying lengths by Rinck himself, arranged according to the order in which they were written. The next ten documents are letters written by others that give us information about Rinck's activities and insights into his teaching.

The third set of documents contains reports of interrogations of Rinck and some of his followers. The first is taken from the court records of the so-called Marburg disputation—in format a debate but in practice an extended interrogation of Rinck's teaching. The next three texts are interrogations of different groups of Rinck's followers, the first of these including Rinck himself. A short final document is a report of the interrogation of an individual Anabaptist. Included with these reports are some letters from the interrogators to their political rulers.

A. RINCK'S WRITINGS

1. Refutation of a text which Johannes Bader, supposed pastor at Landau, recently wrote, holding to infant baptism as being Christian (?1527)

It has fallen, it has fallen, Babylon the Great (Rev 14[:8]; 18[:10]; Isa 21[:9]; Jer 51[:1–58]).

To those only who fear God from the heart, I, Melchior Rinck, a co-partner in tribulation[1] and hope, wish to those who are in Jesus Christ grace and peace from God the Father and our Lord Jesus Christ. Since your most beloved Johannes Bader, supposed pastor in Landau, has maligned the eternal and immutable truth with such pompous and brazen words before the whole world, this demands that I confront him out of love—both of God and of neighbor—defending the truth with the sword of divine testimony against the lies. As Christ says (Matt 10[:37, 38]), whoever loves father and mother more than him is not worthy of him. Indeed, he says, "Whoever does not take up the cross and follow me is not worthy of me"—as if he means to say, Whoever does not bear witness to me with humility, words, and deed, will have no part of me.

Furthermore, since Johannes Bader himself so often acknowledges the innocence of children, it is indeed astounding that he so thoughtlessly [approves] of infant baptism. Baptism is for those who are guilty of sinning, who have acknowledged their guilt through faith, and have faith in God who promises them forgiveness of sins. It is these who are lifted up, as is plain (Matt 3, 28; Mark 1, 16; Luke 3; John 3; Acts 2, 8, 9, 10, 16, 18; Rom 6; 1 Cor 15; Eph 5; Gal 3; Col 2; Titus 3; 1 Pet 3; Heb 10). And what truly is the Gospel other than a covenant of God, within which those who repent are promised forgiveness of sins? (Matt 4, 5, 9, 16; Mark 6, 10; Luke 9, 14, 24; John 1, 6, 10, 14; Rom 1, 4; 1 Cor 15).[2]

Johannes Bader, however, states that outer baptism is not bound to the inner, and wants to prove this by saying that, if this is true, the apostles could not have followed and fulfilled the command of Christ,

1 Margin: Rev 1[:9].

2 Margin: New Testament references on baptism and its meaning, [and] how and whom to baptize.

as regards baptism, since the Lord alone discerns the heart. He also thinks he can use this argument to prove that he has authority to baptize infants, even though he is uncertain of their faith. Is this actually what the Lord wants? In reality Christ (Matt 28[:18–20]) indicates specifically what one who desires to be baptized shall do. He says: "All power has been given to me in heaven and on earth; therefore go and teach all peoples and baptize them in the name of the Father, and the Son, and the Holy Spirit, and teach them to hold to all that I have commanded you."[3] Similarly, he shows specifically (Mark 16[:16]) what one who desires to be baptized shall do, saying "whoever has faith and has been baptized[4] will be saved; whoever does not have faith will be damned."

So now, if Johannes Bader is able to authenticate such a command in relation to infants, he may justifiably baptize them. But if he cannot authenticate such a command and still wants to baptize innocent infants against their knowledge and will—indeed, outside the commandment of Christ!—then he is proving by his action whose servant he is.

In addition, if he can prove that they, even as children, have incurred original sin and possess faith, he can then discuss with their parents whether to allow their infants to be baptized. But if he is not able to do this, and still promises salvation to the infant based on its baptism, which it receives without faith, he is stating something which God has not commanded him to say. He needs to hear what the Lord says through Ezekiel, in the 13th chapter: "Woe to the foolish prophets who follow their own foolish spirit, and still have seen nothing! They envision nothing but vanity, and have spoken lies up to now, exclaiming, 'The Lord has spoken,' when the Lord had not sent them. Still, they wait for the fulfillment of their word! Have you not seen a false vision or uttered a lying divination, when you have said, 'Says the Lord,' even though I did not speak? Woe to you who sew bands on all wrists and make veils for the heads of persons of every height, to capture their souls! When you then have captured the souls of my people, you promise them life. You have profaned me among my people for handfuls of barley and for pieces of bread, damning persons who should not die

---

3 Margin: The one baptizing.

4 Margin: The one baptized.

and granting life to persons who should not live. This you bring about with your lies among my people, for they listen to the lies."[5]

And if he wants to argue that baptism can be compared to circumcision,[6] this is of no help to him, since God established circumcision through Abraham and Moses, his servants; baptism, however, he established through Christ, his son. Furthermore, circumcision was a sign of the yoke of servitude and included those who had not wanted this but had to be coerced and pressured. Baptism,[7] on the other hand, is a sign and confession of the childlike covenant, under which no one is to be either coerced or pressured through the force of compulsion,[8] as may be seen (John 6; Matt 16, 18, 23, 28; Ps 109). Whoever, therefore, receives the servants of God but then rejects the Son of God receives his judgment (Deut 18[:18–19]; John 3, 10; Mark 16).

So, anyone who wants to be a disciple of Moses and does not want to know where Christ—[the one] who opens the eyes of the blind—comes from must in the end be shown, through the eyes of the very least of these, my people, whether he might not also suffer the same [judgment] (John 9). But such a person shall know that it is not Christ, but Moses himself who is the one accusing his disciples before God (John 5[:45]).

It is presumptuous that Johannes Bader insists on the necessity of an explicit [scriptural] proscription of infant baptism, since he denies those [proscriptions] which he already has at hand, priding himself with the claim that what he has, he has received only from God. Yet everything that the command of Jesus Christ (Matt 28) does not permit is forbidden. Since the Lord gave such an earnest command, we are not to add to or take away from his word (Deut 4; Ps 30).[9] We are not to do what seems good to us (Deut 12). We are to deviate neither to the right nor to the left (Deut 17).

To be sure, God speaks through Isaiah (29[:13]): "These people draw near with their mouths and honor me with their lips, while their hearts are far from me, but they serve me in vain, and their worship of me is a human commandment learned by rote." Christ also says (John 14[:21]),

---

5 Margin: Ezek 13[:3, 6–7, 18–19].

6 Margin: Circumcision.

7 Margin: Baptism.

8 Margin: The Christian faith is without coercion. Also: command = something certain.

9 Margin: Nothing to be added to or taken away from God's Word.

"They who have my commandments and keep them are those who love me." Also, (15[:10]), "If you keep my commandments, you will abide in my love." Indeed, he says, Matt 15[:13], "Every plant that my heavenly father has not planted will be uprooted."[10] Those who teach human commandments he also calls "blind, blind leaders." It would seem, then, that he imagines Christ need not be listened to, even though the Father says: This is my beloved Son[11] to whom you are to listen (Matt 17[:5]).

Yes, it is said that he wants to take vengeance on those who would not listen to him.[12] "See to it," says Paul, "that no one takes you captive through philosophy and empty deceit, according to human tradition, according to the elemental spirits of the universe, and not according to Christ" (Col 2[:8]). If Johannes Bader (and his followers) did not have such a prohibition, such blasphemy would not be held against him. But now that such a prohibition makes his sins weightier, he must understand that his path leads to death (if he does not mend his ways).

What, indeed, is infant baptism other than simply the mark [of the beast]?[13] This is what the pharisaical rabble or Roman beasts teach, with the assistance of the rabble of the scribes. This is the total Antichrist.[14] He gives to his own this mark on their brow so that no one can buy or sell who does not have the mark (Rev 3 [see 13:16–17]). But woe to such people, for they will drink the wine of divine wrath (Rev 14[:8]). Also "a foul and painful sore came on those who had the mark of the beast[15] and who worshiped its image." (Rev 16[:2]). And although the ten kings, that is, the scribes, who are to receive authority as kings for one hour, together with the beast, will hate the whore, that is, the Roman church, and make her desolate and naked, banning her and devouring her gathered treasures, giving back the kingdom to the beast, and making war on the Lamb, so will the Lamb still conquer them, for the Lamb is Lord of all lords[16] (Rev 17[:12–14]).

---

10 Margin: Matt 15.

11 Margin: Deut 18; Luke 9.

12 Margin: Deut 18.

13 Margin: What infant baptism is.

14 Margin: Pharisees—scribes, active Antichrists (German: "Phari.—= sreibe, tetig Antichristy"). Throughout Rinck's writings, the Roman church is characterized as "Pharisees," "hypocrites," "work-saints," whereas the Lutheran church is characterized as "scribes."

15 Margin: [a visual sign (cross, within a circle)].

16 Margin: Rev 17.

One might, however, expect Johannes Bader to know the truth, intending to avoid heresy, and to be better instructed in these matters, since he is so adept in debate. I testify—this comes not only from me, but also from others—that in his house he was often convinced of the truth, but then later came to disdain all such matters, maligning to the greatest degree the truth he had recognized, against his own conscience. At that time, I considered him to be my brother in the Lord, [which was] my downfall.[17] I entered into [baptismal] sponsorship, affirming, and [later] lamenting [my decision]. [I did this] in the hope that he would take pity on me and forgive me in a brotherly manner, since the Father of all mercy, through such an atrocious death, with such a powerful hand, has led me. Christ so clearly speaks, "blessed [are] the merciful" (Matt 5), condemning, however, the unmerciful (Matt 6, 13), whereby nothing would be worthwhile. As James says, chapter 2[:13]: "For judgment will be without mercy to anyone who has shown no mercy; mercy triumphs over judgment."[18] As the Lord says (Hos 6), he desires mercy and not sacrifice—to say nothing of Christ, who let an adulteress depart uncondemned (John 8).

Even "the Galileans whose blood Pilate had mingled with their sacrifices" were not the only sinners (Luke 13[:1]). So, also, does the father rejoice in his heart[19] when his son, who confesses his mistakes, returns to him (Luke 15[:6]). And, even though the Pharisee highly lauded his own righteousness, the tax collector will still be the one justified, rather than the other (Luke 18[:9–14]). The Son of Man (says Christ, Matt 18[:11]) has come to save that which is perishing.

Consequently, I had hoped that Johannes Bader would not have maligned the eternal truth and the powerful command of Jesus Christ concerning baptism, which he did to my detriment—not to speak of the evil deeds with which he contradicts the command of Christ, against all truth. May God forgive him mercifully (as soon as he so desires). Amen.

Johannes Bader also says we contaminate the goal of Evangelical truth, since we supposedly say that baptism makes people perfect.

---

17 Zu welcher zeit ich Im dann auch alls mein bruder im herren, mein fall, so ich bei der pattenschafft gethon, bekennet vnd klaget hab, . . .

18 Margin: To be merciful.

19 Margin: Vows (original text: "Vota").

He should be ashamed of stating this untruth, since we actually say: Whoever has faith and has been baptized, will be saved; however, whoever does not have faith will be damned, even if he also submits to baptism a hundred times, as Mark 16 and Paul, in all his writings, will testify.

But whoever says he believes in Christ and extols his blood shall not alter Christ's command, much less hinder those who desire to follow him. He finally, along with all others, must also hear what Christ says (Matt 23[:13]): "Woe to you, scribes and Pharisees, hypocrites! For you lock people out of the kingdom of heaven. For you do not go in yourselves, and when others are going in, you stop them." Is that, however, not altering the Gospel, as the false prophets did in Paul's time, putting baptism first, and thereafter, faith? As for the desire to place water on infants such a long time before the person acknowledges faith, Paul says (Gal 1[:8]): "But even if we or an angel from heaven should proclaim to you a gospel contrary to what we proclaimed to you, let that one be accursed!" Also (Gal 3:[10]): "For all who rely on the works of the law are under a curse." Also (Gal 6 [see 5:3]): "Once again I testify to every man who lets himself be circumcised that he is obliged to obey the entire law. You [who want to be justified by the law] have cut yourselves off from Christ."

Now Paul never baptized first, after which he taught faith. Thus, infant baptism, along with circumcision, is a work of law—that is, devoid of faith.[20] To be sure, those who baptize children, promising them salvation through such a baptism, are consequently under the curse and malediction, and have no part in Christ, as Paul testifies—and this needs no additional commentary—"for whatever does not proceed from faith is sin"[21] (Rom 14[:23]; John 3). And truly, since not all who say to Christ "Lord, Lord" come into the kingdom of heaven, it is certain that those who baptize children are already excluded, since they thereby confess Christ with their mouth, but refuse him the smallest of works.[22] They state that they do the will of God, yet they have not forsaken their own will. They brag about a new life and resurrection through Christ, yet they have not as yet died and been buried with

20 Margin: Infant baptism, a work of law.

21 Margin: Gal 5.

22 dweil sie Christum also mit mundt bekennen, dass sie Inen auch nit geringste Werck verleugnen. *Inen* may well be a mistranscription for *ihm*, and *nit* for *mit.*

him.[23] Such people, however, have to take care to avoid getting what is coming to them in the end times in the lake of fire that burns with sulfur, including the beast and false prophets (Rev 19[:19–21]). God, however, desires that all who want it from the heart and hold blamelessly to the coming of Christ his Son will be graciously saved from such horror. In the Name of Christ, Amen.[24]

2. Admonition and warning to all who are part of the magistracy (?1527)

It has fallen, it has fallen, Babylon the Great (Rev 18; Isa 21; Jer 51).

Greetings to all who are part of the magistracy, whether of high or low rank. I, Melchior Rinck, wish you grace and peace from God the Father and our Lord Jesus Christ.

Every magistracy and power is from God, and a servant of God and of Christians, to punish those who are evil and protect those who are good. This includes Assur, the Turk, Nebuchadnezzar, as Scripture states, along with all godless tyrants—that is, in the case that they are already tyrants and their hearts remain hardened. In this way, God has children who have need of the rod, which is useful and good for them, for we will thereby be driven to God according to his providence. For this reason, he sends and inflicts coercion, persecution, and so on, for our own good, according to his fatherly will and . . . *[one line cut off from original manuscript]*

Meanwhile, in these last and most dangerous times (dearly beloved servants of Christ), much innocent blood of the witnesses and followers of Christ has been shed and spilt everywhere, nonstop. Everyone—not only the pharisaical hypocrites, but also the antichristian scribes—is pronouncing judgment,[25] damning and cursing the children of God as heretics and fanatics, contrary to all honesty and to their own consciences. They miss no opportunity to defame them as insurrectionists against the power of the magistracy, in this manner fulfilling the measure of their fathers before them, and according

23 Margin: "V. D." "God willing."

24 Source: Gerhard Neumann, "Rinck, Melchior. 'A Newly Discovered Manuscript of Melchior Rinck,'" *Mennonite Quarterly Review* 35 (July 1961): 207–11.

25 Margin: [symbol of church edifice, with a cross atop, followed by] "V.D." "God willing."

to the wish of their parents, all of which is innocent blood coming upon them.[26]

It is therefore incumbent to place a current warning and admonition upon you, so that those who desire to act rightly (as far as they understand it) may know what they are to hold to, and also that those who know ahead of time—those who have sinned out of innocence—may thus need to apologize less before God.

The emperor, along with his underlings, is nothing other than a servant of God—who wields the sword on God's behalf to reprimand and punish wrongdoers,[27] but to protect and reward those who do good. For that reason, one also pays him taxes and duties. So, he should ponder and be attentive with the highest diligence to the fact that Christ, including his members, is a child of God. Moses and the prophets testify concerning this in so many ways which the Father clarifies to them. [The emperor] should hold ground and not be convinced by the supposed children of God (namely,[28] the Pharisees and scribes[29]) to attack the Son of his Lord, and become a murderer of the Child, of the very one who made him a powerful servant and granted him this authority of his office (to the degree he embraces His commandments).

And how does it, indeed, always turn out like this? Both the Pharisees and the scribes, who want to give neither taxes nor revenue to the magistracy, but who instead take in much more of these, have great status with the magistracy and are defended with such gravity. At the same time Christ, with his following, who are prepared to render taxes and revenues to the magistracy, has absolutely no space and standing under the magistracy. Will one, then, believe that such a servant, with his hypocrites (if he does not improve), will finally remain without the punishment of his Lord? Woe to the servant who not only does not carry out the known will of his Lord, but also impedes all people as much as he can from doing the will of their Lord, even if they wanted to. He governs and protects those on whom God's wrath has fallen the furthermost—the very same ones who are the greatest and worst enemy. Yes, thereafter he determines without ceasing how he may disguise the Child of his Lord (to whom obedience alone is what is pleasing to the

---

26 Margin: Matt [23:35; 27:25].

27 Margin: Magistracy, what it is [under which is a likeness of a sword].

28 Margin: [two symbols, followed by:] "V. D." "God willing."

29 "Pharisees and scribes" being the Roman and the Lutheran churches.

Father),[30] desiring thereby not only to be known as a faithful servant of his Lord, but also as a child for other pagans.

And if the Turk, along with his fellow members, is indeed a persecutor of Christ (as it is claimed), it is certainly by measure a minor evil deed in comparison to those who now call themselves Evangelical princes[31] and yet desire neither to see nor hear the witnesses of the Gospel, among whom [in their eyes] everything is frenzy and insurrection. Whatever is displeasing to their tender ears they act upon, expelling [such individuals] everywhere. For previously, before they knew anything about Christ, they were perhaps of the opinion that it is enough when one carries out obedience only with the mouth, even if one's behavior is worse than those who are manifestly pagans.[32] It is as if Christ had not said to his own, "You know that the rulers of the Gentiles lord it over them, and their great ones are tyrants over them."[33] As if he wanted to say, concerning those who are pagan bishops and chiefs who defend their teachings with force, that if one [does not accept their teachings] out of love, then one must do so out of fear.

Yes, if a person wanted to teach them concerning truth, he must instead be convinced by them regarding the lies. Also, those among them who are powerful have at their disposal their subordinates as their servants and possessions, wanting to treat these as their inheritance, according to their every pleasure and wantonness. However, "it will not be so among you; but whoever wishes to be great among you must be your servant and whoever wishes to be first among you must be your slave."[34] It is as if he is saying, If anyone among you desires to be a bishop or teacher,[35] such a person shall not govern the church with his own teachings.[36] He shall neither introduce nor maintain his own teachings with coercion.[37] But he is solely a servant of the church, whose teachings the church may judge, rejecting or accepting [the same].[38]

---

30 Margin: Obedience alone pleases God.

31 Margin: "V. D." "God willing."

32 Margin: [symbol].

33 Margin: Matt 20[:25].

34 [Matt 20:26–27].

35 Margin: Bishop or Teacher.

36 Original text adds at this point (with the words crossed out): ("mit keiner gewalt") = "with no coercion."

37 Margin: 2 Cor 2; 1 Pet 5[:2].

38 Margin: 1: [?].

Indeed, whoever desires to be a Christian prince in this land shall consider neither the church nor what it possesses as his own, but rather as owned by the church. He shall not relish as his own the properties of the church, but is rather to make decisions based upon the authorization of the church, except in situations where all such matters would have been determined solely by the spiritual magistracy (as the scribes say) and not at the same time by the general magistracy, which calls itself Christian. God's word is to be abidingly immutable in all places, yet here in this land it is without power and strength, even while people everywhere write, call, sing, and paint: "V.D.M.I.E."[39] Do we think that Christ said in vain, "Heaven and earth will pass away, but my words will never pass away"?[40]

Then (alas) who would not need to call the pagan Pilate holy,[41] if compared to the current [magistrates] who call themselves Christian and Evangelical princes? Yes, was not Jesus outside the emperor's command, riding to Jerusalem without the permission of Pilate and all the magistrates, allowing himself to be greeted as a hereditary king of the Jews after having traversed the land for a long time with such a great multitude of people—yes, entering the temple and ousting the merchants and venders, upsetting the tables of the money changers, scattering the money? Also, this same Pilate states that he finds no reason for decreeing Christ's death, delaying with all diligence as long as he possibly can, hoping that he might possibly preserve Jesus' life, avowing him also to be righteous, even though he would later be condemned by the Pharisees and scribes, that is, by the most devout and best-educated among the Jews.[42]

And where, indeed, among those who boast that they are members or participants of the Roman Empire—yes, even preachers of the Christian faith—remains, currently, that which the pagan Festus states: That it is a Roman custom not to sentence a person to death unless the accused has first been afforded by the accuser an opportunity to refute

39 V.D.M.I.E. = Verbum domini manet in eternum. The Protestant princes used this abbreviation as their motto at the Diet of Speyer in 1526: "The word of the Lord abides forever." It is thus frequently associated with the principle of *sola scriptura*. The slogan was also used, however, by revolting peasants in 1525, and Thomas Müntzer went into battle at Frankenhausen with a rainbow flag bearing this motto.

40 [Matt 24:35; Luke 21:33].

41 Margin: Pilate, holy.

42 Margin: Pharisees and Scribes.

the accusation[43] [Acts 25]? And when Gallio talks to the Jews, after they have accused Paul on account of the Gospel, does he not say: "Oh, you Jews, if it were a matter of crime or serious villainy, I would be justified in accepting the complaint, but since it is a matter of questions about words and names and your own law, see to it yourselves; I do not wish to be a judge of these matters"?[44] [Acts 18:14–15].

And what has the emperor and his staff to do with such matters of faith? Did not God order his Son to proclaim such, and command the same to be heeded?[45] Just as if Christ would have kept his word in such a way, or had commanded it to be kept, and it had not been written, "Do not put your trust in princes,[46] in mortals, in whom there is no help" [Ps 146:3]. And also: "Cursed are those who trust in mere mortals and make mere flesh their strength" [Jer 17:5]. And, "Oh, you wretched masses of God, that you, through such renown, need to be supported and preserved!" But it is certainly true that neither the pope nor Luther have a true Gospel, since both of them advocate in vain with fleshly weapons contrary to the practices of Christ, Paul, and all the apostles.[47] Neither of them will escape a downfall, as they are founded upon sand, since they are building upon Christ, not with gold, silver, or precious gems, but rather with wood, straw, and stubble.[48]

However, if someone would say that they did not know how broadly the office of the emperor's commands extended,[49] who then would not wonder whether that person could come to understand those matters which have to do with faith in Christ? This would certainly be an oddity, since Paul describes the situation so clearly, saying: "For rulers are not a terror to good conduct but to bad. Do you wish to have no fear of the authority? Then do what is good, and you will receive its approval; for it is God's servant for your good. But if you do what is wrong, you should be afraid, for the authority does not bear the sword in vain! It is the servant of God to execute wrath on the wrongdoer. Therefore one must be subject, not only because of wrath but also because of conscience. For the same reason you also pay taxes,

43 Margin: Festus. Acts 25.
44 Margin: Gallio. Acts 18[:14–15].
45 Margin: Scepter [followed by symbol of a scepter].
46 Margin: "Natios g fider in principib g. nos."
47 Margin: All of this is coercion.
48 Margin: "j:".
49 Margin: The extent of [magisterial] power.

for the authorities are God's servants," if they fulfill such law [Rom 13:3–7]. Peter states the same: "For the Lord's sake accept the authority of every human institution, whether of the emperor as supreme, or of governors, as sent by him to punish those who do wrong and to praise those who do right" [1 Pet 2:13–14]. In these passages one clearly sees how matters of faith have nothing whatsoever to do with the emperor, [matters] which are to be planted in the world.[50] God had spoken earlier in his multifarious promise, concerning his most dearly beloved son, Jesus Christ, that he would take revenge upon those who would not listen.

Indeed, it is like a great and reeky presumption whereby the pagan magistracy (as demanded by their office, as they say)—having continued for such a long time, up to the present—convince the people with force to believe this or that, as if faith is not a gift of God, but rather that of the magistracy,[51] or of human power. But the abovementioned verses state that the emperor's magistracy is ordained solely by God, for the purpose that those who do what is evil are punished; those, however, who do what is good are to be protected and sheltered, for which reason one also pays taxes and duties.

But—oh God, Lord of all magistracies—how at this time all this has been reversed to the greatest degree,[52] where those who commit all sorts of evil receive the greatest praise and protection under the magistracy, whereas those who live exemplary lives—or desire so to do—have neither place nor space. And then, such authorities are not even satisfied by any tax or duty. As if it were evil to obey God through Jesus Christ (and this, without any damage to the magistracy), loving God in all things and the neighbor as oneself; and, on the contrary, that it is the only right and proper thing to adhere to the abomination[53] from Rome or Wittenberg, to profess Christ only with the mouth while disavowing him with works. They would have it that either wooden deeds or a faith of straw should be preached: pride, robbery, murder, gluttony, drunkenness, usury, without taking notice of God at all and blaspheming God most atrociously, etc.[54]

---

50 Margin: Christ, the plant of faith.

51 Margin: Faith, a gift.

52 Margin: Everything reversed.

53 Margin: V.D. (God willing).

54 Margin: [symbol].

And actually, since baptism (whereby I am speaking about the very minimum in outward obedience that Christ demands)[55] is a ceremony in which one pays homage to the magistracy of the Son of God, being obedient in appropriating this command through action (Matt 28[:19]), what, then, is the magistracy of the emperor doing now, other than persecuting in the most horrible manner through the inducement of the double abomination, whereby they, the magistracy, trample the Son of God, their Lord, with their feet, protecting the Antichrist, and thus the child of corruption, thereby exterminating the true Christian and Child of blessedness? It is, therefore, a footstool of the Pharisees and scribes[56] that they make, as much as they possibly can, God their footstool, confessing themselves to be either Christians or Evangelicals with their mouths, yet taking pleasure in either the pope's or Luther's command without works, shouting and yelling that there are those who desire to foment insurrection against them.[57] Therefore [the magistrates], to be sure, are not only rising up against God their Lord, but also coercing with force all God's subjects into apostasy and perjury. Consequently, they may well expect—if they take time to so reflect—what kind of punishment awaits them from the Lord and Father of Jesus Christ.

They (the preachers of abomination) say that there is precedent for such baptizing of infants, but my response is therefore: If a murderer[58] had driven out a hereditary prince from his land, bringing his subjects to homage either with cunning or coercion, and this through the pretense of the magistracy, would such a hereditary prince, as soon as he managed to regain his land, be satisfied with the homage which the murderer had earlier received? Yes, and should the subjects also want—as soon as they again receive their true lord—to refuse proper homage? Since we now, in infant baptism, have paid homage not to Christ, who is God, but rather to the pope and Antichrist, albeit under the name of Christ, God has needed to speak abundantly through our messengers, therefore, even standing up to the pope, whose deeds are evidence of such a great evil. Therefore, we now worship our true Lord, the Son of God, according to his command.

---

55 Margin: What Baptism is.

56 Margin: The beast allows the gruesome whore to rage.

57 Margin: Insurrection, the whore.

58 Margin: A parable of a murderer.

And must [our true Lord] consequently now be strangled by the "servant" of his Lord as an insurrectionist? Whoever has ears to hear should listen, for nothing will finally change until one is eager to listen. Yet there is no one to proclaim the will of God to us. One is calling robustly for help, but God is blocking his ears, because now, since one did not want to listen when God did open his ears, there is no one now who desires his help.

Further, baptism[59] is an act of matrimony in which the devout church commits and binds itself to Christ as its true bridegroom, as one may well learn from the eleventh chapter [v. 2] of the second letter to the Corinthians. Yes, through this the church was purified unto Christ as his unblemished bride, Eph 5[:1ff], so it is a great and dangerous presumption for those who boast of being servants of God, who do not in any manner want to suffer as Christ suffered. For, even if we have been baptized in infants' white, according to the command of the ugly abomination, it was certainly no wedding with Christ, but rather a banquet with the great whore, the Antichrist. It is, thus, not unjust that the church now weds itself only to its true bridegroom, Christ, and veers away from old reprobates with whom the church for such a long time had unwittingly been whoring. If a person shows mercy to a poor prostitute[60] who lay in utter sin for such a long time, then desires to take her as his wife, whereby he makes do with the banquets which such prostitutes would have held with her clients, yet does not enter with her into a proper marriage—yes, it would be even befitting that such a prostitute would refuse such a marriage to the same [man]—even a Nero would pronounce judgment.

Further, since baptism is a ceremony in which the person, upon the requirement and power of faith, yields self to God as a sacrifice, as one finds in Rom 6, it can be measured as to what danger and disgrace against God the magistracy stands under if they oppose [such a baptism]. Moreover, since God did not protect his son, in that he [sent] him into all the world as a sacrifice, for reconciliation, the sole basis of atonement, this is nothing other than impeding the eternal, immutable will of God. Not being willing to permit obedience to God—the sole basis of atonement—yet desiring to be a servant of God by driving out God's Son not only from the house, but also even battering him to

---

59 Margin: Baptism, what it is.

60 Margin: A parable or example about a prostitute.

death, results in extoling the "truth" before other pagans, in this manner defending the lies more than other pagans do. They praise Christ in passing, but as soon as he demands that they should follow him, they want neither to see nor hear of him.

For if we are baptized as infants in white, according to the custom of Baal, such is certainly no offering to God, but rather to the devil,[61] even if it took place under the name of God. This was so also in times gone by when the Jews offered their children to demons, and yet without doubt claimed they were doing this just like Abraham, as commanded by God, as one reads in Ps 106[:37] and in the Second Book of Kings, chapter 21[:6].[62]

It is, therefore, not unfair that people, after committing acknowledged errors, repent and submit to God, their Creator and Savior, and do the same through his beloved Son Jesus, as an offering of a pleasing odor.[63] But both the Italian and German murderers, whores and Baal—that is, the whole jumble of muck and horror—set themselves against [such submission to God], and this with the support of the magistracy,[64] claiming thereby to maintain in both lands what [God] has laid at their footstool.[65] May God protect from sacrilege all those who so desire it, for these times are totally sinister and, above all measure, full of danger. Amen.[66]

3. Melchior Rinck to Eberhard von der Tann (1530)

Grace and peace from God our Father and the Lord Jesus Christ. Worthy Ebert, . . . Hans Eckart visited me here in Haina and reported about the petition that you sent to the Hessian prince in Kassel. I am thoroughly astonished at you, how you can reconcile this with a Christian conscience, for you certainly know that what God has joined together, humans are not to separate. Would I not be with my wife, if it were possible? Is it not due to your bloodthirsty pack of false prophets, who damn as fanaticism whatever is not useful to their god, the stomach? Indeed, isn't it your fault, those who abuse the order of God,

---

61 Margin: Sacrificing his children to the devil.

62 Margin: 2 Kings 21[:6]; Ps 106[:37].

63 [Num 15:14].

64 Margin: The beast stoops down, allowing the whore to sit upon it.

65 [A takeoff from Ps 110:1, which reads: "The LORD says to my lord, 'Sit at my right hand until I make your enemies your footstool'" (see also Luke 20:42–43).]

66 Source: *Mennonite Quarterly Review* 35 (July 1961): 211–17.

or magistracy, with frightful wantonness and sacrilege of Christ to the highest dishonor, just as if God were against himself, establishing the mandate of the sword in order to exterminate his children? Indeed, where can one prove that God's mandate concerning the sword has jurisdiction over matters of faith?

Even though I was in the peasants' revolt, no one can prove that I had fomented it, as is now everywhere being bandied about by many people, who cry: "Riot! Riot!" And with no less insistence calling the children of God unfaithful and rebellious against God and Christ.

On the other hand, if someone says I am an anti-baptist, this I could tolerate if those who speak in this way could prove this from even one iota of Holy Scripture. The fact that they strive to coerce me and all who share my faith into accepting their lies—through murder, theft, prison, fire, water, the sword, and other such arguments—is evidence itself that, in fact, it is *their* baptism which is anti-baptist, and it is *they* who are actually the Antichrist about whom all prophets, Christ, and the apostles have previously spoken. I want, therefore, for the sake of God, to admonish, warn, and implore you and all others to abide by the mandate you have received from God, and not, as is often happening presently, for you to be tainted with the blood of the innocent. Otherwise, it would be far better if one had a millstone hanging around his neck, to be sunk into the sea where it is deepest. May God be with you and with all who so desire it from the heart. Amen.

Melchior Rinck, prisoner of Christ, to the worthy and industrious Eberhard von der Tann, Amtmann (official) at the Wartburg, in his own hand.[67]

4. Tract on marriage (1530)

Praise, honor, and imperishable existence to those who with patience and good works strive toward eternal life; but to those who are contentious and are disobedient to the truth and obedient to the wrong, disgrace and anger, tribulation and fear! For a long time now I have been greatly persecuted by both Papists and Lutherans, that is, by the whole desolation and abomination of the Antichrist, not only as a heretic and a fanatic but also as a rebel against all reasonableness, and (as

67 Source: Wappler, *Stellung Kursachsens*, 148–49.

God is my witness and as the actions of my adversaries richly prove) have been pursued from village to village, from city to city, indeed from land to land. Now after this the roguery and unfaithfulness of my supposedly espoused wife and of her parents breaks forth and comes to the light of day (so that nothing may be lacking in my tribulation). She overwhelms me with such wrathful and false accusations that even my judges, if only they would, could, even without my defense, well recognize my innocence and release me from the accusations that have been made.

But God be praised, who until this day has saved me from so many and manifold snares of the flesh, and who shows my adversaries' iniquities and lies by their fruit, forcing them by their open tyranny and deceit to admit to me, before all the world, that which the lovers of truth would hardly be permitted to say even in private. And who might ever have thought that the most learned and widely famous evangelists of Wittenberg, together with their following, would have been so far from the true gospel and the true government if they had not shown themselves before the whole world with such shameful lies, persecution, tyranny, betrayal, and the shedding of so much innocent blood and other greater outrages?

Oh, how long the wolf might have been able to cover himself with the robbed sheep's wool of Scripture, if by his open marauding among the sheep he had not betrayed himself? So the prince of this world, who has changed himself into an angel of light, would even longer have boasted of his tyranny as a magistrate if he had not, with such miserable and pitiful murdering, revealed himself in the light of day for a warning for all who love the truth?

And how could this be any other way, since Christ says: By their fruits you shall know them [Matt 7:16]? He also says: Such they will do to you also, since they know neither me nor my Father [John 16:3]. Yes, and he also says: Beware of people, for they will deliver you before their council houses and will whip you in their schools. You will be led before princes and kings for my sake as a witness over them and over the heathen [Matt 10:17–18]. And did not David speak quite truly when he says: I have spoken in my heart of the roguery of the godless man. There is no fear of God before his eyes. He deceives himself until his deception is found to deserve hate [Ps 36:1–2]? He speaks in the same way again when he says: God says to the godless: How will you be treated if you proclaim my law and take my commandment in your mouth, but hate tutelage and throw my words behind you? If you saw a thief, you ran with him, and you were one with the adulterers. Your mouth you used for evil and your tongue perpetrated deceit. You sat against your brother and brought shame upon the son of your mother [Ps 50:16–20].

To be sure, for a long time my conscience has been consuming me not a little regarding my supposed marriage to Anna, the daughter of Hans Eckhart of Ockershausen. It seems to me to be unjust to prevent her from entering upon a true marriage. Still, I could not admit the truth without terrible scandal and shame. This has caused me to say to some (although with veiled words) that I thought little, indeed nothing at all, of such a marriage. Yet, again, to some I admitted her in writing to be my married wife. However, before all the world and without my doing, she has now with her public behavior proved of what mind she has been toward me from the beginning, that she did not marry me out of love or from a free heart, but for the sake of secure days and because she was forced by her parents. This I have not found otherwise in her from the beginning. Thus, I am compelled, out of love for the truth, by this present writing in the presence of the Most High, henceforth to deny her as my espoused wife. I do this, since it is written: And the two will become one flesh [Matt 19:5]. I do not wish to dishonor anyone with this action but, for fear of lying, I do not deny that which she has proclaimed as truth with her deeds, but wish to confess it as truth with words as well.

If Hans Eckhart wished to give me his daughter in such a way that he could nonetheless keep her for himself, God (to whom alone be praise) has arranged matters differently so that his unfaithfulness and falseness has had to come to the light of day; indeed, it had to come out that he did not wish to give his child in marriage but to sell her. Further, if his daughter Anna also orally agreed to be wedded to me and submitted herself to me, but such was not her will and she nevertheless wanted to remain by herself, then God be praised, who by his effective means saved me from such an unmarried marriage. I should also hope that she would in the future not venture to deceive anyone else with such falsehood to her own great shame.

Christ says: What God has joined, man is not to separate [Matt 19:6]. And he also says: Have you not read that he, who in the beginning made man, caused one man and one woman to be, and he said: Therefore, a man will leave his father and mother and cling to his wife and the two shall be one flesh [Matt 19:4–5]? And should that be [regarded as] joined by God which Satan and his following force together for the desire of temporal honor and utility? Truly, if everything which is forced together were joined by God, then all whores and fornicators who came together for gain or for other dishonorable reason would be joined by God. What then would be the difference between prostitution and matrimony?

Christ also says: Whoever separates himself from his wife, except for adultery, causes her to commit adultery [Matt 5:32]. That is well said. But what if one did not have a wife but a whore under the pretense of marriage and was worse off with his pretended marriage than with open prostitution? Moses permitted a wife to be driven away for any reason so that something worse could be avoided [Deut 24:1]. Christ says: a Christian may divorce his wife for reason of adultery [Matt 19:9]. How much more is it permissible, indeed commanded, that one separate oneself from one who has never been his espoused wife and who under the name of matrimony has deceived him?

If it is contrary to God to separate from prostitution, why then does Paul say: Flee fornication [1 Cor 6:18]? And again: This you must know, that no fornicator or unclean or avaricious person, who is an idolator, has inheritance in the kingdom of Christ and God [Eph 5:5]? And how is it that the world holds to such unmarried marriages so strongly and, for the sake of truth, separates and breaks those marriages which God has joined together? Is it because in this, as in other of its matters, it loves what is its own? In the common whorehouses the whores sell themselves for three pennies. Here one weds in vain unless one has guilders to distribute freely. But that is something she especially hopes to enjoy. She does not want to be a prostitute but wants to be considered a married woman. It is not only that the sale is mutually agreed on, but also that the priest joins their hands together, that there is gorging and swilling, that one respects the blood relatives on both sides. And, to be sure, just as the priests do with their infant baptism and their idol of bread, setting themselves above God and Christ, so they do in the joining of so many unmarried marriages. But the works everywhere give evidence that the masters are neither God nor Christ, but Satan and the Antichrist.

Hans Eckhart (as I hear) charges that inside of six years I have not once been in Ockershausen and that not once in my absence have I sent for his daughter. But, oh God, the audacity of the lie! He knows that he is not able to prove his untruth with a single witness. But thanks be to the kingdom of the Antichrist which not only forces itself knowingly to lie, but without any shame lies to itself so that it will not long continue, but that with its manifold divisions it will collapse, as has happened with all tyrannies that have been from the beginning.

And, even if it were true that Anna were my married spouse, which her doing denies, yet it is manifest that she does not want to follow me, since I have no place to stay. And, even if I were to procure a place to stay, she wants to remain with her parents and not with me, even though she and her people know (and those who persecute me can never truthfully prove otherwise) that it is not for any misdeed that I am pursued here and there. Let anyone who loves the truth, therefore, hear that it is not I who leaves her, but she that leaves me.

I have this word of Paul speaking for me: If now the unbeliever separates himself, let him separate himself. The brother or sister is not bound in such a case [1 Cor 7:15]. If my adversaries say, as they do, that I ought to leave such fanaticism and return to my wife, should they not with such tyranny against me, as also their ancestors have done against Christ, my Lord and their object of ridicule, convict themselves of their own senselessness, that perhaps their senseless senselessness would turn out to be wisdom? But now, since even the infants almost recognize them as the desolation and abomination of which all prophets, apostles and Christ himself also have spoken beforehand, it is fitting that I hold to that which Christ says: Whoever loves wife and child more than me is not worthy of me [Matt 10:37].

And again, if it is wrong to leave wife and child, why then do my adversaries for the sake of truth force so many people away from their wives and children, indeed making many poor widows and orphans? Could they perhaps be desiring to maintain their horror and darkness before Christ and the light? May God reward these jacks and their king according to their works. Amen.

I, for my part, am willing to bear my shame. Even though I have been deceived, but have not myself deceived, I will speak: Father, I have sinned in heaven and before you. I am henceforth no longer worthy to be called your son [Luke 15:21]. May God save all who desire it from error and from this wicked world. Amen.[68]

5. A communiqué from Melchior Rinck and Antonius Jacobs (?1530)

Grace and peace from God our Father and the Lord Jesus Christ. Beloved in the Lord, know that I, Melchior Rinck, and Antonius Jacobs, brethren in the Lord at Haina, imprisoned for the sake of truth, are still alive and well through the strength of almighty God. We hope to remain [true] to the end to both teachings—baptism and the Supper of Christ—and to remain true to Him in all other things, through the support and help of God, although already for a very long time the Papal and Lutheran powers have been working to dissuade us from such teachings. May God save his own from both powers. Amen.

6. Tract on baptism (?1530)

"Let the little children come to me" (Mark 10[:14]).

Just as one cannot damn children because of unfaith, so also one dare not declare them saved on the grounds of faith, since one cannot preach to them, nor can they listen; and likewise, since they neither know nor hate evil, they are also without knowledge and love of the good.

They who love those who are children by nature, yet hate the children of the Spirit and call them fanatics[69]

Whoever brings natural children to Christ [i.e., to baptism], yet does not let the children of the new birth come to Christ [i.e., to baptism], does not love children who are children by nature, but hates them; for he brings them not to Christ but to Belial. He wants to retain through infant baptism what he never had, namely, the blessing, and wants to escape from what is already hanging around his neck, namely,

---

68 Source: Wappler, *Stellung Kursachsens*, 149–52. Also included in Franz et al., *Urkundliche Quellen zur hessischen*, 33–37. This translation was first published in Friesen and Klaassen, *Sixteenth Century Anabaptism*, 55–58. It is reprinted here with the permission of the Institute of Anabaptist and Mennonite Studies.

69 Welcher die Kinder von natur also lieb hat; das er die Kinder des geists Schwuermer heist / unnd hasset. Item welcher die Kinder . . . This sentence, ending with "unnd hasset," is an incomplete sentence, inserted as it is just before "Item," which introduces a new sentence. It thus serves as a heading for what follows.

the curse, because he thereby loves the creature and himself in such a manner as to reject the Creator. And truly, that both the works-saints and the scribes[70] are striving so intensely to uphold infant baptism, is not done out of love for the children, for they are precisely the ones who devour and fatten themselves with the bread that rightly belongs to the children and to the poor orphans. They are doing this, rather, to retain and perpetuate their roguery, conceited honor, power, and false Christendom, which they have already acquired through the establishment of such a baptism. For Satan takes careful note that, as soon as a congregation should arise manifesting obedience to Christ, not only with the mouth and heart, but also with deeds and love, then in the face of such light, his darkness could no longer remain, because it would become obvious that his gospel and Christendom are a groveling abomination.

And, indeed, is there any better way to corrupt a city or lay waste to a sheepfold than to allow the city's enemy into its midst in his early years and raise him up to maturity in the city so that he would have become thoroughly acquainted with all facets of the city? He would thus be able to attack the city, not from the outside in (from where it could not be conquered), but rather from inside out (which no city can endure). Would it then be possible, after the deed, to expel such an enemy from the city (after he—or someone from the outside—had commanded the allegiance of the majority of the citizens through fear)? Or for the city to permit him to remain without his poisoning the city?

Likewise, if a shepherd were to take young wolves, lions, or bears into the sheepfold, raising them with the sheep, would they not eventually (once they were grown) ravage both the shepherd and the sheep? Indeed, they themselves would also want to be shepherd and sheep. And, truly, if the [scribes] were to go in and expel from their [congregations][71] those whom they know with certainty are wolves, bears, and lions, they would surely then experience what infant baptism has brought into being. But the dogs[72] will not do this, as they now have also become silent, but they are instead attacking the sheep

70 [Roman and Lutheran.]

71 Und zwar es gehn nun hin die . . . ierten / unnd treiben aus ihrer ge . . . Here, the original text is illegible.

72 [preachers.]

with greater fury (than hitherto), imploring the lions[73] for help with that which they cannot do themselves, which means that they remain vassals because they cannot gain the upper hand.

May God graciously save the sheep of his flock from their every hand. Amen.[74]

B. LETTERS ABOUT RINCK

1. Governor and domestic councils of Kassel, to Landgrave [Philip] (10 March 1529)

The Schultheiß (mayor) of Hersfeld [Cyriax Hoffmann] reported to us today that Melchior Rinck, who lives there, is very active in spreading Anabaptism, and has been sending the accompanying booklet[75] to his disciples everywhere. It is, therefore, of concern that if he is not opposed and measures are not taken to oppose this unchristian abuse, many subjects in the area will submit to rebaptism. Your Grace may want to command what Your Grace views as just and Christian [. . .] Kassel, on the Wednesday [after] Laetare, in the year [15]29.[76]

2. Report of Elector John to Landgrave Philip of Hesse (4 December 1529)

First of all, [we declare ourselves], as always, at your service . . . . To our highborn and gracious prince . . . . Our dear and faithful Eberhard von der Tann, the Amtmann (official) at the Wartburg, has reported to us what he recently requested from you regarding the imprisoned Melchior Rinck, called the Greek, and what your response was. If this Rinck is not punished at his hearing, due to your reservations, but rather even possibly finding a way that he should be set free, then it is our friendly request that you, in the hearing, at the very least banish him from our principality, land and people, forever, so that through God's grace, our populace—especially the simple and poor—will be more protected

73 [the magistrates.]

74 Source: Geldbach, "Lehre des hessischen Täuferführers," 119–35. A previous translation may be found in John H. Yoder, ed., *The Legacy of Michael Sattler* (Scottdale, PA: Herald Press, 1973), 135–38.

75 Missing from the file.

76 Source: Franz et al., *Urkundliche Quellen zur hessischen*, 19. (The renditions by Franz et al. do not include all the source text verbatim. They have summarized the text in places.)

from his damaging, seductive teachings. And such an oath prior to his release should also include all of us, our lands and such people to whom he might, in time, wish to complain about his imprisonment. This is what we again desire to amiably bring to you. And although we do not anticipate any objections on your part, we still request herewith that you respond agreeably.

Date: Schmalkalden, Saturday, 4 December 1529.[77]

3. Eberhard von der Tann to Elector John (25 November 1531)

Most sagacious, noble, gracious Elector and Lord, Your Grace:

My subjects are prepared with all diligence to serve willingly from this day forth.

Gracious Elector and Lord, it happened approximately in the past year of [15]29, around the Sunday of Quasimodogeniti [first Sunday after Easter: 4 April] in the absence of Your Grace, that your son, the noble prince, Duke Johann Friedrich, my gracious younger lord, graciously notified and sent me orders. According to His Princely Grace's report, a certain Melchior Rinck, also named "the Greek," was said to have repeatedly visited the dominion of Eisenach near Marksuhl,[78] in the bishopric of Hersfeld, and surrounding parts and adhered to the seductive, onerous error against the holy sacraments of the body of Christ [i.e., communion] and baptism and that he was also leading the people astray and impressing upon them such poisonous errors. I was, if this was indeed the case, to diligently track him down and have him brought to prison, etc. Now, although I diligently sought to comply as assiduously as possible, this Melchior was shortly thereafter imprisoned on account of these infractions in a jail belonging to the sagacious, noble prince and lord, Philip, Landgrave of Hesse, etc. This was despite[79] the fact that I, upon Your Grace's command, wrote to His Princely Grace about the same Rinck and his misdeeds and plans, namely, that he was closely attached to Müntzer for a long time while [Müntzer] was still alive, and that he had secretly joined in the Battle of Frankenhausen, wielding his power in this insurrection as a major and leading participant.

---

77 Source: Wappler, *Stellung Kursachsens*, 134.

78 Marksuhl is a village in the Wartburg district of Thuringia. In July 2018, it was incorporated into the municipality of Gerstungen.

79 "This was despite," i.e., the author of the letter thinks the landgrave has shown undue clemency, given the severity of Rinck's infractions, of which the author had informed him at length.

After the uproar was suppressed, rather than expressing regret and choosing to renounce this error—which he never did—he instead was often heard to say in his speeches that God had helped him at Frankenhausen, that he was to fulfill Müntzer's unchristian actions and bring them to their conclusion. Since that time, up till now, he has abandoned his wife here in this province and has traveled around in various lands, using his secret hideaway and proclaiming, against the public prohibition of all magistracies, the harmful poison of the riotous Anabaptists among many poor, simple, ignorant people, men and women, spreading the same openly in broad daylight and on the basis of his own writings—in part published, in part in his own handwriting. These had been sent to His Princely Grace, so that these same writings—the message on his "shield"[80]—may be adequately comprehended.

In submissiveness I also reported this to His Princely Grace [the landgrave] and suggest that he should order the often-mentioned Melchior, on the grounds of his infractions, to be interrogated under torture. I have therefore requested that the same statement be graciously sent to Your Grace so that Your Grace might also consider such perilous and dangerous matters with timely counsel and understanding. Furthermore, after I had received a deficient answer to my report, Your Grace kindly directed a response from Schmalkalden to be written regarding my report [to] His Princely Grace,[81] requesting that, should the decision be reached that the imprisoned Melchior was not to be punished but to be set free on account of [the landgrave's] reservations, [the landgrave] should banish Rinck permanently from Your Grace's land, and to include this ban in the oath [upon his release]. Consequently, none other than this often-mentioned Melchior, on the basis of His Princely Grace's policy, was banned approximately half a year ago from the land and thereupon again set free, unpunished, according to reports. He took the opportunity to systematically crisscross Hersfeld, Vacha, and other places—also at times in Your Grace's land—remaining hidden and spreading his poison seductively, resulting in the visible corruption of many simple people.

Because this often-mentioned Melchior, along with another eleven Anabaptists, was arrested and imprisoned once again in His Princely

80 In other words, for whose side or for what cause Rinck is fighting.

81 See letter above, Primary Sources B.2.

Grace's principality in the city of Vacha, through the efforts of Martin von der Tann, my brother, a councilman there, on the most recent St Martin's Day, and might now escape just punishment for the second time—and because this recent offense should be considered worse than the first, and this evil less under control than before, I ordered said councilman, my brother, to inform me of his[82] Princely Grace's disposition in the matter and under no circumstances to release Rinck without my advance knowledge. And as he is harming Your Grace's land and people, I thought it prudent to write to Your Grace to point this out and ask for further instruction. I have now notified Your Grace concerning these matters as your most humble servant. You will no doubt consider this issue with the great understanding of an Elector and relay to me how I should handle this matter in Your Grace's humble service, as I will, of course, view as my allocated duty.

Written in my own hand, in haste. From the Wartburg, Saturday, Katharine [25 November], 1531. Your Grace's willing servant, Eberhard von der Tann, Amtmann (official) at the Wartburg.

First Attachment

Most gracious Elector and Lord, since I have been informed that Your Grace and my gracious Lord from Hesse are to meet at Nordhausen, I have the following additional thoughts concerning the profusion of the abovementioned transactions. I do not want to refrain from revealing further concerns to Your Grace regarding these matters that need to be investigated: [first], whether these matters concerning the imprisoned Rinck were addressed and acted upon by My Gracious Lord from Hesse, so that he might for once be punished as a former rebel leader and main instigator of the Anabaptists, and that this insidious evil might be countered, which is difficult and impossible [as long as he remains unpunished]. Second, since offenders, both male and female,[83] are being held in prison at great cost and expense, [I have wanted to report on these things] so that Your Grace may better know how to proceed, and which commands to issue. I write in obedient confidence

82 The translation here assumes, based on the context and other instances of the forms of address, that the "M. G. F." is a mistake in the original or the transcription and should in fact read "S. G. F."

83 Nach dem die beide vbeltheter Mhan vnd weibe schwerlich vnd mit grossem vnkoest gefengklich enthalten werden, . . . "Mhan vnd weibe" can also be translated "husband and wife" or "man and woman."

that Your Grace will graciously receive this somewhat hasty letter due to the circumstances outlined above.

Datum ut supra in litteris. [Date as above in the letter.]

Eberhard von der Tann, Amtmann (official) at the Wartburg.

(If His Grace is absent, the current commissary at Nordhausen is to open.)

Second Attachment

Most gracious Elector and Lord, I am hereby sending to Your Grace two copies of Melchior Rinck's writings—one which he presented to me in prison, the other which he wrote since that time, and both in his own handwriting. From these Your Grace can take note of [the nature of] his remorse, and the harm done by his infractions and his plans.

Datum ut supra in litteris. [Date as above in the letter.]

Third Attachment[84]

Concerning the Anabaptists who are imprisoned at Eisenach and Hausbreitenbach: due to their persistence [i.e., refusal to recant], my gracious Lord has until now been more inclined regarding their imprisonment to engage in sharp punishment, rather than to retain them in jail. However, the Elector has not been able to go through with this on account of the Landgrave, who shares jurisdiction in these areas, and His Grace commanded Ludwig von Boyneburg and me, near Schmalkalden, to speak about this with the Landgrave, so that these same Anabaptists might receive their due, [a command] which we carried out, also with His Princely Grace himself. But His Princely Grace, as previously, was unwilling to pronounce the death penalty. His Princely Grace, however, offered to carry half the costs which have been incurred up to now on behalf of the prisoners; one proposition was discussed which indeed is unfitting, based on all manner of considerations. As there are more Anabaptists at Hausbreitenbach who are not imprisoned, whom Your Graces, the Elector and the prince, are also rounding up, these persons should be divided evenly according

84 Although Wappler, *Stellung Kursachsens*, places this here as a "Third Attachment," it may have come from another (unknown) source. Franz et al., in their summary of this, note only two attachments. And whereas the first two attachments utilize the second-person form of address (E[ure] Ch[urfürstliche] G[naden]), the third uses the third-person (S[eine] Ch. G.)

to number, with each prince being free to determine how he chooses to punish, or not to punish, his portion [of Anabaptist prisoners], and even though the councilors are currently at Nordhausen to speak with the Landgrave about this, I am worried that the Hessians will stick fast to their previous opinion. But as to the question whether the prisoner from Eisenach should be sent to Hausbreitenbach, I do not consider it advisable, for in Hausbreitenbach there is no particularly good prison. This is what I have wanted to report to you, not desiring that it remain unreported.

Datum ut s[upra]. (Date, as above).[85]

4. Elector John to Landgrave Philip (21 December 1531)

Highborn and friendly prince . . .

When we were recently together at Nordhausen, some of our council members presented to your governor of Kassel and your chancellor a whole array of charges against Melchior Rinck, imprisoned in Vacha on account of Anabaptism and other matters. Although your chancellor promised our councilors to convey this information to you and bring back to us your response, due to other matters which occupied you and us at the time, this did not happen. For this reason, we do not doubt that you will now consider the charges made by our councilors and our request with your aforementioned chancellor.

As the above-named Melchior Rinck had already been expelled from your and our lands as a spokesman and teacher of the onerous and seductive Anabaptist sect, and (according to what [we were] told) pledged his word that he would not again cross over the Westerwald Mountains into your or our principalities, we are, therefore, of the amiable confidence that you, in order to shield your and our—and other—principalities and people from such unchristian activities, will exercise the death penalty against him in the light of his noncompliance [with this vow and the law] and his unchristian teachings and actions as an old insurrectionist and leader in your and our principality, leading astray ignorant people.

For we approved the open mandate of the Roman Imperial Majesty, pronounced at Speyer in [15]29, as did other electors, princes, and other ranking officials of the kingdom. The same is true for our open

85 Source: Wappler, *Stellung Kursachsens*, 145–47.

declaration against this sect, which later appeared publicly through our councils and scholars, which we are sending you for your consideration, attached, which shows that we as a magistracy, under God and on the basis of conscience, may not on our part skirt punishing such teachers, activists, and the like. If this were to continue to exist in our principalities (may God protect us!), we would then to the same extent desire to embrace and determine said punishment.

Consider also that we on our part, along with you, should also decree such punishment and justice for such a person, so that he is charged—and held accountable for—his actions in our principality. And so our official at the Wartburg, our councilor and trusted servant, Eberhard von der Tann, is ready and instructed, so that he may follow through with orders from you or your delegate. We did not want to refrain from expressing this reasonable opinion to you, inclined as we are to be of service.

Date: Torgau, 21 December 1531.
To Landgrave at Hesse, etc.
[from] John, Elector, etc.[86]

5. Elector John to Eberhard von der Tann (21 December 1531)

Dear councilor and loyal servant, we have taken note of your letter concerning the imprisoned Anabaptist Melchior Rinck, and after that have written to . . . the Landgrave of Hesse, as you will see in the attached copy. If he or his delegate should write to you concerning this matter, you are to go to them and report on how Rinck behaved within our principality. We also want to decree that, having received our instructions regarding the other Anabaptists, you understand you are to hold to the same. We did not want to leave you uninformed about these matters.

Date: Torgau, 21 December 1531.
To the Amtmann (official) at the Wartburg.[87]

6. Landgrave Philip to Elector John (3 January 1532)

First of all, our amiable service to you, and the good we are able to do. Dear highborn prince . . . , We have cordially noted in its totality your letter concerning Melchior Rinck and your councilor's suggestion

---

86 Source: Wappler, *Stellung Kursachsens*, 152–53.
87 Source: Wappler, *Stellung Kursachsens*, 153–54.

regarding how to punish those who adhere to the sect of Anabaptism. And, as far as Melchior Rinck is concerned, we do not want to withhold from you that we have had him brought to a convenient location far enough away from your and our lands. He himself is to be held in prison for the rest of his life so that he no longer can seduce or make anyone a follower. We have also established an ordinance proposing how to proceed against such people, as you will see, attached.

We still cannot find it within our conscience to punish someone with the sword on account of faith, where we do not otherwise have other infractions sufficient to justify [the penalty]. For if we were to hold to such an opinion, we then would not be able to tolerate Jews or Papists, who blaspheme Christ to the highest degree, but would need to judge them in the same manner.

But you should have no doubt that, regarding this sect, we still want to respond with such earnestness and understanding, hoping to God that our own people remain from now on unchallenged by such seduction. This we did not want to hold back from you in this our friendly, well-meaning response, and we trust that you may understand our position for the best.

Date: Kassel, Wednesday, the third day of the month of January, in the year [15]32.

To the highborn prince, Lord John, Duke of Saxony, Archmarshal and Elector of the Holy Roman Empire, Landgrave in Thuringia and Margrave of Meissen . . . .[88]

Attachment: Landgrave Philip's Ordinance regarding the Anabaptists (1531)

Since there is much bewilderment at present on account of the Anabaptists, it will be necessary to maintain a meticulous vigilance so that the scourge does not make further inroads. Therefore, we have concluded that a person found to be suspect shall be thoroughly interrogated by his pastor. And if he admits to this [i.e., being an Anabaptist], and the pastor cannot convince him to repent and mend his ways, he

88 Source: Wappler, *Stellung Kursachsens*. Wappler places the introductory letter after the text of the ordinance, as this reflects the chronological order. The title "margrave" had originally applied to military commanders but it had become a designation for a member of the minor nobility, roughly equivalent to a landgrave.

is to send for the superintendent of his district, writing to him about how the person is minded. He should then summon the individual to appear before him and, should, along with two or three learned pastors, attempt to instruct him. If he accepts instruction, professes the faith, and if this is the first occurrence, nothing more should be done. If it is the second time, one is to tell him that he is to acknowledge before the church his error and sin and that, since he has riled the church of God, to ask for forgiveness and to promise from now on to mend his ways and to remain, obediently, within the Christian church, and not to take into his house any Anabaptist, or to have fellowship with them. If it is the third time, he shall be treated as if it is the second time but, in addition, he is to sell one half of his possessions—whether or not he has children, is rich or poor—giving this into the coffers for the destitute. And the local official shall carry this out on his own, when asked, and is obligated to do so.

Whoever is unwilling to mend his ways or to be instructed, whether he be an Anabaptist preacher or a baptizer, since he has consequently misused the church's office of preaching and service—an office which he has audaciously assumed on his own, without having been called—shall be expelled from the principality and my gracious lord's region forever, under the threat of beheading, not to return until he mends his ways and, as noted above, repents in the presence of the church. At this point he is again to be accepted, as noted above. If he is a rebaptized [individual] who is not preaching, or has not preached, [and] who also has not organized meetings, since he has forsaken the Christian church, he also is not to be tolerated, but rather his house and property, farmland and meadows, and all the rest of his possessions are to be sold, and in this case [he is] not to be dealt with differently than the Jews, who are not to own inherited estates in the principality or region.

If, however, the wife and children of this same person again enter our community, they are again to be accepted and to have the privilege of owning property.

If one or more who has been expelled returns, not holding to his oath, such are to be placed before the worldly magistracy and that should occur which is [considered] just.[89]

---

89 Source: Wappler, *Stellung Kursachsens*, 154–55.

7. Elector John to Landgrave Philip (15 January 1532)

Dear friendly Highborn Prince . . . We have read the total contents of your response concerning Melchior Rinck, along with the attached ordinance on how you intend to deal with such Anabaptists, etc. All that which we have already written to you concerning Rinck has been upon the advice and reservations of our scholars up to now, for every magistracy has the responsibility, under God and conscience, to punish such teachers and seducers. Meanwhile, as we note—that you have reservations regarding the consideration of our scholars on how to punish [them], which we sent, and [that] you informed us that the same Rinck has been brought to a place far enough away from your and our lands, where he is to be held for the rest of his life, condemned, in prison—we cannot force you to deal otherwise in this matter.

Since, however, a number of other Anabaptists who are followers of the same sect have been arrested by your warden and official in Hausbreitenbach, and we gave our official at the Wartburg orders as to how to respond concerning them, it is our cordial request that you instruct the aforementioned warden to contact our official and his deputies to agree upon a specific punishment. For not punishing heretics and despisers of the Word of God would oppose the written law, which one is obligated to enforce. And we desire to hold to this and, above all, by means of divine grace, to contend against these same Anabaptists with their seductive teachings, to the extent that we may be free in regards to God and our consciences. We do not doubt that you too, no less than we, will also hold to such a grave understanding, so that, from now on, no one may be tarnished or infected with such seduction. This we did not want to hold back from you, with whom we are inclined once again to amiably serve.

Date: Torgau, Monday, 15 January 1532.

To the Landgrave of Hesse.[90]

8. Elector John to Eberhard von der Tann (15 January 1532)

Dear Councilor and loyal servant, in the attached copy you will see how we have just now responded to the letter of our dear Prince, the Landgrave of Hesse, regarding the imprisoned Melchior Rinck and other Anabaptists. We thus desire that you, along with all the other

90 Source: Wappler, *Stellung Kursachsens*, 156.

subordinates who deal with these matters, carry out this received instruction and command, and when you are prevented from doing so by the [shared] Hessian [jurisdiction], see that appropriate punishments are imposed against these Anabaptists. The above is in keeping with our previous counsel. This we did not want to hold back from you.

Date: 15 January 1532.

To the Amtmann (official) at the Wartburg.[91]

9. The Hutterites to Matthias Hansenhan (1537)—an excerpt

Our dear brother Christoph Gschäl has come to you once more and has told you of our love, our life, and our work in Christ Jesus, which has moved many to join us here. But many of these, may God have mercy, left us again; they were taken away by the false servant Hans Both, who wanted to mix his false leaven among God's people. When we refused to allow this, he said we were trying to cut him off from the springs of living water. But we acted rightly and in the fear of God and replied that we could not tolerate such talk; but if he would agree to be silent, we would bear with him in love. Thereupon he insisted all the more that we were trying to keep him from the living springs.

We replied that his was not the wholesome teaching of our Lord Jesus Christ, but a false leaven; he persisted, however, and said that Melchior Rink took the same position. Our answer was that even if Melchior Rink did say and teach this, it still was not right. We did not believe Melchior took this position, however, and thought Hans Both and his followers might have misunderstood him. They then said we were calling Rink a false prophet and were furious (that is typical of Hans Both). By influencing those who had recently joined us, they stole their hearts from us, with the result that they would no longer listen to us but went with Hans Both and Valtin Schuster, who drew the people after them and grew more and more hostile. Finally, in our pain, we laid it all before God and left it in the hands of him who knows us and sees us as we are . . . .

Would to God we could confer with you, my Matthias, and especially with Melchior Rink, and open our hearts to one another; but if

91 Source: Wappler, *Stellung Kursachsens*, 156–57.

it cannot be, we lay it in the Lord's hands. But we never made accusations against Melchior Rink, for why should we slander a man we do not even know? The Lord forbid! If someone quotes Rink in order to prove his own wrong ideas, we cannot agree with it but must say that even if an angel from heaven were to try to bring us an alien teaching, we would with God's help neither follow it nor weaken our position.

Melchior Rink will bear the responsibility for whatever he says or does, but we only hear about his integrity and constancy in affliction, for which we heartily rejoice and praise God in heaven. God grant that we shall meet and speak with him in the Lord, but Hans Both's thinking is alien to us; we do not know his voice, and he will have to face judgment for spreading slander about us.[92]

10. Martin Bucer to Landgrave [Philip] (17 March 1540)

[. . .] Regarding the prisoner [Melchior Rinck], for the sake of the Lord I, too, ask Your Grace, as George Schnabel and Herman Bastian [have done]: it is one thing to jail someone, but another thing to also impose harsh conditions. We are all poor sinners.

The Landgrave answered on 22 March 1540: [. . .] As far as the incarceration of Rinck is concerned, we have once again, as has often happened in the past, commanded that he be comfortably confined and have thus provided for the construction of a room just for him.

Bucer expressed his thanks on 25 March 1540 for [Philip's] Christian pronouncement.[93]

92 Source: This extract is found in Franz et al., *Urkundliche Quellen zur hessischen*, 182–83. It is translated in *The Chronicle of the Hutterian Brethren*, vol. 1 (Rifton, NY: Plough Publishing House, 1987), 127–28. Copyright © 1987 by Plough Publishing House. Used with permission.

93 Source: Franz et al., *Urkundliche Quellen zur hessischen*, 270.

C. INTERROGATIONS

1. Marburg Disputation (1528)

Files concerning the articles and the interrogation of Melchior Rinck by Balthasar Raid[t] at Marburg, 17 to 21 August, 1528: (a) "Mr. Balthasar [Raid's] text and the accompanying articles which Mr. Melchior Rinck is said to have preached." (b) Interrogation of Melchior Rinck on 17 August 1528. (c) Rinck's confession of faith. (d) Raid's closing statement on 18 August 1528. (e) "Mr. Balthasar's answer to writings Mr. Melchior introduced, including on baptism," on 18 August 1528. (f) Balthasar Raid to Landgrave Philip on 21 August 1528.

a.

Mr. Balthasar [Raid's] text and the accompanying articles which Mr. Melchior Rinck is said to have preached.

Proceedings, the Monday after the Assumption of Mary [17 August] [15]28.

Your gracious, honorable, and learned lords! Melchior Rinck met in secret near Hersfeld with a few people, taking it upon himself to teach them concerning the Holy Gospel differently than what has until now been preached here. And he has introduced a new insurgency into our gracious prince's holy land by reportedly rebaptizing some of his followers, as if infant baptism should not be considered [a proper] baptism, and has gathered people around him and won a number of followers, of which two are present here: Mr. Claus Schiffman and Jörge Zedell, barber. Having brought together a following in secret, he subsequently sought to preach in the local church in Hersfeld. This desire, along with his writings, became known to our gracious lord [the landgrave], who responded that if Rinck would submit in writing the content of his teaching, together with his position on the sacraments of baptism and the altar, along with their practice, our gracious prince[94] would provide a time and place for him to speak with our gracious prince's

94 The original text—here, and found as well throughout this paragraph—reads: "S. F. G." an abbreviation for "seine fürstliche Gnade," literally translated as "his royal grace," a term of high honor, here translated as "our gracious prince."

scholars on the basis of Scripture, allowing everyone to be informed. However, failure to do so would result in his being banished from our gracious prince's land.

Meanwhile, my gracious lord [i.e., the landgrave] came to Friedewald, asking for the named Melchior and commanded that he be brought to him—speaking with him personally and interrogating him amicably. In this way it has been established that Melchior Rinck has erred in his teaching, seducing the people and convincing them with Scripture, with the consequence that our gracious lord banished him and those who follow him from this land unless they were to recant and condemn in writing their errors before the congregation at Hersfeld, or to defend the same articles before his university here at Marburg on the basis of Scripture. And if these articles cannot be proved correct, they shall recant them, in writing and orally, before the congregation at Hersfeld, and then send the same in writing to our gracious prince. Alternatively, if they are not willing to do this, none of them shall come to Hersfeld and shall be promptly banished from the entire principality. And since our gracious prince then found out that they were willing to come to this place, our gracious prince sent me here to report such to you, dear lords, so that you may know what took place at Friedewald. The articles which they taught among the people, and are found in their books, which were known in part at Friedewald—on which basis they have been expelled from our gracious lord's land—are:

The first article

Melchior Rinck blasphemes and maligns the holy Gospel of Jesus Christ, which God has revealed to us at this time, stating that such is a false, pharisaical, hypocritical gospel, and all who follow Martin Luther, and who teach as he does, are leading the people to the devil. For although Luther had God's Spirit at the beginning, he has now become a devil and the true Antichrist. (They thereupon ask, desiring to know from [Rinck] in which article of faith Dr. Luther and his followers have taught erroneously and where this opposes Scripture.) [R-B: he disagrees and refers to his own articles.[95]]

95 In all twelve articles which follow, "R-B" (Balthasar Raid) appends his own summary in Latin of Rinck's response to each of the charges. Wappler places this in brackets.

The second article

Melchior Rinck says, original sin from Adam damns no one until a person reaches the age of accountability and willingly sins. [R-B: he agrees.]

The third article

Melchior Rinck disavows that children die on account of sin and says that the passage (Gen 3 [see 2[:17]), "in the day that you eat of it you shall die," has to do with spiritual death, and not that of the body. [R-B: he agrees.]

The fourth article

Indeed, children, before the age of accountability, and before they consciously enter into sin, are neither just nor unjust, neither redeemed nor unredeemed, but rather carry within themselves from the time of birth, good and evil seed. [R-B: he agrees.]

The fifth article

All who receive the sacrament—as Luther has shown us up till now from divine Scripture—always receive a devil, for they say, we do not have the correct sacramental rite. Therefore, we desire them to show us another and better rite on the basis of Scripture. [R-B: he disagrees but he wants to express disapproval of how it is practiced.]

The sixth article

All sayings in Scripture where God damns the flesh, sin, and the human being, says Melchior, have nothing to do with children, and are not speaking of children, for they do not possess reasoning, which precludes sin. [RB: he agrees.]

The seventh article

At Friedewald he denied the predestination of God, contrary to chapter 9 of Romans. [R-B: he disagrees.]

The eighth article

He has said, Christ was not obedient to the Father according to the flesh, but rather, flesh strove against Spirit and was disobedient, yet without sin. [R-B: he disagrees.]

The ninth article

He writes that he disagrees with Luther and the pope on baptism and the sacrament [of the Lord's Supper], in that in baptism all children are offered to the devil, and all those who take communion are receiving a devil. [R-B: he agrees.]

The tenth article

He also says, children are not able to listen to the preaching of repentance and forgiveness of sin, so one cannot preach repentance to them, for they have not departed from the good, since they know neither good nor evil, for which reason [infant] baptism is also blasphemy. Therefore, it is necessary that a person submit to [adult] baptism, thereby forsaking the first baptism, and then confess anew as if it [the baptism] had just now occurred.[96] [R-B: he agrees.]

The eleventh article

Also, the abovementioned Melchior has also persuaded several people at Hersfeld that Christ's body and blood are not present in the sacrament of the altar, who then spewed blasphemous words against it to the dismay of many people. [R-B: he admits this.]

The twelfth article

They also teach that a person may prepare himself and come to faith and the Spirit of God through forgiveness, repudiation, and rejection of his endeavors, creatureliness, and self (this is nothing other than through one's natural strength, given from God at the time of creation). In this way, God's grace through Christ is completely disavowed, when to be sure it is faith in Jesus Christ alone which leads mankind to God and away from creatureliness and self-love, making everything else useless, since one discerns in faith that there is no creature who is of service and useful unto Christ, leading to salvation, unless there follows in the heart a willing unmindfulness and yieldedness [*Gelassenheit*] in all things, which is the rightful Sabbath.

This is what I know, your gracious, honorable, learned lords, concerning this matter, which I wanted to share with you, so that you may

---

96 Darumb sei es not, das man sich oder anders laß teufen oder der ersten tauf sich verzeihen und darnach von newem, als ob sie itzt gescheen were, bekennen. *Oder* can mean "aber" (but)—here translated "thereby."

be able to confirm such—with Scripture, where this be the case—or desist from and condemn that which is false, to proceed with the judgment pronounced by our gracious lord and of which everyone is aware. [R-B: he disagrees.]

b.

On the Monday following Mary's Assumption [17 August], Melchior Rink was interrogated and examined on the basis of the following presumed articles, in the year [15]28.

Concerning the first article, that our gospel is a false, pharisaical gospel, Mr. Melchior responded that he does not at all own up to having blasphemed the Gospel of Christ, but hopes to testify with his body that his is a true gospel, and that there can be no forgiveness of sins outside of the Gospel of Christ. However, concerning what Luther holds as gospel, the articles which he presented yesterday indicate and testify to this, and he still desires to hold to the same articles.

Concerning this article he was requested, again, to present a clear answer, upon which he said basically: He does not own up to [having blasphemed the Gospel of Christ]; Luther taught erroneously in the matter concerning the two articles, the sacrament and infant baptism, confirmation of which will be shown at the appropriate time.

Concerning the second article, he says, his answer is the same as that at Friedewald, that original sins do not result in damnation until a person reaches the age of accountability and willingly sins.

Concerning the third, he again said that children do not die on account of sin, and that the passage, Gen 3 [2:17], does not speak of bodily but of spiritual death.

Concerning the fourth, he says he still confesses that children, from the time of birth, are neither just nor unjust, neither redeemed nor unredeemed, etc.

Concerning the fifth article, he says: That I am said to have said or written that a person receiving the sacrament is receiving the devil, this he did not say, nor does he confess it. However, that Luther in this case is teaching erroneously, this he hopes to adequately verify.

Concerning the sixth article, he says and admits that the passages of Scripture which damn the flesh have nothing to do with children, as pointed out in the article.

Concerning the seventh, he denies having stated that he had disavowed predestination, contrary to the ninth chapter to the Romans; instead, he holds to predestination as it was taught there.

Concerning the eighth, he says: he had thus spoken to my gracious prince and lord at Friedewald, that in the garden Christ strove against the flesh with the spirit, causing him to sweat bloody sweat. More than this he did not admit to, regarding any other such allegations. But our gracious lord continued to press him on this, asking him whether he has said and preached that in the garden Christ was not obedient in the flesh to his Father. But he did not respond or confess to our gracious lord otherwise than what is indicated here now. Nothing otherwise will be found.

Concerning the ninth article, he says he confesses it once again as follows: he does not admit to having said that those who receive the sacrament are imbibing a devil. However, he does admit to not agreeing with Luther or the pope and is mindful that children who are baptized are being offered to the devil. This he confesses and wants to prove.

Concerning the tenth, he reaffirms, regarding infant baptism, what is stated in the article.

Concerning the eleventh article, he says the following: that he is not aware at this time of having persuaded several people that the body and blood of Christ are not present in the sacrament of the altar. If, however, someone who had heard this from him would come forward, he could be convinced otherwise. Yet [that the body and blood of Christ are not present in the sacrament of the alter] is nevertheless not an incorrect, but rather a correct teaching, and he might well have so spoken, somewhere. Yet he is not aware as to whether or not several people heard this from him. In summary, after much coaxing, he confessed it to be true.

Concerning the twelfth, he says that man, according to the testimony of Scripture, cannot prepare himself and come to the Spirit, to faith, and to the Father through forgiveness, repudiation, and the rejection of his own efforts, etc., as quoted [in article twelve]. This he again confesses. That he, however, had preached that humans, through their own capacity, can do this, and not through God's strength, this he completely denies having said.

[In Raid's handwriting:] Thereafter the rector of the University of Marburg instructed Mr. Melchior Rinck to take his articles in hand

and to elaborate on each, individually, as to how he understands them, and he listed with each article the Scripture which he had given [as basis]. They were able to agree upon the first three according to reason; there are five articles which follow in "c."

c.

[In Melchior Rinck's handwriting] Account of my Faith toward God through Jesus Christ, which I have prepared as requested.

The first article

Since God is love (1 John 4), which is not self-seeking (1 Cor 13), it is certain that man, created in the image of God (Gen 1), was created in the image of love, that is, that man was of one mind with God, as can be seen in the firstborn of love, Jesus Christ [Luke 2:7], whereby he is also called an image of God (2 Cor 4; Col 1; Heb 1).

[In Raid's handwriting] This first article he exegeted thus: man was created to love God with his whole heart, whole soul, etc., and the neighbor as oneself.

The second article

However, after man, on account of unfaith and contempt of the divine word, became an image of false love, resulting in love of conflict, it is certain that he is not able to return to the original image except through true faith and conversion to the word of God, which mankind had at some point rejected (Gen 3, 12; Deut 18; Isa 28, 40; John 1, 10, 14).

The third article

When this became obvious everywhere that God had not lied when he said that on the day someone will eat from the tree of the knowledge of good and evil, that this person will die, with every mouth silenced, God gave the Law, which Paul later in several places interprets (Rom 5, 7; Gal 2, 3; 2 Cor 4). For just as mankind, at the beginning in paradise, having dominion over God's creatures, transgressed and became disobedient, so also at the time of the Law, mankind transgressed, not only as regards works, but also as regards themselves. Humans became either Pharisees or Scribes, arguing that those works or the faith which they have, and which are demanded by Scripture, emanate from themselves, as Paul clearly shows, where he speaks to the Romans in the fifth chapter. For this judgment sprang from a single sin that resulted in condemnation; "but the free gift following many trespasses brings justification."[97] And [Paul] says, law came in because sin had taken the upper hand.[98]

The fourth article

Infant baptism is truly against John the Baptist's baptism, and those which have been commanded by Christ, in view of the fact that this baptism has been established for those who mend their ways, quit sinning, desire to repent, believe in the forgiveness of sins, as is obvious: Matt 3; Mark 1, Luke 8, Acts 2, 10 and 19. And children are without guilt of sin, even though they were born in original sin, as the following scriptures indicate: Ezek 18; Deut 24; 2 Chron 25; John 3, 9, 15; Paul in Rom 1, 2, 5; 1 Cor 15; Mark 16; and they are also without faith: Rom 10; Deut 1.

The fifth article

Whoever says that Christ declared his natural and adopted body and blood to be in bread and wine as food and drink is truly against Christ, John 6, and cannot maintain such an interpretation with divine and unfalsified scripture.

Whoever desires to deal with me regarding the above-written articles should begin with the first one and then proceed with the next, combatting untruths with the entirely sufficient and unfalsified Holy Scripture. In this way, much unnecessary and scattered talk will be avoided and those listening may all the sooner come to understand the matter. It is also my greatest and highest request that my interrogators and antagonists not be overly hasty with the verdict, but rather ponder the matter most diligently, since it is not mine, but God's. Amen.

d.

[In Raid's handwriting] After Melchior Rinck clarified the first three articles as he wanted to have them understood, Balthasar Raid, early on Tuesday [August 18], gave this closing statement, in order to avoid much rewriting, speaking:

---

97 [Rom 5:18.]

98 [Rom 5:20.]

To the first: Dear Mr. Melchior, so as not to quarrel with you about matters upon which we agree, I will repeat in short what yesterday you have explained in your first three conclusions, and how I have understood them. As to the first, you have in your conclusion said and confessed yesterday that God created humankind according to his likeness, that is, that he is wise, devout, just, and holy—that is, that he loves God and his neighbor with his whole heart, clinging solely to God as the highest good and without self-love. Is this correct? Melchior's answer: Yes.

To the second: You have avowed that mankind created in the image of God, was led astray by the devil, fallen through unfaith, becoming an image of the devil—that is, [possessing] full and complete egotistical love, that is, a sinner and a condemned person. Is this right? Melchior Rinck answers: Yes, it is so.

To the third: You have avowed that mankind cannot come to the image of God and God's kingdom—that is, to divine wisdom, devoutness, righteousness, and holiness—except through faith in Jesus Christ, as God promised to Adam out of grace in the first book of Moses [Gen], in the third chapter; for the same Christ, as promised there, is created by God for all believers unto wisdom, justice, holiness, and salvation.

To the fourth, you have avowed that in order to come to faith and the Spirit, no work of the law helps, nor does relinquishment of possessions, of works, of sensual desires, or of one's self, for through the law comes the knowledge of sin, bringing a person to repent and sorrow for his or her sins. Therefore, the law also precedes the Gospel, but this in accordance with the image of God, namely, in order to become devout, just, and holy before God, the only thing which helps is a genuine and true faith—which alone trusts and depends on God's grace and mercy—offered to us in Christ as a gift. The same faith receives the Holy Spirit, which works and brings "love that comes from a pure heart, a good conscience, and sincere faith" (1 Tim 1:[5]). Is this correct, Melchior? Answer: Yes, this I have stated and avowed.

Answer, Raid: Since we are one in understanding with one another, it is not necessary for us here to quarrel. But tell us then, dear Mr. Melchior, why do you blaspheme Dr. Luther and all of us so very much, even yesterday, as being phonies, hypocrites, seducers? [Can you] point to someone else among us who has taught differently, or since you also teach this in the same way we do, why do you and your horde not reprimand yourselves? Come now! We accept the confession which we in the main have correctly taught, and hope that the other two articles will also reveal that they are retained correctly, as regards our own conventions, as we until now have taught, in line with Christ and his apostles.

That you say, however, that humans were created in the likeness of God, and that one is to see the same in Jesus Christ, who for this reason also is to be named an image of God, to this I say that Paul (2 Cor 4; Col 1; Heb 1) did not so speak, but himself taught that Christ is truly and innately God, and does not say that he was created in the image of God, as other humans. Nor does he say that he was referred to as an image of God, but rather that he is, says [Paul], the image of innate divine essence, as true God, but likewise, a human being is not a divine image. To which Melchior answered: in what he had said, he certainly had not denied the divinity of Christ, but rather had affirmed it. In addition, I would like to prove that God has given the law, upon which it becomes evident that he had not lied, etc.

After this, Mr. Melchior was informed that, since they had reached agreement on the first three articles, he was now to provide evidence for his fourth article, which he was willing to do, and this now follows.[99]

Proof of the fourth article by Melchior Rinck:

1., 2., Biblical References: Matt 3[:1–2, 5–6]: "In those days John the Baptist appeared in the wilderness of Judea, proclaiming, 'Repent, for the kingdom of heaven has come near.' . . . Then the people of Jerusalem and all Judea were going out to him, and all the region along the Jordan, and they were baptized by him in the river Jordan confessing their sins."

3. Matt 28[:18–19]: "And Jesus came and said to them, 'All authority in heaven and on earth has been given to me. Go therefore and make disciples of all nations, baptizing them in the name of the Father and of the Son and of the Holy Spirit.'"

4. Mark 1[:4]: "John the baptizer appeared in the wilderness, proclaiming a baptism of repentance for the forgiveness of sins." Mark 16 [:15–16]: "Go into all the world and proclaim the good news to the

---

99 Source: The following section, mainly biblical texts, is not included in Wappler, *Täuferbewegung in Thüringen*, but is in Franz et al., *Urkundliche Quellen zur hessischen*, 10–16.

whole creation. The one who believes and is baptized will be saved; but the one who does not believe will be condemned."

5. Acts 2[:37–38]: "Now when they heard this, they were cut to the heart and said to Peter and to the other apostles, 'Brothers, what should we do?' Peter said to them, 'Repent, and be baptized every one of you in the name of Jesus Christ so that your sins may be forgiven; and you will receive the gift of the Holy Spirit.'" Acts 8[:12]: "But when they believed Philip, who was proclaiming the good news about the kingdom of God and the name of Jesus Christ, they were baptized, both men and women." Item. [8:29–32, 35–36]: "Then the Spirit said to Philip, 'Go over to this chariot and join it.' So Philip ran up to it and heard him reading the prophet Isaiah. He asked, 'Do you understand what you are reading?' He replied, 'How can I, unless someone guides me?' And he invited Philip to get in and sit beside him. Now the passage of the scripture that he was reading was this: 'Like a sheep he was led to the slaughter, and like a lamb silent before its shearer so he does not open his mouth' . . . He preached to him the good news about Jesus and the eunuch said 'Look, here is water!'"

Acts 9[:17–18]: Ananias, concerning Paul. [". . . Then [Paul] got up and was baptized . . ."]

Acts 10[:44]: "While Peter was still speaking, the Holy Spirit fell upon all who heard the word." Here the Spirit is given before baptism, so that the kingdom of Christ can be seen to pertain even to the Gentiles.[100]

Acts 16[:15]: concerning Lydia. "When she and her household were baptized," etc.

Item. Acts 16[:31–33]: "'Believe on the Lord Jesus, and you will be saved, you and your household,' and they spoke to him the word of the Lord, and all who were there were baptized without delay, he and his entire household." Acts 18 [8]: Crispus ["the official of the synagogue, became a believer in the Lord, together with all his household; and many of the Corinthians who heard Paul became believers and were baptized."]

Acts 19[:1–6]: The Ephesians, who had not received the Holy Spirit, because they had been erroneously baptized with John's baptism, had to be baptized in the name of Christ.

---

100 Margin: Because we know this is given in baptism.

Rom 6[:3]: "Whoever of us has been baptized has been baptized into his death."

And children are still innocent of innate sin, as the following Scripture shows:

Ezek 18[:1–5, 19f]: "The word of the Lord came to me: What do you mean by repeating this proverb concerning the land of Israel, 'The parents have eaten sour grapes, and the children's teeth are set on edge'? As I live, says the Lord God, this proverb shall no more be used by you in Israel, etc. . . . It is only the person who sins that shall die. If a man is righteous and does what is lawful and right, etc. . . . Why do you say, 'Why should not the son suffer for the iniquity of the father?' . . . when instead, it is the person who sins who shall die. A child shall not suffer for the iniquity of a parent, nor a parent suffer for the iniquity of a child."

Deut 24[:16]:[101] "Parents shall not be put to death for their children, nor shall children be put to death for their parents; only for their own crimes may persons be put to death."

2 Kings 14[:6]: "The parents shall not be put to death for the children, or the children be put to death for the parents," wherefore the king killed the slaves who killed the king's father, but he did not kill their sons. Also, "the children shall not be put to death for the parents, but all shall be put to death for their own sins." So: 2 Chron 25[:4].

John 3[:18–19]: "Those who believe in him are not condemned; but those who do not believe are condemned already. . . . This is the judgment, that the light has come into the world, and people loved darkness rather than light."

John 9[:39]: "Jesus said, 'I came into this world for judgment so that those who do not see may see, and those who do see may become blind.'" 9[:41]: "Jesus said to them, 'If you were blind, you would not have sin.' But now that you say, 'We see,' your sin remains."

John 15[:22]: "If I had not come and spoken to them, they would not have sin."

John [16]: "He convicts the world of sin because they do not believe in me."

Mark 16[:16]: "The one who does not believe will be condemned."

---

101 Margin: Punishment by the sword.

Rom 1[:18, 32]: "For the wrath of God is revealed from heaven against all ungodliness and wickedness of those who by their wickedness suppress the truth. . . . They know God's decree, that those who practice such things deserve to die."

Rom 2[:2]: "We know that God's judgment on those who do such things is in accordance with truth."

Rom 5[:12]: "Therefore, just as sin came into the world through one man, and death came through sin, and so death spread to all because all have sinned."

1 Cor 15[:21–22]: "For since death came through a human being, the resurrection of the dead has also come through a human being; for as all die in Adam, so all will be made alive in Christ."

Children are without faith: this he also wants to prove:

1) Rom 10[:14, 17]: "How are they to call on one in whom they have not believed? And how are they to believe in one of whom they have never heard? And how are they to hear without someone to proclaim him?" Item. "So, faith comes from what is heard, and what is heard comes through the word of Christ."

2) Acts 8[:31]: "The eunuch replied, 'How can I, unless someone guides me?'" And so, if hearing were not essential for faith, why then does the Father say, Matt 17[:5], "This is my Son, the Beloved; . . . listen to him . . ."[102] Christ also does not speak in vain, "You have already been cleansed by the word that I have spoken to you" John 15[:3].

3) Luke 9 [10:42; 11:28]: One thing is essential, "Blessed are those who hear the word of God." "Children, however, know neither good nor evil." Deut 1[:39]. 1 Cor 14[:20]: "Do not ascribe reason to children."

Scripture tells us that baptizing infants is truly against John [the Baptist] and Christ: I ask you to refute this, if it is God's will, to refute this with clear, unfalsified Scripture.[103]

e.

Mr. Balthasar's answer to the articles Mr. Melchior introduced and in regards to baptism. Proceedings, Tuesday after the Assumption of Mary [August 18], afternoon, [15]28.

---

102 Two illegible words in parentheses.

103 In the handwriting of Raidt. The conclusion is cut off. This part is designated as "D-4." On the backside of the page: "In the afternoon Balthasar Raidt responded as follows herewith in 'F.'"

Today it has been heard, my Christian lords, that we are of one mind concerning the main point of our holy faith in the teaching which has to do with mature adults. May the almighty God also grant the grace to prosper with fruit, to the honor of his holy name. Amen.

However, there is still a schism between us concerning infant baptism and the sacrament of the altar. We now want also to examine this, since Mr. Melchior Rinck is of the opinion that infant baptism lies in opposition to the order and command of Christ. His first reason for surmising this is:

Infants are still without the guilt of innate sin. In establishing his assertion, he quotes Ezekiel [18:20]: "The person who sins shall die. A child shall not suffer for the iniquity of a parent, nor a parent suffer for the iniquity of a child," stating, as regards corporal punishment, that this saying stands on our side, since Christ through his death took away original sin, that after his arrival no one was condemned, except for whoever does not believe—that is, for whoever does not discard original sin, as Christ says [Mark 16:16] "The one who believes . . . will be saved; but the one who does not believe will be condemned." And John [15:22]: "If I had not come and spoken to them, they would not have sin." Now such a sermon of grace did not take place solely through Christ, but also first through Adam, and then Abraham, then David and others who believed, having their sins taken away through Christ, who also preached this, and also had done enough for the sin. Out of this it does not follow that children are without the guilt of innate sin.

Furthermore, [Rinck] points out the passage in Deut 24; and likewise, 2 Kings 14[:6]; 2 Chron 25[:4], where the context has to do with bodily punishment in accordance with the law of Moses, and, in our case, through the worldly magistracy.

Item: he points out the passage John 3[:18]: "Those who believe in him are not condemned; but those who do not believe are condemned already." Item: John 9[:39]: "Jesus said, 'I came into this world for judgment so that those who do not see may see.'" Item: John 15[:22]: "If I had not come," etc. Item. John 16[:8–9]: "The Holy Spirit will punish the world for their sin, for they do not believe in me," and regarding all the other passages which follow, Mark, last chapter, Rom 1, Rom 2, Rom 5, here, I am in agreement with him that unfaith alone is sin before God, that faith through Jesus Christ is righteousness. But it does not follow that children are without the guilt of innate sin and that original sin does not condemn them.

Item: the passage 1 Cor 15[:21–23]: "For since death came through a human being, the resurrection of the dead has also come through a human being; for as all die in Adam, so all will be made alive in Christ. But each in his own order: Christ the firstfruits, then at his coming those who belong to Christ." Therefore, it is forever clear that Paul is speaking of the bodily resurrection of the dead and not of the guilt of sin. For all will arise, good and evil, but not all will be saved, as Christ says Matt 25[:46]: "And these will go away into eternal punishment, but the righteous into eternal life."

If, however, someone wanted to say: If this were so, it would follow that Christ's grace is smaller than Adam's sin, since in Christ not all are saved, who are condemned in Adam. To this I answer: It is not for us to set a quota for God as to whom he desires to save. He is God and Lord, may he be blessed in eternity, Amen. [Such setting of a quota] has no place here. Whoever holds to this should read chapters 9, 10, and 11 of the [Book of] Romans.

And I conclude, therefore, that it is still unproven that children are without the guilt of innate sin, but will, with God's help, prove that all who are born from Adam are sinners and guilty and condemned through Adam's sin, until they are saved through the faith of Jesus Christ, namely:

1. Through Christ (Matt 12[:33]) "Either make the tree good, and its fruit good; or make the tree bad, and its fruit bad." So, all humans have been Adam's fruit, who is after all evil.

2. Eph 2[:1–3]: "You were dead through the trespasses and sins in which you once lived, following the course of this world, following the ruler of the power of the air, the spirit that is now at work among the children of unfaith." (Here it is clear that those who have no faith have the devil; so, if children have no faith, they also have the devil.) "All of us once lived among them in the passions of our flesh, following the desires of flesh and senses, and we were by nature children of wrath like everyone else." What does "by nature" mean? Nature is indeed nature, before a person comes of age.

3. John 3[:6–7]: "What is born of the flesh is flesh, and what is born of the Spirit is spirit." In my view, however, all of Adam's children have been born of the flesh.

4. Rom 8[:6–7]: "To set the mind on the flesh is death, but to set the mind on the Spirit is life and peace. For this reason, the mind that is set on the flesh is hostile to God; it does not submit to God's law—indeed it cannot."

5. Rom 5[:12]: "Therefore, just as sin came into the world through one man, and death came through sin, and so death spread to all because all have sinned." Thus, children also die, therefore the guilt of sin must also be in children, for death is the payment of sin. Rom 6, Gen 2 and 1 Cor 15[:56]: "The sting of death is sin," and Rom 5[:14]: "Yet death exercised dominion from Adam to Moses, even over those whose sins were not like the transgression of Adam." For this reason are all of them condemned, as also in Rom 5[:16, 18] where the judgment is: "Out of one sin came condemnation," and "Through one person's sin came condemnation for all people."

6. John 3[:5] "No one can enter the kingdom of God without being born of water and Spirit"—as if Christ is saying: all those born of the flesh (which of course applies to *most* children!) cannot enter the kingdom of God unless they are born anew out of the water and the Holy Spirit.

7. On this point, everyone should read the fourth chapter of Isaiah.

8. Gen 6, 7, 8[:21]: "Every desire within the thoughts of the human heart is disdainful and evil for all eternity." And so, I believe, children are a part of the human heart—and note: Moses says: "for all eternity." "Eternity"! An hour and a day is also part of eternity.

9. Ps 51[:5]: "In sin I was born, in sin my mother conceived me."

10. Such is also found in the ninth and tenth command of Moses: "You shall not covet." Now, children also covet, which proves the point that children are sinners, and, according to Scripture, condemned if they do not come to Christ, who is Redeemer of all people who come to him.

The second reason of Melchior Rinck is that children have no faith. My answer: When Melchior speaks of the children of nature, who have not yet come into the Christian church and to its head [Christ], I have now also proven that this is so. However, when he makes this claim regarding children who are brought to Christ, I say no, for he has not proven this one iota, nor would he be able to prove it. That Melchior has much to say about bodily listening, the word, and outward confession, and acts of reason, this is of no concern to me. Reason is of no avail in divine matters. Isaiah places reason far below faith [43:10[104]]: He is not saying unless you can understand you cannot believe, but rather is saying, first believe, then come to understanding. This was stated in the testimony which Mr. Melchior gave today.

That baptizing infants is the right thing to do, and forever Christian, this I want to prove, as follows . . .

[*Beyond this point, in Raid's own handwriting:*] At this point, [when Raid desired to continue his argument justifying the legitimacy of infant baptism,] the rector said it would not be necessary. So Balthasar Raid stopped speaking, and the lords of the university carried on bravely and honestly concerning infant baptism, with many fine arguments which are written down, as far as I know, by the chancellery's scribe. But Melchior would not be convinced, as had also been the case at Friedewald. He did not want to dispute or clarify his position concerning the fifth article, even with one word, but instead said they had not convinced him otherwise as regards infant baptism. And so the matter ended on Tuesday night [18 August 1528].

f.

Balthasar Raid, preacher at Hersfeld, to Landgrave Philip:

Just as Your Majesty's Grace had commanded the Schultheiß (mayor) of Hersfeld, I rode to Marburg on the Thursday after Laurentius [August 13], to appear before the Anabaptists. And so that Your Majesty's Grace may know what took place there, I am sending the same, as much as I have, to Your Majesty's Grace to examine. Whatever is missing, I believe, Your Majesty's Grace will find at Marburg in the chancellery. Through all this I am greatly amazed that people place so great an emphasis on such things, as they did not bring up one point of proof which would have served their purpose, except for proving that the apostles had baptized some adults, which indeed everyone well knows.

And I pray fervently for Your Majesty's Grace in God's name that Your Majesty's Grace may take serious measures, assigning public penitence to those who want to remain in the land as a warning to others, for there are without doubt others out there. May the almighty God

---

104 [Isa 43:10: "You are my witnesses, says the Lord, and my servant whom I have chosen, so that you may know and *believe me and understand* that I am he." Emphasis added.]

and Father protect Your Majesty's Grace and Your Grace's poor subjects, that they do not experience [these matters]. Amen.

Dated at Hersfeld on Friday after the Assumption of Mary [21 August], in the year [15]28.[105]

2. Interrogation of Rinck and other Anabaptists in Vacha (1531)

Documents concerning the detained Anabaptists and Melchior Rinck at Vacha (12 November 1531 and 1 March 1532). (a) Amtmann (official), Rentmeister (bursar), Schultheiß (mayor) and Council at Vacha to Landgrave Philip on 12 November 1531. (b) "Examination and interrogation of the Anabaptists who were discovered to be with Melchior Rinck, called 'the Greek,' at Vacha, and imprisoned on St. Martin's Day [11 November] 1531." (c) The Amtmann (official) from the Wartburg, Eberhard von der Tann, to Landgrave Philip on 1 March 1532. (d) Eberhard von der Tann to Landgrave Philip, concerning "The transgressions of Melchior Rinck, 'the Greek'" (without date [probably 1 March 1532]).

a.

Amtmann (official), Rentmeister (bursar), Schultheiß (mayor) and Council at Vacha to Landgrave Philip:

Your Grace has commanded us in all seriousness to watch out with the greatest vigilance for those who hold secretive meetings with preaching. And furthermore, Your Grace has also recently and at various times commanded us, and especially me as Amtmann, to expel from Your Grace's principality those who have been besmirched with rebaptism, who do not submit to scriptural instruction and to recantation—which we have already done with several persons.

In this regard, gracious Prince and Lord, it was reported to me that those whom we expelled this past summer have repeatedly gathered in the city, in gardens and also other places. And now we were notified that they are coming here, especially on market day, to meet in their houses, and also into those whose residents are part of their sect, and not alone, but including one of the strangers of their sect,

105 Sources: Wappler, *Täuferbewegung in Thüringen*, 294–302; Franz et al., *Urkundliche Quellen zur hessischen*, 10–16.

for secret gatherings and preaching. With this in mind, at the recent St. Martin's Day market [11 November] in the evening after the gate closed, we conducted house searches in the suspicious locations and found, gathered there, Melchior Rinck, called "the Greek," along with twelve others (whose names Your Grace may find on the attached note). We found that they had been preaching in secret, with special emphasis on the Gospel of Mark, the last chapter, where Jesus Christ, our Savior, established baptism, preaching in line with their sect's interpretation. They were therefore accosted as to why they were doing this contrary to Your Grace's order and command. They responded with all sorts of defiant words. For these reasons we apprehended them and took them into custody.

Request for instructions on how to proceed. Date: Sunday after St. Martin's Day [12 November], in 1531. [Attached] Note [as referred to, above]:

Melchior Rinck, called "the Greek."

Hans Werner and his wife, citizens here at Vacha, both of whom recanted rebaptism in your presence, Your Majesty, and who also renounced it a year ago in our presence, upon which they were permitted to be in the city, and now have held this [Anabaptist] meeting in their house.

Jörg Grusselbach and his wife, citizens here, who had recanted rebaptism earlier, but then, a second time affirmed [rebaptism], upon which they were expelled from Your Majesty's principality, and now discovered in this meeting.

Adam Angersbach from Nidernhaun[106] near Hersfeld.

Hermann Adam, a farm worker [*Hofmann*] at Springen, belonging to the cloister at Kreuzberg.[107]

Kontz[108] Mulher from Ausbach, within the administrative jurisdiction of Friedewald.

Heinz from Kathus said that he had from time to time refrained [from taking communion in the town church] and had a wife and children at Dorndorf at his mother's place.

---

106 Today, Unterhaun.

107 Most likely the Benedictine convent on the Werra in the town known today as Philippsthal. The convent was ravaged in the Peasants' War and given up entirely in the second half of the sixteenth century.

108 Kontz, or Kunz, shortened for Konrad, was a common name in the sixteenth century. This same person, below, is for some reason named "Cort."

Bilg[109] "from the mountain," from Motzfeld.

Anna and Ursel Zoberin, sisters, who say they are two poor maidservants, born in Großenbach, who are currently employed in Treischfeld, within the administrative jurisdiction of Haselstein.

b.

Examination and interrogation of the Anabaptists who were with Melchior Rinck, called "the Greek," apprehended and imprisoned at Vacha on St. Martin's Day [11 November] 1531.

Hermann Adam, from Springen, says that he, at the suggestion of Jörg Grusselbach, went to Hans Werner's house for no reason other than that he desired to see Melchior Rinck, since earlier, some years ago at Eckardtshausen, he had attended Rinck's wedding. He says that he has not been rebaptized, nor has he until now been a follower of [the Anabaptist teaching]; and from now on he intends to put all this behind him. He has no desire to comment on the Anabaptist articles and said that, had he not been put in prison with Rinck, he would not have exchanged two words with him since the time of the revolt [i.e., Peasants' War], etc., and will swear an oath of allegiance and post bail—upon which he was dismissed.

Cort [Kontz] Mulher from Ausbach says he entered Hans Werner's house during the Martin's Day market to purchase cloth, and came upon [Rinck,] the Greek. He remained in order to listen to his teaching, but did not submit to baptism, nor does he desire to be baptized, nor to follow the [Anabaptist] teaching—to which he formally took a vow, and to avoid imprisonment, swore an oath of allegiance, upon which he was dismissed.

Adam Angersbach, the blacksmith from Unterhaun, has submitted to rebaptism, and said that what moved him to do so was that he heard the Lutheran ministers in Hersfeld preaching many objectionable things concerning baptism. These were, namely, that [even] if they knew children did not have their own faith, they still wanted to baptize them; but, in addition, at another time, within the pope's teaching and province, someone had taken a child to be baptized, where he [Angersbach] had heard the preacher say that if no godparent, other than one's chums, can

109 This is perhaps the same person as Gilg Scherer, called "Gilg am Berge." Gilg is later mentioned as a leader of the Anabaptists, but a total illiterate.

be found, they will not baptize the child, since they are baptizing the child upon the faith of the godparent until the time that children come into their own faith. And several other incidents he remembered, etc. In this manner he has seen little good coming from the preaching of the Lutheran preachers, just decadence, freedom, licentiousness—far worse and more evil than under the Papacy. But where God's word, the truth, and the Holy Spirit are taught, it yields fruit; people cease sinning and mend their ways. For this reason, he cannot observe that God's word is being taught truthfully, for they, the preachers themselves, openly lead sinful, decadent lives. As Christ says: "By their fruits will one know the false teachers, for grapes are not gathered from thorns."[110] Therefore, he does not believe that they have the Holy Spirit, for the Holy Spirit does not waver as they do, and is not greedy, etc., as is currently found among the Lutherans, as well as earlier under the Papacy, etc. And now, where the Holy Spirit does not reside and is not taught, there the truth also cannot be taught and acknowledged.

In this manner he recognized in Melchior Rinck's teaching and life—and could not help but recognize—that [Rinck] has been teaching the truth. For Christ says "By their fruits one will know a false prophet."[111] Also, he [Angersbach] said that [Rinck] began by teaching them about *Gelassenheit*, that is, that one must yield oneself completely before God, not connecting one's own life and heart to the temporal; that a person who loves something more than Christ is not worthy of him;[112] and that one must avoid sinning and resist the devil and evil, etc.—upon which [Angersbach] committed himself to living out the divine good, abstaining from cursing, gluttony, boozing, and other sins. He also said that baptism is a covenant of a good conscience with Christ, among people who begin a good life and desire to abstain from sin.[113] Also, since Christ commanded and said to his apostles, "Go into the whole world, preach the Gospel to all creatures; whoever believes and is baptized will be saved."[114] And further, at another earlier command, teaching and saying: "Whoever believes and is baptized . . ."[115]

110 [Matt 7:16.]
111 [Matt 17:15–16.]
112 [Matt 10:37.]
113 [1 Pet 3:21.]
114 [Mark 16:15–16.]
115 [Matt 28:19.]

In this manner Melchior Rinck taught him that he needs to be instructed ahead of time [i.e., before baptism] by God, for faith comes from hearing; and now, since baptism without faith is nothing, therefore he had no report or knowledge of his having faith or having a clear conscience before God. Therefore he, through his infant baptism, had experienced no abstaining from sin (which he also observed in others who were baptized as infants). Consequently, Brother Melchior offered many times, before all the brothers and sisters, to prove this with his blood, and to prove this vis-à-vis the whole world, with hundreds of writings. And Rinck had offered to face Balthasar Raid in a disputation [on the matter], inviting him to Sorga near Hersfeld, but Balthasar did not come.

After that, his conscience did not have any instruction other than the command of Christ, and the correct, veracious teaching, and he submitted to baptism. For true baptism follows the cross, as one then sees, that among those who submit to this baptism, as a consequence, many have been killed and persecuted, witnessing, on account of such baptism, with their blood. Had they not been right and lacked the Holy Spirit, it would not have been possible for them to remain so steadfast. So, Brother Melchior Rinck taught them that infant baptism was a human statute, arranged by the pope, at the time when clergy were forbidden to marry. This he wanted to prove with Scripture. Hence, such human statutes are forbidden through Christ, etc. Furthermore, children have committed no sin or evil before the time they willfully enter into this. For this reason, they have no need of baptism. Furthermore, if the sacrament of baptism is needed for infants, who are to be brought for this purpose, why are they not as infants given the sacrament of communion, etc.? The same for Christian tithes and offerings, etc.

He submitted to instruction through Scripture, recanted, and affirmed from now on not to be a follower; he is willing to swear an oath of allegiance.

Bilg [Gilg][116] Scherer, previously a resident in the district of Landeck, submitted to rebaptism, for which reason he was expelled from the

---

116 Franz et al. have "Gilg" (p. 44). This "Gilg/Bilg Scherer" may be the same as the "Gilg Schneider," who emigrated to Moravia in 1533 and was subsequently involved in a controversy with the Anabaptists there. For a discussion of this possibility, see Heinrich Beulshausen, *Die Geschichte der osthessischen Täufergemeinden*, Beiträge zur deutschen Philologie 53 (GieBen: Wilhelm Schmitz Verlag, 1981), 263ff.

district, and for some time has been wandering about. He stated that it was his decision [to be rebaptized], for he recognized that this was correct and that his conscience had not taught him otherwise. If he had considered it wrong, he would not have done it. He stated his reasons, in line with those reported above by Adam Angersbach, etc., stating in addition that Brother Melchior had taught that one baptizes no one in order to bring about the salvation of the soul, but that baptism ought to be entered into solely because it is the command of Christ, not for the sake of salvation or for the forgiveness of sins, but rather out of love and obedience to the command of God, upon the goodness of Christ, or, because God is good, and not that a person should seek salvation therein.

He submitted to instruction, recanted, and is also willing to swear an oath of allegiance.

Heinz Ot from Kattes, near Hersfeld, submitted to baptism upon the command of God—as he said—stating his reasons, similar to those of Adam Angersbach, that he had been taught by Brother Melchior, teachings which he accepted as correct, and that Brother Melchior many times had substantiated this to him in a hundred writings, which need to be referenced. If the Reformers can make their case based on Scripture, [he said,] that he could be won over. They all answered this article in the same way, etc., and Brother Melchior especially said that as long as it has not been shown with Scripture, he will continue to consider infant baptism wrong, etc. Item: He says he believes that Christ blotted out and took away all original sin on the trunk of the cross. This he also heard preached publicly at Hersfeld, and that children have no original sin. Item: Every human who comes to knowledge has two spirits: one which is good, the other, evil. The good spirit spurs one to do good, the evil, to do evil.

Item: Regarding the Lord's Supper, they all answered that they have not yet been well taught, but all of them were deferential and warned adamantly and with great sighs about it. They say that one should feel oneself worthy to go to communion, but they perceive themselves as being completely unworthy of this, and that it is a great mystery of God, etc. And this Heinz Ot said that the Lord's Supper is no sacrament, also that there is no forgiveness of sin therein, and calls it the breaking of bread. He wanted to warn every person about this for the sake of God, especially anyone who has land and possessions, saying that the current practice could be dangerous and onerous in harming the neighbor, and an encumbrance to a rich person, etc.

Item: He also says that one is to obey the magistracy, as long as it does not act in opposition to God's commandments. He also did not know what he would do if this or another state were overrun, for he held that a Christian is prepared to suffer injustice, and if someone took his coat, he would also allow his cloak to be taken, and the coat means temporal goods and the cloak, the body; nor does a Christian sue in court.

When he professed his view of the Lord's Supper, he was moved to a private interrogation. He then expressed this opinion: Where has God commanded that one should make an image out of the bread that needs to be so fine, delicate, and white? God is in one loaf of bread just as he is also in another loaf—just as he is otherwise also in other creatures. Therefore, one cannot bind God in bread and so receive God, as we think, but rather, that God broke the bread, saying one is to take it, and the eating of it is his body. [He admitted] that they have[117] occasionally broken such bread and eaten it, as the apostles did, and on occasion heard God's Word proclaimed and taught in [private] houses, for his Word is Life and Spirit and grants Life and Spirit. When [the bread] is received through preaching and the Spirit, it brings with it life [everlasting], as Christ clarifies and interprets in John, chapter six. Many [of those interrogated] cited this passage as a source of consternation, [stating] that it was not the Lord's Supper which we observe and hold to today, warning everyone about this, etc., and I assume that one may find further rationale on this in Rinck's books which were presented at Friedewald to My Gracious Prince, where much regarding the bread of God may be found in the margins.

He submitted to our teachings, recanted, and was willing to swear an oath of allegiance.

Hans Werner, citizen of Vacha, says that baptism does not save, but is a covenant of a good conscience with Christ, out of which good and blessedness follow those who have faith and who abstain from sin. Item: Brother Melchior taught that infant baptism was conceived by Satan and mankind in the era when clergy were forbidden to marry. Item: children have no faith; therefore, they are not to be baptized.

117 Wappler has "Das sei," which is most likely a transcription error for "Das sie."

Item. No child is a Christian, but rather a lackey[118] of Christ, who, however, ought to be trained to be one, etc., and should, as should adults, be taught through the Word, out of which follows faith, and then baptism, etc., for faith has to do with the heart, and through confession one comes into salvation. Item: Children have no sin until the time when they will to sin. Item: Brother Melchior has not wanted to teach him anything about the Lord's Supper, saying he wants to understand the large matters but does not yet know the small, and that Brother Melchior holds it to be a high mystery and work. Item: Since he [i.e., Hans Werner], however, is to give his testimony about the Lord's Supper, he considers it to be a sacrament, and whoever is worthy in his heart may receive it. But he is unfortunately not able to do so. He says he hosted this meeting because Christ commanded us to show mercy, to feed and shelter the poor, etc., and that most within the group came to seek out Brother Melchior. It was for this reason that he hosted Brother Melchior.

And he hosted Brother Melchior because Jorg [Georg] Witzel had suggested that he would like to discuss baptism with him, hoping he might be able to convince him to recant. He had always thought a lot of Mr. Georg, and, had Mr. Georg been able to do this, he [Werner] hoped it would satisfy his conscience and [he could] distance himself from that [i.e., the Anabaptist movement].

He has been rebaptized, along with his wife. They recanted the same [for the first time] at Friedewald in the presence of our gracious prince and lord; and then again when he and she, on the basis of their own words, were again suspected and cautioned and also shown the decree of our gracious lord concerning the Anabaptists; and now, in this third instance, held an [Anabaptist] meeting in his house. Upon the basis of the decree he was commanded to sell his possessions, conforming to the written content of the decree, and swearing to conform to the content of the written command to move to the other side of the Rhine River, with wife and children, etc.

Greta Werner, his wife, also indicated the same rationale and reasons as specified above, saying in addition that she, too, followed the example of Christ, and also that as soon as the Father in heaven sent the Holy Spirit upon Christ, saying, "This is my beloved son, with whom I

118 Original: "midling."

am well pleased," etc.,[119] here she could not understand otherwise than that such a baptism which Christ received there—being an example from that point on—was pleasing to God. Item: Furthermore, that in the Acts of the Apostles, only adults were baptized. The same in Acts [9:18],[120] where Paul was baptized as an adult, etc.[121] Item: Original sin harms no one, unless a person wills to sin, and that children know of no sin. Item: that Adam had sinned; this he did willfully. Item: children sin after being baptized, which is why [infant] baptism brings forth no fruit, for [baptism] is a covenant of a good conscience[122] which avoids sins, etc. She said she would in the end agree that infant baptism is all right; however, that it rests on the godparents, since no one can believe on behalf of children.

She was expelled, with her husband, upon the basis of the decree and commandments.

Jörg Grusselbach and his wife, local citizens, had once recanted and then in a second case had been expelled from the land and now was apprehended in this meeting. He admitted having come again into the city at the request of his child, who asked him to abide by the decree, for if he did not abandon his error, his possessions would be sold and he would be sentenced according to the decree. Thereupon he came into the city, desiring to answer this [letter from the child], etc.—and when he found out that Brother Melchior was there, he went to him in order to speak with him about this, etc.

He was ordered to sell his possessions, in line with the decree, and expelled with his wife to the other side of the Rhine.

Anna and Ursel Zoberin, sisters, from Großenbach from the district of Hasselstein, became acquainted with rebaptism from a person named Jorg,[123] whose last name they did not know. They recanted and were on this basis set free.[124]

---

119 [Matt 3:17.]

120 Original has "Actorum 13. cap. 12."

121 Von Paulo widergetauft worden etc.

122 [1 Pet 3:21.]

123 Possibly Jörg Zaunring.

124 Source: Wappler, *Täuferbewegung in Thüringen*, 326–33.

c.

The Amtmann (Official) from the Wartburg, Eberhard von der Tann, to Landgrave Philip (1 March 1532)

Your princely grace, I hereby humbly send you this petition regarding what I know about the infractions of the imprisoned Melchior Rinck—"the Greek." And the reason I do so is that, in the land under my command, he has seduced many pious, gullible, simple folk to their disadvantage and damnation, both in soul and body, and has not allowed for other opinions. For I have nothing to gain from his or anyone's demise but rather I am sincerely interested in the welfare and betterment of each [individual]. But, because I have no hope of this in this case, and in addition have heard how he should be let go or kept unpunished in your grace's prison for all the days of his life, I am concerned that many of his followers might conclude that the authorities are unwilling or unable to punish this unchristian rebellion. Rinck also thinks the same: that because he was imprisoned under threat of death many times before, but each time was found not guilty, his cause must be a good and just one, and so he was able to wander from village to village and, with these and other embellished, secretive reasons, to lead lots of folk into error.

In this manner I seek to inform Your Princely Grace, so that you might act on this matter in accordance with your understanding as a Christian and praiseworthy sovereign, to deter others with public punishment after having graciously proclaimed his transgressions, and know how to preside piously in your office in these and other matters to the glory of God and to maintain a common peace. . . .

Date: Wartburg, the Friday after Reminiscere [1 March], [15]32.[125]

d.

Eberhard von der Tann to Landgrave Philip concerning "The infractions of Melchior Rinck, 'the Greek.'"[126]

125 Source: Wappler, *Täuferbewegung in Thüringen*, 333.

126 Wappler, *Täuferbewegung in Thüringen*, 333–36. He notes: "printed, but incomplete and full of errors, in Hochhuth, *Der Landgraf Philipp und die Wiedertäufer*, XXVIII, 547–49."

First of all, it is evident, apparent, and undeniable, that the same Melchior Rinck, called the Greek, was involved in the recent peasants' uprising as a particular agitator and captain alongside Müntzer and Pfeiffer, and more active than these and others within the mob at Frankenhausen.

And although he, along with others who had participated in the same uprising, more unwittingly than willfully, ought to be shown mercy in the hope of his betterment, he has, however, never sought this improvement nor shown a desire for forgiveness or asked the magistrates for such, and has yet to express regret for such evil deeds and other abuses, as others have done. Rather, immediately thereafter, and in more than one place, [he was active in preaching Anabaptism]—even though Müntzer, who renounced his actions [at Frankenhausen], was publicly tried in order to scare [the populace], receiving no grace, but punished for his seditious venture.

Also, immediately after he was set free, he left his wife behind and wandered about, seeking, under the name of that unchristian beguiling rebaptism, to foment another uprising, time and again, for more than six years secretly slithering about and passing around his poison.

Whether or not this same rebaptism should be understood as mere mistaken faith, a matter solely of the heart that justifies punishment with the worldly sword, this I will not expand upon here, since it is not my vocation, but rather I leave that to the experts in Scripture and legal scholars to find out.

When, however, these people act in words and deeds against the visible Holy Scripture and the prohibition of the magistracy, and do not heed many a friendly and stern admonition and warning, then according to my simple understanding they ought to be punished simply on account of [being associated with] Anabaptism—whether they explicitly promote rebellion or not—by the magistracy, for their public blasphemy of God, which it really is.

For where such punishment is not forthcoming, then one must equally allow all the unbelieving blasphemers of God dwelling among us—those who blaspheme and malign our faith and the honor and majesty of our Savior Jesus Christ—to practice this depravity unpunished, whereby many simple hearts will be led astray and tainted.

And, since, as it is said, a prince should show less mercy in forgiving and forgetting attacks against his honor than in damages done to his subjects, the Christian prince ought all the more to wield the power of the magistracy to defend God's honor, with a view to the betterment and love of the neighbor, to which all the members of the other Christian estates are dedicated and strive.

However, the Anabaptists' teaching and life—and especially that of Melchior Rinck—prove in this regard that they embody the greatest public blasphemy, are also rebellious, standing in opposition to the magistracy, as may be discovered in the following clarifications:

First of all, the aforementioned Rinck has been teaching openly that there should be no magistracy; secondly, telling this to the poor, simple [people] that they have been punished in particular on the basis of this and similar articles coming from the recent peasants' revolt, but also emphasizing as well that, in the place of participating in such a revolt, a Christian shall not be an overlord—also teaching openly that the congregation should have the power to appoint and dismiss the magistracy—which is two ways of saying the same thing: two pairs of pants but one cloth.

In this way he from the outset denigrated the magistracy in the hearts of the people. It follows that if this attack were to succeed in felling the magistracy and giving the community the power to appoint and dismiss "such an unchristian and contemptuous magistracy," as he regards and calls it, it would in the end result in the total collapse of this institution and, in its place, summon a Müntzer-like horde, devoid of government. For where there is no magistracy, or where it is without honor, there can be no peace; where there is no peace, there is no food, and no one is able to live protected from crime, thievery, robbery, coercion and vice, etc. There would thus be far less possibility of teaching God's word, and raising children unto God's fear and discipline, but rather this would finally lead to the destruction of both regiments—the spiritual and the worldly—resulting in a forsaken horde extending throughout the whole wide world.

In addition, it is further evidence [of his rebellious spirit] that the often-mentioned Rinck publicly disdains Your Majesty's multiple merciful admonitions and clemency, as well as the penalties and banishment [to which he was previously sentenced]. And recently, according to reports, when Your Majesty's councilman at Vacha asked why he had disdained these same commands, he is said to have responded, insolently, "The earth is the Lord's," for which reason he absolutely will not give in at all to these, Your Majesty's frequent commands requesting his submission.

And by way of solid justification that his intention has been solely to again resurrect an insurrection with a view to an overall break-up and destruction of the magistracy and the social estates, let it be noted that in this regard he has acted against the magistracy as an insurrectionist, acting as much as he could to bring down all worldly political orders, Christian regulations and estates, delegitimizing and destroying both [the Christian and the magisterial] regiments—without which, however, the world would be a desolate waste, in no way able to survive—and in turn to introduce here on earth a fictive equality and fellowship of all people and possessions—which we hold and anticipate to be Christian [but only] in the future life.

Out of all this, then, it follows in fact that in the principality of Saxony and elsewhere, through [Rinck's] inspiration and seduction, many simple people have followed him, taking themselves down the fallacious path of erring desolation, in an inhuman manner forsaking their vocation: the parish ministers forsaking their office of pastoral care, husband and wife—often both; at times, one of the two—forsaking their children and infants, occasionally themselves forsaking one another. This is counter to divine law and all reason. What, then, finally would eventuate out of all this other than an insurrection and a desolate, disorderly mob of unreasonable and preposterous people? This is a question for each to consider.

And if [Rinck] denies all or part of what is touched upon above, he can easily be disproven, if necessary, on the basis of his own books—in part published, in part written with his own hand—which he has circulated, some of which I had previously sent to Your Majesty, some of which I still have at hand.

Out of all this, as touched upon above, it is manifest that [Rinck's] teachings and those of Müntzer are in complete agreement, apart from the fact that the one emphasizes rebaptism, and the other emphasizes Christian brotherhood. Although the first seems to be shielded with a better appearance, both, however, are intent on instigating a common insurrection.

Likewise, now, just as the magistracy is not charged to oversee matters of faith, but rather to pronounce judgment concerning the ensuing actions of this same brotherhood, so also shall this same [magistracy] anticipate this teaching of rebaptism as a public blasphemy, an insurrection in the making, to be punished and judged, and in no manner allowing them, through their action, to gain the upper hand upon which they then would be blessed and accepted.

For what can indeed be more inflammatorily set, written, stated, and acted upon than the common rabble's active assault couched under the façade of rebaptism, as recounted above, [in the testimony] of that person [Rinck], who claims that no overlord can act in a Christian manner. And yet these same people set and dismiss [rules and law], and in short, desire to act and do what they want according to their own fancy, completely free and without boundaries, leading to the disadvantage and ruin of many poor, simple people. This should be considered attentively by the overlords to the highest degree, in advance, and then acted upon as a top priority when such acts, with concomitant harm, take place, tending [to these concerns] by giving help and advice in the light of German custom.

Now it has recently happened that Melchior Rinck, named "the Greek," a previous arouser and instigator of the recent peasants' insurrection, which he did not get enough of, is still impenitent, ever persevering, and actively diligent, carrying out the same [insurrection] again under the pretense of promoting rebaptism. Through all of this he has also in manifold active ways proved himself to be an unbelieving, blaspheming, disobedient, intractable insurrectionist, not willing to confess. I therefore [recommend] to Your Majesty to have [Rinck] punished to the highest degree, first of all, as a blasphemer, and secondly as an inconvincible, stubborn, unrepentant insurrectionist and a despiser of every divine and human order, given his transgressions. This should be done to the honor of God and to maintain a common peace, for the improvement of [Rinck] himself, and as an abominable example to others.[127]

127 Source: Wappler, *Täuferbewegung in Thüringen*, 333–36.

3. Interrogation of Anabaptists at Berka (1533)[128]

Files from Berka, produced by commissaries of the elector and princes concerning the Anabaptists, 1533 . . .

Heintz Cleue from Herda. He freely and openly acknowledged being Anabaptist and gave the following report. First of all, he held infant baptism to be wrong for the reason that nowhere did God command that infants be baptized; second, that infants are not able to believe; third, that infants are blessed and saved without [infant baptism]. He said that a man named Jörg[129] from Moravia baptized him at Sorga in Heinz Lutter's house on the 14th day before Shrove Tuesday of this year.

Regarding the Lord's Supper, he says that Christ's body is not, nor will be, in the Supper. Item: he knows of no Lord's Supper that Anabaptists observe. He says the magistracy is a divine order and that one is to be obedient to it. But he also says, if the magistracy ordered him out of the land, he might go away, but perhaps not, depending on the circumstances. He also says that he will not go to [the local] church as long as the current preacher and vicar remain at Herda. He says that Christians may own their own house and farm.

Concluding report: he desires to remain with the Anabaptists.

Hans Kessel from Herda. He acknowledges that he had also been baptized a year ago at Sorga near Hersfeld by Jörg Zwinck [Zaunring] in the home of Heinz Hutter. He says they have a main leader who occasionally comes to them from Sorga, whose name is Gilg. Hans also says that infant baptism is an abomination and atrocity in the eyes of God, out of which nothing good has ever come, but rather all forms of sin. He says that infants are blessed on account of their innocence, and indeed, that they are not able to believe.

He does not believe that Christ's body and blood are in the Lord's Supper, saying that one can see what body and blood are; since, however, one cannot see [body and blood in the sacrament], so [body and

---

128 The source of this section is Staatsarchiv-Marburg 22a-1–11, as transcribed by Ellen Marie Yutzy Glebe. It is a report sent to Landgrave Philip. The substance of the report overlaps with Wappler, *Stellung Kursachsens*, 168–76, apparently a report sent to Saxon authorities—which has also been referenced.

129 Presumably Jörg Zaunring.

blood] can [not] be therein. He says, whoever is living out God's righteousness is eating his body and drinking his blood.

Concerning the magistracy, he says he does not understand the article, that he has not yet been given instruction about it. However, he considers God to be his magistrate. He also states that no Christian may kill another human being, and he will not attend preaching services in the churches. No Christian dare own property; he believes, above all, that all humans have been created for good.

Concluding report: he cannot and will not desist.

Peter Leinweber from Herda. He acknowledges that on the most recent Shrove Tuesday he was baptized at Sorga, along with the two just mentioned above, by Jörg Zwinck. Also, that he was taught by two of their teachers, Gilg and Alexander. Gilg was said to be a tailor and Alexander a sexton. He says infant baptism is wrong, since Christ never commanded it. As for the Lord's Supper he says that bread is bread, wine is wine, and Christ did not place his body and blood in the elements, since one can neither see nor taste these. All who hold to his views and faith have as much right to his possessions as he does. He did not share [in this manner] with others. Regarding the magistracy, he says that God has said that they are not to name themselves "lords" here on earth, for there is one [Lord] in heaven, whom one is to acknowledge.

Concluding report: this person desires to remain with the Anabaptist teaching.

The old Hans Zwingen from Wünschensuhl had twice recanted and repented, affirming to refrain from his errors, and has now for the third time defected. He was questioned intensively as to who and what caused him to fall again, but in short, he was unwilling to answer, except that his own conscience had moved him. He has now finally resolved that he would, in short, no longer agree to accept or tolerate any other instruction.

This person was not present when the concluding report was given.[130]

Hans Heylman, called Black Hans, from the village of Breitenbach. He acknowledges that around two years ago, at Rengers, he was baptized by Jörg Stein, and since that time was with him once in a field. However, he will not say who else was present. He says that infant baptism is wrong,

---

130 The minutes of the hearings printed in Wappler suggest that this individual "did not appear for the group instruction."

since God has not commanded that infants be baptized. Item: That no one is to be baptized unless he or she has been taught and brought to faith, and that [infants] are not able to believe. He cannot and will nevermore believe that Christ's body and blood are in the sacrament.

A Christian is not to own anything, but those who desire to be true Christians need to hold all possessions in common, and if a prince enters their order [i.e., their community of faith], he also needs to hold all possessions in common. A Christian cannot occupy the office of magistrate with good conscience, although he is committed to suffer the magistrate's use of force and remain subservient.

Concluding report: he desires to remain with the Anabaptists.

On the Sunday after . . . Apostolorum [i.e., on July 20] the following were interrogated:

Hermann Adam from Springen acknowledges that he submitted to an additional baptism but did not say where and when he was baptized. His baptizer was supposedly named Jacob Schmidt, about whom he could not or would not say from where he came.

As for infant baptism, he says he respects the opinion of others: whoever is satisfied with [infant baptism] may remain with that opinion. He himself, however, was not able to be at peace with it. For this reason, he submitted instead to be baptized again.

As for why he considers infant baptism wrong, what he thinks of the sacrament of communion, and [his opinion concerning] community of goods, he did not want to give any answer and claimed that he was under no obligation to answer.[131] He says one should obey the magistracy, yet he desires . . . to abstain from doing wrong and will not allow himself to be forced by the magistracy to attend church services . . .[132]

He was not present for the general instruction and pronouncement of the sentence.

Hermann Adam's wife, named Barbara. She says she does not know whether or not she is baptized, or is a heathen, since she knows nothing of any baptism. As for infant and adult baptism, she says she does not know which is right or wrong. Concerning the sacrament, she says she remains with God's words and had nothing more to say about it. Regarding going to church, she knows of no church outside of her own heart.

---

131 Manuscript defective. Filled in with Wappler.

132 Text defective, only partially legible.

She was not present for the general instruction and pronouncement of the sentence.

Lentz Rüdiger called "Swab," from Hausbreitenbach. He acknowledges that he was baptized earlier this year at Herda by someone named Christoffel, in Hans Kessel's house in the presence of Hans Kessel and Peter Leinweber. He says infant baptism is wrong, since infants cannot believe. But he says that infants can still be saved, for they are already saved on account of their innocence, since they are without sin and pure. He does not believe that Christ's body and blood are in the bread and wine, since one cannot see or taste or grasp [body and blood therein]. He says further that he holds that the words concerning the Lord's Supper apply to any eating and drinking, for Christ spoke, "do this in remembrance of me."[133]

Regarding possessions, he says that a Christian is obligated to help another person with his own [possessions]. Concerning the magistracy, he says the head leader of his community forbade him to go to our churches and from attending our baptismal or Lord's Supper services. He says further that a true Christian, whom he esteems as his brother in the faith, cannot wield the princely magisterial power over other Christians and still be or remain a Christian. But he also says, he does not know, if a prince were to come into their brotherhood desiring to be baptized, whether such a person would need to relinquish his princely office.

Concluding report: he desires to remain Anabaptist.

Tyle from Rengers. This man had also recanted twice, repenting publicly at Eisenach. He says he was again received into the brotherhood by Jörg Zwinck at Sorga, and that he was prohibited from attending our church services, including baptisms and the sacrament. He acknowledges also that since that time he has often demeaned both sacraments. He says that at Bamburg, Jörg Zwinck witnessed with his blood, as several brethren from Sorga have in recent weeks reported to them.[134] He says, in short, that his position on baptism and the Lord's Supper is the same as before. But he does not want to elaborate.

---

133 [Luke 22:19.]

134 This is most likely Jörg Zaunring, an Anabaptist leader from Tyrol. See "Zaunring (*Martyrs Mirror*, Zaunringerad; Loserth, Zaunried) Georg (Jörg or Juriaen) (d.1531 or 1538) an early Tyrolean Anabaptist and co-worker with Jakob Hutter," *Mennonite Encyclopedia*, vol. 4, 1018–19. According to the testimony here, Zaunring's death came not in 1531 or 1538, but in 1533.

Concluding report: he desires to remain Anabaptist.

Hans Zwinger, the younger, from Wünschensuhl. He was also present earlier at Eisenach, and at that time did not profess Anabaptism . . . although his wife and father were attached to the movement. Even though he had never confessed to being rebaptized,[135] he still recanted and was punished along with the others.

His wife ran away [from home] three years ago, leaving behind a seven-week-old child, for she otherwise would have needed to recant her error and repent.[136] And meanwhile, his wife[137] resided at Sorga until this past Easter, where another child was conceived which will be raised at Sorga by Heinz Hutter, and who is to remain unbaptized. He [Zwinger] acknowledges freely that he does not want to bring the child home, because he does not want to be forced to have the infant baptized.

As to why he considers infant baptism wrong, he says that he can give no reason—the same, also, for the Lord's Supper. In short, he will not accept any other interpretations, but rather wants to remain with his current tenets.

Concluding report: he desires to remain Anabaptist.

Young Hans Zwinger's wife, named Gela. This woman acknowledges that everything said about her is correct. She says she desires to remain with her tenets and in short will not accept any other instruction. She continues to hold to her position on the sacrament and wants to remain thereby.

Concluding report: she desires to remain Anabaptist.

The wife of Hans Kessel, named Margret. She is greatly pregnant, soon to deliver. She acknowledges having been baptized by Christoffel from Moravia, approximately four weeks ago, in her own house at Herda, in the presence of several brethren from Herda, when several others were also baptized, such as Lentz, Osanna, Groß-Hans's daughter from Awenheim, Beautiful Kethe from Wünschensuhl, and Peter Leinweber['s wife].[138]

---

135 Text defective, only partially legible. Supplemented with notes from Wappler's account.

136 According to Wappler's account, the child was placed with another woman to be nursed and died soon thereafter.

137 und mitteler weib . . .

138 Wappler says "Lentz Rudiger." Wappler also suggests that Osanna is an appositive here, which gives the name of Groß-Hans's daughter, and Wappler lists the third person as Peter Leinweber's wife, which corresponds to the subsequent text.

She says that infant baptism is wrong since infants cannot confess their faith. Item: that they are pure and saved within divine creation. She does not believe that Christ is in the Lord's Supper, since he is in heaven, and no human [can] . . . bring him into the nature and essence of bread and wine.

She says that all possessions among Christians are to be held in common—as she has been taught by her brother . . . that no one has power over the other person. . . . She says one is to obey the magistracy, yet she refuses to go to church.[139]

Concluding report: she intends to remain Anabaptist.

Anna, Peter Leinweber's wife. She acknowledges that she was baptized in Hans Kessel's home by Christoffel at the time and in the presence [of others], as Kessel Hans's wife has reported. She says that infant baptism is wrong, since infants have no faith. She does not believe that Christ's body and blood are in the sacrament. She says she knows of no reason to indicate why she does not believe so. She says she has been taught that Christians are to have and utilize all possessions in common. She says she does not want to give a further answer as to whether a Christian may be a magistrate, or whether a Christian must be subject to the magistracy. She says she concurs with her husband and wants to remain with her convictions.

In sum, she desires to remain Anabaptist.

Margret, Casper Schneider's wife, in the village of Breitenbach. This Casper has been ill for almost three years, his wife says. She knows nothing about his baptism; one may ask him about it. Item: she acknowledges adult baptism, having been baptized by Jörg von Staffelstein at Rengers, in Albrecht's home in the presence of Albrecht and his wife and children. She says that infant baptism is wrong, that no one should be baptized who has not first come to faith. She does not believe that Christ's body and blood are in the Lord's Supper, since she cannot see it.

She says Christians are to have all possessions in common, where one may partake of the other's possessions to meet one's own needs. She says that whoever desires to be a true Christian shall hold no magisterial office, no commanding power over other Christians, but also says that one should submit to the magistracy. She rejects instruction to the contrary.

---

139 Defective text.

Concluding report: she desires to remain Anabaptist.

Könne, Hans Wilhelm's wife from the village of Breitenbach. She says that more than a year ago she was baptized by Jacoff Schmiden of Breitenbach in Casper Schneider's house in the presence of both. She says infant baptism is wrong, since infants cannot believe. She says she does not believe that Christ's body and blood are in the bread and wine.

She says a Christian is not to own possessions on earth. She says she does not know what to think about the magistracy, having heard many differing views. They are thirsty for [Anabaptist] blood, which they are getting by the bucket-full.[140] She finally concluded that, in short, she desires to remain with her convictions. She acknowledges that her husband is not in agreement with such errors but has punished and beaten her for her views.

Concluding report: she desires therewith to remain.

On the Monday after . . . the following interrogations took place:[141]

Margret Garköchen. She acknowledges that two years ago, at Hersfeld, she was baptized by Melchior Rinck. She says that infant baptism is wrong, since Christ never commanded it. This person is currently imprisoned at Hausbreitenbach and had been expelled from the principality of Hesse . . . and will absolutely not accept instruction. She says that the revolt in which Müntzer and Melchior Rinck were involved was a divine occurrence and those who punished them will receive their own punishment. She is completely hardened like the devil himself.[142]

Elsa, wife of Fritz Erben. She acknowledges that about three years ago she was baptized by Claus Schreiber at Herda. This is a poor . . . and crazy woman who cannot say anything about baptism or the sacrament, except that she disdains and blasphemes both—infant baptism and the sacrament—and that she will not be convinced to change her mind, reasoning that Christ did not submit to baptism until he was thirty-three years of age.

Concluding report: this woman also desires to remain Anabaptist.

---

140 . . . man sie ["sei"] durstig nach iren plut, das wird man maul und nasen vol kriegen, . . . Literally, "One is thirsty for their blood; this, one will get [by the] mouth- and nose-full . . ."

141 Defective text.

142 Defective text.

Alheit, Simplicious Wagener's wife, at Hausbreitenbach. This person says she has not been otherwise baptized, but rather that she only listened to one of the [Anabaptist] teachers in Peter Leinweber's house, whose teaching she appreciated. . . . She [admitted to having] not attended the local parish church for some time. She was forewarned not to attend Anabaptist meetings and to ignore such and was then questioned if she would do so, and hold obediently to the other common Christian decrees, upon which she answered that she wanted to behave properly, except for [avoiding contact with][143] her biological siblings who are Anabaptists.

Katharina, Young Hans Paul's wife from Wünschensuhl, acknowledges that she was baptized by a man whose name is unknown to her, in Langen Tiln's house, in the absence of her husband. She will not state when it happened. She submitted to baptism without the consent of her husband. She says infant baptism is wrong and that she does not believe that Christ's body and blood are in the sacrament of the altar, but would give absolutely no reason or answer as to why for any of it.

She says that if one is to do rightly, one should have all temporal goods in common, to be used equally with other Christians. She says that no Christian is to exercise power and dominion over other people, or to punish delinquents physically, but rather to forgive—as often as they sin and ask for pardon.

Concluding report: she also chooses to remain Anabaptist.[144]

4. Interrogation of Anabaptists at Sorga (1533)

1533 August. Interrogation of the Anabaptists at Sorga near Hersfeld.

Baptism. Attendance at sermons and the sacrament. Acceptance of the magistracy. The law concerning taxes and military service. Participation in the Peasants' War. Community of goods.

---

143 Defective text.

144 Source: Staatsarchiv-Marburg 22a-1–11 (German text transcribed by Ellen Marie Yutzy Glebe). A parallel source, Wappler, *Stellung Kursachsens*, 168–76, was also referenced.

a.

2 August 1533. Abbot Kraft of Hersfeld to the Landgrave. Actions against the Anabaptists at Sorga.

[Franz summarizes[145] Kraft's report as saying that] *although he had proceeded against the Anabaptists in the Hersfeld region of Sorga according to the mandates of* "past Imperial Diets," *i.e. by* "sentencing them to imprisonment, . . . and banishing them from our lands," *the local residents are becoming* "only more obstinate and malevolent." *He had already—to no avail—asked Philip's councilors in Kassel for advice* "several times" *as to* "what form the countering of such iniquity within the region might take. So" *as not to be accused of supporting the Anabaptists, he asks urgently that instructions on how to proceed be sent back via the messenger bringing this letter, and also that your grace's [servant], Ciriax Hoffmann [Schultheiß (mayor)] of Hersfeld, should be instructed to be helpful and supportive in this matter, as you, our prince protector [Verspruchsfurst], see fit . . . Hersfeld, the Saturday after the* [*Feast of the*] *Liberation of St. Peter,* in the year [15]33.

b.

Articles for the interrogation of the Anabaptists.

1. Whether they also attend our preaching services and desire to receive the sacrament with us in fellowship?

2. Whether a Christian may hold and exercise secular authority?

3. Whether they are also willing to pay taxes for military campaigns?

4. Whether they are also willing, alongside my gracious lord of Hesse and the abbot of Hersfeld, to enter into battle against their enemies and more particularly to defend the fatherland, counter danger, and, if necessary, kill in battle?

5. Whether the recent rebellion of the peasants was godly or ungodly?

6. Whether a person may take another person's possessions in case of need?

7. Whether a Christian may own personal possessions?

---

145 Franz's summarization is marked here in italics.

8. Whether you have fellowship with individuals outside your own community?[146]

9. Whether the magistracy may justifiably demand payment of interest and taxes?

c.

The interrogation.

Proceedings with the Anabaptists on the Saturday after [the Feast of St.] Ciriacus, 1533 [9 August] at the Petersberg near Hersfeld, in the presence of my gracious lord from Hersfeld, Ciriax [Hoffmann], the Schultheiß (mayor) of that place; Lord Melchior [Schwind] of Gudensberg; Lord Balthasar [Raidt], pastor at Hersfeld; and Chancellor [Feige], along with other pious people. What took place is clearly herewith reported:

Hans Koch, a miller, (and Elsa, his wife) desires to remain with his beliefs, as does also his wife.

1. He says, with his wife concurring, that he has heard nothing in Melchior's sermons that he objects to, but he still does not attend his preaching services. God has forbidden it, [he says,] for God said, beware of the scribes, etc. He considers [the preachers] to be the scribes of whom Christ speaks, since they are acting against God's command concerning baptism and the sacrament—saying that, whether God does or does not so desire, he wants to have no fellowship with us.

2. He says he does not understand the article, but that he has until now not broken away from the magistracy.

3. He could not provide an answer of which he felt certain.

4. He would not do it.

5. This he recognizes as ungodly. He himself, however, had participated, hoping God will forgive him. He was not a leader [of the insurrection].

---

146 Warumb habt ir mit einem beurschen in usserlichen dingen gemeinschaft? ("Why do you have fellowship with a man in external matters?") The answers to this question, as noted below, suggest that the intent of the question was to identify those outside of the Anabaptist circle who were sympathetic to the Anabaptist cause, who, thus, could also be held liable. The way the question was answered by most of those queried—which at first seems highly unfriendly—therefore makes good sense. The Anabaptists were extremely careful not to implicate their neighbors.

6. He says no.

7. He says one may not own possessions, which, however, may be used for the needs of the poor.

8. He does not want to have fellowship externally, but in times of need, he would want to help them.

9. He says he will not refuse.

This person had earlier recanted. He hopes God will forgive him; he regrets having recanted. He will not take the oath of banishment, nor himself sell off his possessions.

Hans Plat from Sorga, [and] Greta, his wife, both rebaptized. He sees no flaws in Melchior's teaching.

1. Where preaching takes place as Melchior preaches, he will listen. As for participating in the sacrament, he does not know how to position himself. He would like to say that he would, but also to say, he would not. Summing up, he does not want to participate, for he says they preach according to their self-interest.

2. He does not want to be against the magistracy, but they should kill no one. And if he were a Christian prince, he would call no one into military action. Item: a Christian prince will not go into battle or murder. He thinks he should pay taxes, for it is written [Luke 20:25], Give to God what belongs to God—but the magistracy should arrange things so that they do not need this.

3., 4. He will not do it—protecting [the fatherland] militarily.

5. He will leave it up to God; he was told that it was good and right. He was there, Master Adam [Kraft] and Curt had done it, and they said, there should be no magistracy and also that it was fully justified and they should press on. He does not claim that the rebellion was justified. He was also punished because of his participation.

6. He does not know about this. He does not understand what this means.

7. He is allowed to own property but yet should act as if he had none, and that no one should own possessions.

8. He bids such a person good morning and good evening and considers him a needy person.

9. He does not understand, he wants to give the prince of the land what he is due, but he does not know what this is.

He does not desire to stay away from my gracious lord's land for they could not honorably do so. The wife says that she wants to remain with the children.

Hans Zisen from Sorga and Elsa, his wife.

1. No, he does not want to do it.

2. They are taught daily that they should [have] a Christian magistracy, that they are to be subject to the magistracy, and both allow for such things as hanging a thief.

3., 4. They do not want to do it.

5. He participated, but he does not know whether it was right or not. He had been punished.

6. He said no and answered the question correctly.[147]

7. A Christian should not own anything, for he needs simply to be like Christ.

8. They have absolutely no fellowship with him; however, in times of need they help him.

9. He says yes, if they so request. As to whether they have the power to demand such, this he does not know.

Heinz Hutter and Konne, his wife.

1. Both state: no. When asked why, [they say] God will show it.

2. He says he thinks the magistracy is to be obeyed and states that he cannot say with a good conscience whether a Christian may or may not be a magistrate.

3., 4. In his view, a Christian should not fight. He had no intentions of fighting. They had once been incited with good words [to fight], namely Master Adam [Krafft] and Conrad in the peasants' revolt, and of Balthasar Raid. It would have been better had it not happened. Whereupon, says Balthasar, this could not possibly be true. For he had not even known at that time where Hersfeld was situated, and that [Hutter's] words toward him were therefore coercive and unjust. [Hutter] then acknowledged having spoken of him unjustly.

5. He wants to leave this up to God. He has no intention of being one who starts such things.

---

147 sagt nein, sagt recht. *Recht* probably means having answered the question in a manner not arousing suspicion.

6. They say no; whoever is a Christian will leave another's possessions alone.

7. He may surely have possessions of his own, but they are to be used as God commands, and for those in need.

8. No. They have no fellowship with him, but in times of need they do not want him to suffer.

9. This he leaves up to God. When magistrates rule according to God's command, one is justified to pay taxes. If they do not, this they have to answer to God.

Heinrich Lutz and his wife, Catharina. His wife was not interrogated, but Heinrich says his wife shares his views.

1. He says no. When asked why, regarding the first article, he says: Ask me in such a manner that I can respond.

2. He says he does not know; he does not understand the meaning.

3., 4. He says he cannot understand this question, but it is natural that one hangs a thief.

5. This he does not know, whether it was godly or ungodly. It was a revolt, and he says he had participated.

6. He says no. He would not want to seize his brother's possessions unless he [his brother] allowed it.

7. He says yes. He may certainly have his own possessions, if he then also shares them.

8. If they request something from him, they help them. Otherwise they totally avoid them.

Groschen and Margarethe [his wife] from Sorga.

1. Both say no. They desire to attend preaching services where Christ is preached. Our [i.e., the established church's] Christ does not bring us suffering.

2. They say they do not understand it [the article].

3., 4. They say no, that the Ten Commandments do not allow it.

5. The recent rebellion had to do with temporal goods, for which reason it was ungodly. If it had taken place for the sake of the Gospel, they do not know [if it would be godly].

6. They believe a Christian does not do it. But if the need is present, they allow this to happen, for love does not permit one to tolerate [another's] suffering.

7. They are managers of them [i.e., their worldly possessions] and do not take them from one another against the other person's will.

8. They have no fellowship with him, nor do they initiate [such contacts] with him; but if such a person makes a request, they do help him.[148]

Endres Lober, whom Claus Schreiber baptized.

1. He says he cannot at this time do this, basing his answer on freedom of the will. He says the pastor cannot help him, but that it depends upon himself to overcome depravity and find salvation. For what can God do about that fact that he acts wrongly?

2. There is nothing he can say about this. As for matters wherein he has an obligation, he will do what he considers to be acceptable, but not do things he considers harmful.

3., 4. He would not want to go to battle against his neighbor; he would much rather that they do it to him than that he do it to them.

5. He had participated in the recent rebellion. He says no, it was not godly. Had he known then what he knows now, he would not have participated.

6. It might well be.

7. One may well make use of his own possessions, but he needs to share with his brother.

8. He says he has no fellowship with him, but when they ask for help, help is given, but apart from the times they ask for help, there is no contact.

Hen Schmidt says, yes, he was baptized three years ago. He has no problem with Lutherans nor Anabaptists nor Papists, but wants to go anywhere where he recognizes that truth is being preached.

1. Since autumn he has not concerned himself with the Anabaptists.

2. He does not know. He does not intend to save anyone with his hands [i.e., using physical force]. Other than that, he has nothing more to say. He cannot reject the magistracy.

---

148 8. Sie haben kein gemeinschaft mit ime, sie komen ime auch nicht zuvor, aber wan er sie pittet, so helfen sie im nicht. Given the context, the last *nicht* has to be a mistake.

3., 4. He believes it is one's duty to pay taxes, but he would not consider actually going into battle bodily, for God has forbidden him to kill.

5. He was also in the peasants' rebellion, for which he is sorry. Adam Kraft and Lord Henrich Rab taught them, stating it was pleasing to God, whereas the entire court would say it was not godly. He also never again intends to do that, since God does not so desire.

6. A person dare not make use of someone else's possessions without the other person's consent.

7. He may certainly have belongings, if he makes proper use of them.

8. For reasons [unspecified], this question was not posed.

Marx Baumgart and Herda, his wife.

1. He says no, since their sermons are not from God. For they do not want to attend preaching services where actions, according to their opinion, do not follow. If the sacrament is from God, they would let it stand; if it is not from God, they would once again let it stand. Claus Schreiber had baptized the women.

2. Whoever is a Christian does not pronounce the death penalty, for God says, "Vengeance is mine, I will repay" [Rom 12:19].

3., 4. He says no. He would not do it.

5. He had not participated. He does not know whether it was justified or unjustified, but he would not participate.

6. He says yes. A person of faith still has needs.

7. He says yes, if he makes proper use of them.

8. He does not concern himself with them, unless it was necessary.

Herman Stalpf from Laches, Heinz Bill and Osanna, his wife.

1. They acknowledge their own [faith] as the truth and desire to remain therewith. They say the sermons do not move anyone to improve [i.e., repent, stop sinning] and do not want to attend.

2. Their conscience does not speak to them about this. They say, the Ten Commandments do not give instruction on this point.

3., 4. They do not know how to answer this. Stalpf, however, says that what he is required to give from his possessions, that he desires to do.

5. Stalpf had participated. They do not know [whether the peasants' rebellion was godly or ungodly].

6. He says yes, if he takes it out of need. If he is an upstanding Christian, he will not take more than what is needed. Stalpf says, however, that he cannot answer, since he has not heard anything about this.

Item: Claus Schreiber had baptized these three.

7. He may certainly have belongings, but he may not consider them to be only his own. Stalpf says that possessions do not damn him if he makes use of them appropriately.

8. He has nothing to say about this.

Gilg and Anna, his wife. He is their leader, having baptized eleven of them at Angerspach: Jacob, his wife, two of Jacob's sisters, the other names he cannot name. Melchior Rinck had baptized him.

1. He, along with his wife, says no.

2. He says the magistracy is a servant of God, and he allows for the fact that they administer their calling. He participated in the rebellion. Asked further about his conscience, he says he remains with his opinion.

3., 4. He will not go into battle, but he is willing to pay taxes for matters of war, for the sword has been given to the magistracy.

5. This he hands over to God as to whether it was just or unjust. He says if he is expelled from the land, he would leave.

6. He says a Christian may take things out of need, but that he would not do this in the manner of a thief.

7. [As for] having, or not having possessions, they hold nothing as their own as long as this is pleasing to God. But when God or a neighbor requests, then they give it over.

8. They consider such to be a pagan and tax collector [Matt 18:17].

Young Hen Lutz and Else, his wife; Cunz Hutter and Gele, his wife.

1. They say no.

2. Young Hen and his wife, and Cunz say they do not understand the question. But his wife Gele says one must pull out the weeds.

3., 4. They say no. Cunz Hutter says yes.

5. They say no.

6. They also say no.

7. They may certainly have [possessions], but they should not place too much importance on them.[149]

---

149 Mags wol haben, soll aber gelassen stehen.

d.[150]

11 August 1533. Chancellor Feige to the Landgrave. Report concerning the interrogation.

[. . .] I came this past Friday, along with Lord Melchior [Schwind] from Gudensperg, and dealt with the Anabaptists at Sorga diligently yet gently in accordance with your grace's ordinance and opinion, in the presence of my gracious lord from Hersfeld, to whom the men and women are accountable.

Although we earnestly sought to instruct them for the better, we instead found them to be obstinate and determined people who know nothing, or at least almost nothing, of Scripture. They can provide no evidence of our preachers' wrongdoing and must admit that their teachings are correct, but despise them nevertheless. They openly denounce them, stating that they do not practice what they preach. And when asked why they believe this, they can only point to the fact that fruits do not appear among the listeners. This is not the way those from Hersfeld perceive the situation, for one actually finds there for the most part a well-mannered people. I therefore conclude that it is purely hate and self-interest which motivates their movement. They see themselves alone as righteous and chosen, and they hold us all, as long as we do not convert to their [faith], for heathen. They say that we deny Christ with our works, and that our baptism is not from God.

There were twelve resident men with their wives at Sorga who were discovered publicly. In addition, there were many present with their wives, and single women, as well, all of whom had fled from more distant regions: from Franken, the Abbey of Fulda, the Riedesel territories,[151] and Ludwig von Boyneburg's jurisdiction.[152] That which cannot remain anywhere else, ends up here in Sorga. And as one would like to be rid of these strangers, I was hoping that they would also be open to counsel.

None of them are willing to come to our sermons or fellowship, as reported above, and they hold our preaching, especially as concerns

---

150 Franz et al. have *E.* rather than *D.* (which does not exist in Franz).

151 The noble Riedesel family had territorial holdings around Lauterbach.

152 The von Boyneburgs were a Hessian noble family with holdings around Felsberg and Lengsfeld.

baptism, not to be from God. The other sacrament was not dealt with very much.

The majority are of the opinion that a Christian may not wield or employ the authority of the magistracy. Some say, they do not understand this [question]. If a lord came to them who would claim to be Christian, he himself would certainly know what he should do, for he would kill no one. No more than two say that a thief should be hanged. But all state, with one exception, that a Christian is not to fight on the battlefield, whether offensively or defensively, and that God would shelter them in such instances. But one person said he would participate in battle—who, if I am not mistaken, will recant.

None of them publicly praised the peasants' rebellion, but a few said they do not know whether it had been right or wrong. A few said it was unjust, to the extent that it was about temporal matters, but that they did not know how they would judge it if it had been for the sake of the Gospel. Several said it was wrong, and that the people had been seduced by the preachers.

As far as possessions and their use is concerned, they did not answer inappropriately.

I, therefore, find that these people err, holding to many an opinion, with each judging according to his own discretion. But they all agreed that our preaching is not from God, and that theirs is true, and if they were to come into our congregation they would be sinning against God. They damn our position and religion absolutely. Item, that no one is willing to carry the burden of a military campaign, believing a Christian prince will not order anyone into military combat, including himself. Some, such as their leader, say they would be willing to give money for this reason if requested, leaving the responsibility, then, in the hands of the magistracy.

Their leader, named Gilg, is the mildest concerning the magistracy, but he strongly opposes our sermons and form of baptism. He is, however, purely a layperson who is unable to write or read.

My lord from Hersfeld vehemently protested, desiring harsher treatment, especially for the top leaders such as Hans Plat, Hans Koch, Hans Zisen and Heinz Hutter, but Lord Melchior and I have indeed abided by the instructions issued to us and ordered the Schultheiß (mayor) to banish the outsiders, and to treat, first of all, the four aforementioned persons, and then also the others, if need be, in accordance with your order, if they are unwilling to change [their opinion]. Indeed, we stated to all of them many times that, since they are not present in our congregation, and are also not willing to defend the fatherland, Your Grace cannot tolerate such renegade and disobedient subjects. Still, one is to exercise with them every bit of compassion that is possible, so that they will have no reason to complain concerning the current matters at hand and their fairness.

The preachers are still desiring that they be treated a bit more severely—but still short of shedding of blood—with imprisonment and other such tactics, with a view to changing their minds. The abovementioned peasants have for the most part recanted before and then once again fallen. We have allowed them three weeks to sell their possessions. We will see what they do. This is all I can report at this time, and I am of the firm opinion that it will be necessary to get rid of these people, for it is impossible to dissuade them once they latch onto their opinions, otherwise than with the sword.[153] Nor do they listen to any instruction, for whatever the wandering preachers teach them, that they believe.

Hersfeld, on the Monday after Laurentii, [11 August 15]33.[154]

5. Interrogation of Margret Garköchin (1537)

22 May 1537. Balthasar Raid, pastor at Hersfeld, Georg Ruppel, pastor at Vacha, Casper Mosebach, pastor at Heringen, and Ciriacus Ortlieb, pastor at Friedewald, to the Landgrave.

Garköchin does not recant.

[. . .] On the basis of the verbal instructions of Your Princely Grace's commissioner in Kassel, given to the magistrate, we came to Friedewald on the Friday after Exaudi [18 May], and spoke with, interrogated, and responded faithfully to Margret Garköchin [Koch], the Anabaptist, outlining our faith based on Scripture, and also her errors, including her sins and the danger to her soul and conscience if she persists therein. Thereupon she requested a day or two to consider [these

---

153 Franz et al. note that "otherwise than with the sword" is crossed out in the original handwritten text. It is left in the current translation, since it is unknown whether it was Feige himself who crossed out the words, or someone who did so at a later date.

154 Source: Franz et al., *Urkundliche Quellen zur hessischen*, 64–71.

matters]. Thus, we gave her until the Tuesday after Pentecost [22 May], and came back here today with friendly and trusting conversation, as before, desiring an answer from her. In the end she was resolute, concluding that she had listened to roughly three types of teachers and preachers, namely, the Papists, the Evangelical or Lutheran, and finally Melchior Rinck, but she had recognized the latter to be a righteous preacher and still considered his teachings to be true—which she had made known at Berka some years ago. Her desire is to still remain steadfast and persevere. Consequently, we parted from her, telling her that she is harming her soul and outlining her sins and iniquities, whereby we lamented her blindness and misery of the soul. [. . .] Friedwalt, on the Tuesday after Pentecost, 1537.[155]

155 Source: Franz et al., *Urkundliche Quellen zur hessischen*, 152–53.

Bibliography

Bauman, Clarence. *The Spiritual Legacy of Hans Denck*. Leiden: Brill, 1990.

Baylor, Michael, ed. *The Radical Reformation*. Cambridge: Cambridge University Press, 1991.

Bender, Harold, and C. Henry Smith, eds. *The Mennonite Encyclopedia* Volumes I-IV. Scottdale, PA: Mennonite Publishing House, 1955.

Bender, Harold S., and Paul Wappler. "Thuringia (Germany)." Global Anabaptist Mennonite Encyclopedia Online, 1959, last modified May 13, 2021. http://gameo.org/index.php?title=Thuringia_(Germany).

Beulshausen, Heinrich. *Die Geschichte der osthessischen Täufergemeinden*. Beiträge zur deutschen Philologie 53 (GieBen: Wilhelm Schmitz Verlag, 1981).

Breul, Wolfgang. "Celibacy—Marriage—Unmarriage: the Controversy over Celibacy and Clerical Marriage in the Early Reformation." In *Mixed Matches: Transgressive Unions in Germany from the Reformation to the Enlightenment*, eds. David Luebke and Mary Lindemann. New York: Berghahn Books, 2014.

———. "Von Humanismus zum Täufertum: Das Studium des hessischen Täuferführers Melchior Rinck an der Leipziger Artistenfakultät." *Archiv für Reformationsgeschichte* 93 (2002): 26–42.

Bucer, Martin. *Concerning the True Care of Souls* (trans. Peter Beale). Edinburgh: Banner of Truth Trust, 2009.

Burnett, Amy Nelson. "Martin Bucer and the Anabaptist Context of Evangelical Confirmation." *Mennonite Quarterly Review* 68 (1994): 95–122.

The Chronicle of the Hutterian Brethren. Rifton, NY: Plough Publishing House, 1987.

Coutts, Alfred. *Hans Denck*. Edinburgh: Macniven and Wallace, 1927.

Dirrim, Allen. "The Hessian Anabaptists: Background and Development to 1540." *Mennonite Quarterly Review* 38 (1964): 61–62.

Dyck, Cornelius. *An Introduction to Mennonite History*. Scottdale, PA: Herald Press, 1967.

Dyck, Cornelius, William Keeney, and Alvin Beachy. *The Writings of Dirk Philips*. Scottdale, PA: Herald Press, 1992.

Estep, William. *The Anabaptist Story*. Grand Rapids, MI: Eerdmans, 1996.

Franz, Günther, Eckhart Franz et al., eds. *Urkundliche Quellen zur hessischen Reformationsgeschichte: Volume IV: Wiedertäuferakten, 1527–1626*. Marburg: Elwert, 1951.

Friedmann, Robert. "The Schleitheim Confession (1527) and Other Doctrinal Writings of the Swiss Brethren in a Hitherto Unknown Edition." *Mennonite Quarterly Review* 16 (1942): 82–98.

Friesen, Frank, trans., and Walter Klaassen, ed. *Sixteenth Century Anabaptism: Defences, Confessions, Refutations*. Waterloo, ON: Institute of Anabaptist and Mennonite Studies, 1981.

Furcha, Edward. *Selected Writings of Hans Denck*. Pittsburgh, PA: Pickwick, 1976.

Geldbach, Erich. "Die Lehre des hessischen Täuferführers Melchior Rinck." Trans. Leonard Gross. *Jahrbuch der hessischen kirchengeschichtlichen Vereinigung* 21 (1970): 119–35.

———. "Towards a More Ample Biography of the Hessian Anabaptist Leader Melchior Rinck." Translated by Elizabeth Bender. *Mennonite Quarterly Review* 48 (1974): 371–84.

Glebe, Ellen Yutzy. "Anabaptists in Their Hearts? Religious Dissidence and the Reformation in the Landgraviate of Hesse." ProQuest: UMI Dissertation Publishing, 2011.

———. "Landgrave Philipp's Dilemma: The Roots of Tolerance and the Desire for Protestant Unity." In *Politics and Reformations: Histories and Reformations*, eds. Christopher Ocker, Michael Printy, Peter Starenko, and Peter Wallace, 293–312. Boston: Brill, 2012.

Goertz, Hans-Jürgen. *The Anabaptists*. London: Routledge, 1996.

Greengrass, Mark. *Christendom Destroyed: Europe 1517–1648*. London: Penguin, 2015.

Gritsch, Eric. *Thomas Müntzer: A Tragedy of Errors*. Minneapolis: Augsburg Fortress, 1989.

Gross, Leonard. *The Golden Years of the Hutterites*. Scottdale, PA: Herald Press, 1980.

Hammann, Gustav. "Lindenborn: A Typical Incident in Early Anabaptist History in Upper Hesse." *Mennonite Quarterly Review* 51 (1977): 67–69.

Hancock, Alton. "Philipp of Hesse's View of the Relationship of Prince and Church." *Church History* 35, no. 2 (June 1966): 157–69.

Hege, Christian. "The Early Anabaptists in Hesse." *Mennonite Quarterly Review* 5 (1931): 157–78.

———. "Hesse (Germany)." Global Anabaptist Mennonite Encyclopedia Online, 1956. http://gameo.org/index.php?title=Hesse_(Germany).

Hill, Kat. *Baptism, Brotherhood, and Belief in Reformation Germany: Anabaptism and Lutheranism, 1525–1585*. Oxford: Oxford University Press, 2013.

Hochhuth, Karl. *Mittheilungen aus der protestantischen Secten-Geschichte in der hessischen Kirche: 1. Theil: Im Zeitalter der Reformation.* Leipzig: J. A. Barth, 1858–64.

Klaassen, Walter. *Anabaptism in Outline*. Scottdale, PA: Herald Press, 1981.

Klaassen, Walter, and William Klassen, *Marpeck: A Life of Dissent and Conformity*. Scottdale, PA: Herald Press, 2008.

Littell, Franklin. *The Anabaptist View of the Church*. Boston: Starr King Press, 1958.

———, ed. and trans. "What Butzer Debated with the Anabaptists at Marburg: A Document of 1538." *Mennonite Quarterly Review* 36 (1962): 256–76.

Matheson, Peter. *The Collected Works of Thomas Müntzer*. London: T & T Clark, 1980.

Melloni, Alberto, ed. *Martin Luther: A Christian between Reforms and Modernity (1517–2017)*. Berlin: de Gruyter, 2017.

Moore, John. *Anabaptist Portraits*. Scottdale, PA: Herald Press, 1984.

Neff, Christian, and Richard D. Thiessen. "Philipp I, Landgrave of Hesse (1504–1567)." Global Anabaptist Mennonite Encyclopedia Online, April 2007. https://gameo.org/index.php?title=Philipp_I,_Landgrave_of_Hesse_(1504-1567).

Neumann, Gerhard. "Rinck, Melchior. 'A Newly Discovered Manuscript of Melchior Rinck.'" *Mennonite Quarterly Review* 35 (1961): 197–217.

Ocker, Christopher. "Between the Old Faith and the New: Spiritual Loss in Reformation Germany." In *Enduring Loss in Early Modern Germany*, ed. Lynne Tatlock. Leiden: Brill, 2010.

Oyer, John. "Anabaptism in Central Germany 1: The Rise and Spread of the Movement." *Mennonite Quarterly Review* 34 (1964): 219–48.

———. "Anabaptism in Central Germany 2: Faith and Life." *Mennonite Quarterly Review* 35 (1965): 5–37.

———. "Bucer Opposes the Anabaptists." *Mennonite Quarterly Review* 68 (1994): 24–50.

———. "Luther and the Anabaptists." *Baptist Quarterly* 30, no. 4 (October 1983): 162–72.

———. *Lutheran Reformers against Anabaptists: Luther, Melanchthon and Menius and the Anabaptists of Central Germany*. The Hague: Martinus Nijhoff, 1964.

Packull, Werner. "Early Contacts between Anabaptists in Hesse and Moravia." In *The Contentious Triangle: Church, State, and University: A Festschrift in Honor of Professor George Huntston Williams*, eds. Rodney Petersen and Calvin Pater. Kirksville, MO: Truman State University Press, 1999.

———. "An Early Hutterite Account of Anabaptist Founders." *Mennonite Quarterly Review* 72 (1998): 53–68.

———. *Mysticism and the Early South German-Austrian Anabaptist Movement*. Scottdale, PA: Herald Press, 1977.

Payton, James. "Reformation Ecumenism Reframed." *Post-Christendom Studies* 2 (2017–18): 20–41.

Schad, Elias. "True Account of an Anabaptist Meeting at Night in a Forest and a Debate Held There with Them." *Mennonite Quarterly Review* 58 (1984): 292–94.

Schowalter, Paul. "Menius, Justus (1499–1558)." Global Anabaptist Mennonite Encyclopedia Online, 1957. http://gameo.org/index.php?title=Menius,_Justus_(1499-1558).

Scott, Tom. *Thomas Müntzer*. New York: St. Martin's Press, 1989.

———. *Thomas Müntzer: Theology and Revolution in the German Reformation*. London: Palgrave MacMillan, 2014.

Scott, Tom, and Bob Scribner, eds. *The German Peasants' War*. Atlantic Highlands, NJ: Humanities Press, 1991.

Shenk, Wilbert. *Anabaptism and Mission*. Scottdale, PA: Herald Press, 1984.

Simons, Menno. *Complete Works, 1496–1561*. Scottdale, PA: Herald Press, 1956.

Snyder, C. Arnold. *Anabaptist History and Theology*. Kitchener, ON: Pandora Press, 1995.

Stalnaker, John. "Anabaptism, Martin Bucer, and the Shaping of the Hessian Protestant Church." *The Journal of Modern History* 48, no. 4 (1976): 601–43.

Stayer, James. *Anabaptists and the Sword*. Lawrence, KS: Coronado Press, 1973.

———. *The German Peasants' War and Anabaptist Community of Goods*. Montreal: McGill-Queen's University Press, 1991.

Stayer, James, and Werner Packull, eds. *The Anabaptists and Thomas Müntzer*. Dubuque, IA: Kendall/Hunt, 1980.

Wappler, Paul. *Die Stellung Kursachsens und des Landgrafen Philip von Hessen zur Täuferbewegung*. Münster: Druck und Verlag der Aschendorffsehen Buchhandlung, 1910.

———. *Die Täuferbewegung in Thüringen von 1526 bis 1584*. Jena: Gustav Fisher, 1913.

Wenger, John. "Rinck, Melchior. 'Letter and a Note: Allow the Children to Come to Me, etc.'" *Mennonite Quarterly Review* 21 (1947): 282–84.

Whitford, David. *A Reformation Life: The European Reformation through the Eyes of Philipp of Hesse*. Westport, CT: Praeger, 2015.

Williams, George. *The Radical Reformation*. Kirksville, MO: Sixteenth Century Journal Publications, 1992.

———. "Sanctification in the Testimony of Several So-Called *Schwärmer*." *Mennonite Quarterly Review* 42 (1968): 5–25.

Williams, George, and Angel Mergal. *Spiritual and Anabaptist Writers*. Philadelphia: Westminster Press, 1957.

Wright, David. *Martin Bucer*. Appleford, UK: Sutton Courtnay Press, 1972.

———. *Martin Bucer: Reforming Church and Society*. Cambridge: Cambridge University Press, 2002.

Yoder, John Howard. *The Legacy of Michael Sattler*. Scottdale, PA: Herald Press, 1973.

Notes

Introduction

1 James Stayer, *The German Peasants' War and Anabaptist Community of Goods* (Montreal: McGill-Queen's University Press, 1991), 78.

2 Walter Klaassen, *Anabaptism in Outline* (Scottdale, PA: Herald Press, 1981), 87. Less well known is the rest of this statement: "no one can follow him unless he first know him."

3 William Estep, *The Anabaptist Story* (Grand Rapids, MI: Eerdmans, 1995).

4 Hans-Jürgen Goertz, *The Anabaptists* (London: Routledge, 1996).

5 Cornelius Dyck, *An Introduction to Mennonite History* (Scottdale, PA: Herald Press, 1967).

6 Werner Packull, *Mysticism and the Early South German-Austrian Anabaptist Movement 1525–1531* (Scottdale, PA: Herald Press, 1977).

7 Werner Packull, "An Early Hutterite Account of Anabaptist Founders," *Mennonite Quarterly Review* 72 (1998): 53–68.

8 George Williams and Angel Mergal, *Spiritual and Anabaptist Writers* (Philadelphia: Westminster Press, 1957), 208. Obbe Philips, a contemporary of Menno Simons, had been an Anabaptist but later renounced this allegiance. A similar list of Anabaptist "false prophets" appears in an early eighteenth-century catalog of heretics by an unknown author, *The Devil of Delphos*, in which Rinck features alongside Hubmaier, Hut, Müntzer, Hofmann, and the Münsterite leaders.

9 In a letter to Philip on 17 March 1540. See Primary Sources B.10.

10 In a letter to Elector John of Saxony on 25 November 1531. See Primary Sources B.3. The term *Amtmann* refers to a senior clerk in the middle grade of the German civil service.

11 Paul Wappler, *Die Täuferbewegung in Thüringen von 1526 bis 1584* (Jena: Gustav Fisher, 1913), 326–333.

12 C. Arnold Snyder, *Anabaptist History and Theology* (Kitchener, ON: Pandora Press, 1995), 125.

13 See John Oyer, *Lutheran Reformers against Anabaptists: Luther, Melanchthon and Menius and the Anabaptists of Central Germany* (The Hague: Martinus Nijhoff, 1964), 64.

14 Snyder, *Anabaptist History and Theology*, 124.

15 See, for example, Walter Klaassen and William Klassen, *Marpeck: A Life of Dissent and Conformity* (Scottdale, PA: Herald Press, 2008).

16 Paul Wappler, *Die Stellung Kursachsens und des Landgrafen Philip von Hessen zur Täuferbewegung* (Münster: Druck und Verlag der Aschendorffsehen Buchhandlung, 1910); *Täuferbewegung in Thüringen*. The first 227 pages of the latter work tell the story; the remaining 300 pages contain a reproduction of archival materials. Wappler's work is generally regarded as fair, accurate, and thorough, and has not been superseded, requiring only some minor revisions.

17 Günther Franz et al., eds., *Urkundliche Quellen zur hessischen Reformationsgeschichte: Volume IV: Wiedertäuferakten, 1527–1626* (Marburg: Elwert, 1951). There are also several articles in German providing summaries of Rinck's life, teaching, and influence, including Erich Geldbach, "Die Lehre des hessischen Täuferführers Melchior Rinck," trans. Leonard Gross, *Jahrbuch der hessischen kirchengeschichtlichen Vereinigung* 21 (1970): 119–35; Erich Geldbach, "Towards a More Ample Biography of the Hessian Anabaptist Leader Melchior Rinck," trans. Elizabeth Bender, *Mennonite Quarterly Review* 48 (1974): 371–84; Werner Packull, "Rinck, Melchior," *Theologische Realenzyklopädie* vol. 29 (1998), 215–18; and Wolfgang Breul, "Vom Humanismus zum Täufertum: Das Studium des hessischen Täuferführers Melchior Rinck an der Leipziger Artistenfakultät," *Archiv für Reformationsgeschichte 93* (2002): 26–42.

18 Oyer, *Lutheran Reformers against Anabaptists*, 47. Oyer's earlier articles are "Anabaptism in Central Germany 1: The Rise and Spread of the Movement," *Mennonite Quarterly Review* 34 (1964): 219–48; and "Anabaptism in Central Germany 2: Faith and Life," *Mennonite Quarterly Review* 35 (1965): 5–37.

19 Ellen Yutzy Glebe, "Anabaptists in Their Hearts? Religious Dissidence and the Reformation in the Landgraviate of Hesse" (ProQuest: UMI Dissertation Publishing, 2011). See also Ellen Yutzy Glebe, "Landgrave Philipp's Dilemma: The Roots of Tolerance and the Desire for Protestant Unity," in *Politics and Reformations: Histories and Reformations*, ed. Christopher Ocker et al. (Boston: Brill, 2012).

20 Kat Hill, *Baptism, Brotherhood, and Belief in Reformation Germany: Anabaptism and Lutheranism, 1525–1585* (Oxford: Oxford University Press, 2013).

21 David Whitford, *A Reformation Life: The European Reformation through the Eyes of Philipp of Hesse* (Westport, CT: Praeger, 2015). The landgrave is named Philip in some sources, Philipp in others.

22 John Wenger, "Rinck, Melchior. 'Letter and a Note: Allow the Children to Come to Me, etc.,"' *Mennonite Quarterly Review* 21 (1947): 282–84.

23 Frank Friesen, trans., and Walter Klaassen, ed., *Sixteenth Century Anabaptism: Defences, Confessions, Refutations* (Waterloo, ON: Institute of Anabaptist and Mennonite Studies, 1981), 55–58.

24 *The Chronicle of the Hutterian Brethren*, vol. 1 (Rifton, NY: Plough Publishing House, 1987), 127–28.

Chapter 1

1 Mark Greengrass, *Christendom Destroyed: Europe 1517–1648* (London: Penguin, 2015), 314.

2 Glebe, "Anabaptists in Their Hearts?," 234, 237.

3 A landgrave was equal in authority to a duke, owing allegiance directly to the emperor.

4 Glebe, "Anabaptists in Their Hearts?," 60. For a detailed study of Philip's career as a Protestant prince and the principles that undergirded his unusually tolerant stance, see Alton Hancock, "Philipp of Hesse's View of the Relationship of Prince and Church," *Church History* 35, no. 2 (June 1966): 157–69.

5 Spiritualism in the Reformation era was a loose movement of those who prioritized interior spiritual experience and were less interested in doctrinal and ecclesial details. Leading figures were Caspar Schwenckfeld and Sebastian Franck. Anabaptists and Spiritualists engaged in dialogue in various places throughout this period.

6 Glebe, "Anabaptists in Their Hearts?," 238.

7 In a letter to his sister, Duchess Elizabeth of Saxony, in February 1530. Quoted in Christian Hege, "The Early Anabaptists in Hesse," *Mennonite Quarterly Review* 5 (1931): 157. Source not provided.

8 See Primary Sources B.6.

9 Glebe, "Anabaptists in Their Hearts?," 243–46.

10 Glebe, "Landgrave Philipp's Dilemma," passim.

11 See further Glebe, "Anabaptists in Their Hearts?," 67–72.

12 "Report of Eberhard von der Tann concerning the misgivings of the councils of the elector and landgrave regarding the meeting at Nordhausen," in Wappler, *Stellung Kursachsens*, 148. "Nemlich es seind zubedenkn, das dieselben schedlich Sect einbrechen, wo nit mit Enst darzu gethan vnd dyjenigen, so auf irem jrthum verharren, am leib vnd zum todt gestrafft wurden, wie dan Vnser G. Herrn vermog kay. M. der Neulichistn Neuen ausgangen constitucion vnd ordnung, auch sonst der gemein Recht verordnung nach zutun gneigt weren. Dorgegen haben Vnsers G. Herrn des landgrauen Ret furgewandt, wo sich dieselbn widerteuffer von jrem jrthum nit wollen lassen abweisen, das man ynen das Feur ausleschen sol. Das wurden sie nit leiden konnen vnd sich selber hinwek wenden, oder vfs Eusserste sol man ynen jre heuser zunageln, aber dy person an jren leiben anzutasten, des hab jr herr bedenken, etc."

13 Details in Christian Neff and Richard D. Thiessen, "Philipp I, Landgrave of Hesse (1504–1567)," Global Anabaptist Mennonite Encyclopedia Online, April 2007, https://gameo.org/index.php?title=Philipp_I,_Landgrave_of_Hesse_(1504-1567).

14 Glebe, "Anabaptists in Their Hearts?," 295.

15 Franz et al., *Urkundliche Quellen zur hessischen*, 47.

16 Quoted in Neff and Thiessen, "Philipp I, Landgrave." Source not provided.

17 Hancock, "Philipp of Hesse's View," 157.

18 Quoted in Neff and Thiessen, "Philipp I, Landgrave." Source not provided.

19 Hege, "Early Anabaptists in Hesse," 158.

20 George Williams, *The Radical Reformation* (Kirksville, MO: Sixteenth Century Journal Publications, 1992), 667.

21 The text of this sermon can be found in Williams and Mergal, *Spiritual and Anabaptist Writers*, 49–70; and in Peter Matheson, *The Collected Works of Thomas Müntzer* (London: T & T Clark, 1980).

22 His tract on this subject is as intemperate as the title indicates: "Against the

Murderous, Thieving Hordes of Peasants" (May 1525). This tract is included in E. G. Rupp and Benjamin Drewery, *Martin Luther, Documents of Modern History* (London: Edward Arnold, 1970), 121–26.

23 See further on the peasants' movement, Tom Scott and Bob Scribner, eds., *The German Peasants' War* (Atlantic Highlands, NJ: Humanities Press, 1991). On Müntzer's role, see Eric Gritsch, *Thomas Müntzer: A Tragedy of Errors* (Minneapolis: Augsburg Fortress, 1989) and Tom Scott, *Thomas Müntzer: Theology and Revolution in the German Reformation* (London: Palgrave MacMillan, 2014).

24 The Swiss Anabaptists had attempted to open a dialogue with Müntzer, recognizing him as a fellow dissenter on various issues but disagreeing with him on the use of violence. Two letters from Conrad Grebel and his companions in September 1524 highlight these areas of agreement and disagreement, but there was no response from Müntzer, who may not have received the letters. The text of the letters is in Williams and Mergal, *Spiritual and Anabaptist Writers*, 73–85. See further James Stayer and Werner Packull, eds., *The Anabaptists and Thomas Müntzer* (Dubuque, IA: Kendall/Hunt, 1980).

25 Glebe, "Anabaptists in Their Hearts?," 249.

26 Glebe, "Anabaptists in Their Hearts?," 264.

27 Hill, *Baptism, Brotherhood, and Belief*, 7, 15.

28 *Der Widdertauffer lere und geheimnis, aus heiliger schrifft widderlegt* (1530). This had a foreword written by Luther and was dedicated to Philip of Hesse.

29 Quoted in Paul Schowalter, "Menius, Justus (1499–1558)," Global Anabaptist Mennonite Encyclopedia Online, 1957, http://gameo.org/index.php?title=Menius,_Justus_(1499-1558). Source not provided.

30 Quoted in Schowalter, "Menius, Justus (1499–1558)." Source not provided. The sixth statement probably indicates Menius had some contact with Hans Denck.

31 Oyer, *Lutheran Reformers against Anabaptists*, 68–71.

32 See Primary Sources B.6.

33 See Primary Sources C.3.

34 See Primary Sources C.4.

35 See Primary Sources C.4.d.

36 Oyer, *Lutheran Reformers against Anabaptists*, 162.

37 Franz et al., *Urkundliche Quellen zur hessischen*, 90. "daß sich inzwischen die widerteufer an etlichen enden im Lundorfer grunde bei Saufenberg und itzo neulich bei Gemunden an der Wora im walde in einer wusten kirchen us vilerlei stetten, flecken und dorfern versamlet, daselbst ire gesprech und rat gehalten, auch etliche getauft." Translated in Gustav Hammann, "Lindenborn: A Typical Incident in Early Anabaptist History in Upper Hesse," *Mennonite Quarterly Review* 51 (1977), 67.

38 Karl Hochhuth, *Mittheilungen aus der protestantischen Secten-Geschichte in der hessischen Kirche: 1. Theil: Im Zeitalter der Reformation* (Leipzig: J. A. Barth, 1858–64), 594. [Zeitschrift für die historische Theologie, 1858, 538–644] "Uebrigens solle man Gott bitten, sich selbst bessern und die Täufer gütlich und freundlich ermahnen. Wenn auch Alles was Dieselben im Schilde tragen böse sey, müsse man doch Vorsicht gebrauchen und, ehe man zu dem Schwerte greife, alle Mittel vorher versucht haben."

39 Hochhuth, *Mittheilungen aus der protestantischen*, 594. "In der Wiedertäuffer-Secte zeige sich eine Heimsuchung Gottes; deßhalb müsse ein Landesgebet angeordnet, fleissig gegen die Sectirer gepredigt, das Volk zur Besserung ermahnt,

auch darüber gehalten werden daß die Laster nicht ungestraft bleiben, damit die Wiedertäufer von uns keine Ursache nehmen eine neue Kirche aufzurichten. Der Obrigkeit liege die Pflicht ob, alle Uebel zu strafen; und zwar, wie einer gesündigt, danach solle er gestraft werden."

40 Hege, "Early Anabaptists in Hesse," 162. Hege (162–78) gives a detailed account of this Order and its aftermath.

41 A translation of this document can be found in Friesen and Klaassen, *Sixteenth Century Anabaptism*, 74–86.

42 John Stalnaker, "Anabaptism, Martin Bucer, and the Shaping of the Hessian Protestant Church," *The Journal of Modern History* 48, no. 4 (1976), 609.

43 Franz et al., *Urkundliche Quellen zur hessischen*, 62.

44 Franz et al., *Urkundliche Quellen zur hessischen*, 76. "gotfurchtigen . . . mann" "er solt euch den rechten weg und von euerm widerglauben weisen, damit ir zu rechtem erkentnis gotlicher warheit kommen mochtet, wilchs wir herzlich gern sehen und vil lieber vernemen wolten dann mit der scherpfe, wie wir dan des guten fug haben und auch gescheen möchte, gegen euch zu handlen, do ir solcher euerer verfurischen, widerchristlichen secten nit absteen woltet."

45 Bucer had been engaged there in dialogue with the Anabaptist leader Pilgram Marpeck, and had recently (1536) published a lengthy treatise, *Enarrationes Perpetuae, in Sacra Quatuor Evangelia*, in which he noted and criticized the Anabaptists' perspectives on various issues, including baptism and the magistracy.

46 Franklin Littell, trans. and ed., "What Butzer Debated with the Anabaptists at Marburg: A Document of 1538," *Mennonite Quarterly Review* 36 (1962): 256–76.

47 In his German Mass (January 1526). English text available via the Hanover Historical Texts Project at https://history.hanover.edu/texts/luthserv.html.

48 Littell, "Anabaptists at Marburg," 265.

49 Littell, "Anabaptists at Marburg," 266.

50 Littell, "Anabaptists at Marburg," 276.

51 Glebe, "Anabaptists in Their Hearts?," 316. Franz et al, *Urkundliche Quellen zur hessischen*, 241: "Es sind der teufer meer in E.F.G. landen, dann ich imer gemeinet hette, und under denselbigen fil gutherziger leut."

52 Glebe, "Anabaptists in Their Hearts?," 104. Franz et al, *Urkundliche Quellen zur hessischen*, 210: "das dises irtumbs des widertaufs die groste ursach ist die ungeschicklickeit der predicanten und sie also ungelert, das sie den widerteufern nit widersprechen khunden, und hochlich von noten ist durch die oberkheit und superintendenten ein einsehens zu haben, sunst wurdt unsers erachtens wenig hoffnung sein, on grosse plutvergiessen disem irtumb zu steuern."

53 A translation of this confession, written by Tasch and signed by several others, can be found in Friesen and Klaassen, *Sixteenth Century Anabaptism*, 103–12.

54 Williams, *Radical Reformation*, 675.

55 Stalnaker, "Anabaptism, Martin Bucer," 601, 607.

56 Stalnaker, "Anabaptism, Martin Bucer," 625.

57 Quoted in Christian Hege, "Hesse (Germany)," Global Anabaptist Mennonite Encyclopedia Online, 1956, http://gameo.org/index.php?title=Hesse_(Germany).

58 *Chronicle of Hutterian Brethren*, 127. See also Oyer, *Lutheran Reformers against Anabaptists*, 104; Friesen and Klaassen, *Sixteenth Century Anabaptism*, 98–102.

59 Oyer, *Lutheran Reformers against Anabaptists*, 104. Oyer describes Anabaptism in this region, by comparison with Anabaptism elsewhere, as an "undisciplined stepchild" (107).

Chapter 2

1 The suggestion of Glebe, "Anabaptists in Their Hearts?," 256.

2 Variations of his name appear in the sources and are reproduced here as written: Rink, Rinck, Ring, Ringk, and Reick. It is not known when or why he changed his name.

3 For example, Wappler, *Stellung Kursachsens*, 134, 145–47.

4 Gustav Bossert, ed., *Quellen zur Geschichte der Wiedertäufer*, vol. 1 *Herzogtum Württemberg* (Leipzig: 1930), 56, quoted in Breul, "Von Humanismus zum Täufertum," 29.

5 *Staatsarchiv Marburg, Politisches Archiv des Landgrafen Phillip des Großmütigen*, no. 1961, Best. 3, no. 1961, fol.1[v], "Anzeigung wo durch sich die auffrur der pfaffen halber hier zu hirsfelt erhaben hadt geschehen vff donnerstag nach lucie v[ir]ginis Anno etc. xxiij," quoted in Wolfgang Breul, "Celibacy—Marriage—Unmarriage: the Controversy over Celibacy and Clerical Marriage in the Early Reformation," in *Mixed Matches: Transgressive Unions in Germany from the Reformation to the Enlightenment*, ed. David Luebke and Mary Lindemann (New York: Berghahn Books, 2014), 38–39.

6 Breul, "Celibacy—Marriage—Unmarriage," 40.

7 It has been suggested (in an article in the 1911 edition of the *Encyclopedia Britannica* and repeated in other places) that in 1524 Rinck accompanied Melchior Hofmann and Bernt Knipperdollinck (who was later involved in the uprising in Münster) on a trip to Stockholm, ostensibly on business but also with a reform agenda. But evidence to confirm this trip is lacking.

8 On Strauss, see further Joachim Bauer and Michael Haspel, eds., *Jakob Strauss Und Der Reformatorische Wucherstreit* (Leipzig: Evangelische Verlagsanstalt, 2017).

9 Geldbach, "More Ample Biography," 373.

10 Wappler, *Täuferbewegung in Thüringen*, 51. Translation by Leonard Gross. "Thomas Münzer aber, der were ein rechter held mit predigen, durch welches wort die kraft Gottes gewaltig wirkete; der sollt in einem jare mehr ausrichten den tausent Luther ihr ganzes leben lang."

11 Snyder, *Anabaptist History and Theology*, 73.

12 Tom Scott, *Thomas Müntzer* (New York: St. Martin's Press, 1989), 149.

13 See Primary Sources C.2.d.

14 Together with Conrad Grebel, Hans Hut and possibly Balthasar Hubmaier, according to Thomas Nipperdey, "Theology and Revolution in Thomas Müntzer," in Stayer and Packull, eds., *Anabaptists and Thomas Müntzer*, 105.

15 Geldbach, "Lehre des hessischen Täuferführers," 124.

16 See Stayer, *German Peasants' War*, 80–82.

17 Packull, *Mysticism*, 46

18 Packull, *Mysticism*, 195.

19 See Primary Sources A.1.

20 Clarence Bauman, *The Spiritual Legacy of Hans Denck* (Leiden: Brill, 1991), 15.

21 According to the chronicler of Worms, Friedrich Zorn: see Packull, *Mysticism*, 57.

22 Stayer, *German Peasants' War*, 78.

23 A detailed comparison between the structure and content of Denck's tract and Rinck's articles is provided by Geldbach, "More Ample Biography," 378; "Lehre des hessischen Täuferführers," 120.

24 Oyer, *Lutheran Reformers against Anabaptists*, 111–12.

25 See Primary Sources A.2.

26 Geldbach, "More Ample Biography," 377.

27 Oyer, *Lutheran Reformers against Anabaptists*, 128.

28 See Primary Sources C.1.

29 Oyer, *Lutheran Reformers against Anabaptists*, 56.

30 See Primary Sources C.1.f.

31 See Primary Sources B.1.

32 See Primary Sources A.5.

33 See Primary Sources B.2.

34 See Primary Sources A.4.

35 Unhappy marriages were not uncommon among early Anabaptists, especially if one spouse did not share the convictions of the other, or was unwilling to risk persecution, or if the husband traveled frequently.

36 See Primary Sources B.3.

37 See Primary Sources A.6.

38 Hans Arbeiter, for instance, a Hutterian missionary captured in 1568, "asserted that no earthly magistrate had the right to forbid God's missioners from setting foot on their land, for the earth was the Lord's (Ps. 24:1), and the Lord had called the church to mission." Quoted in Wilbert Shenk, *Anabaptism and Mission* (Scottdale, PA: Herald Press, 1984), 111. *The Chronicle of the Hutterian Brethren* repeats this claim: "You cannot deny us a place on the earth or in this country. The earth is the Lord's, and all that is in it belongs to our God in heaven. Besides, if we promised you to go and planned to do so, we might not be able to keep our word, for we are in God's hands and he does with us whatever his will is" (139).

39 See Primary Sources C.2.d.

40 See Magister Elias Schad, "True Account of an Anabaptist Meeting at Night in a Forest and a Debate Held There with Them," *Mennonite Quarterly Review* 58 (1984): 292–94.

41 See Primary Sources C.2.a.

42 See Primary Sources B.3.

43 See Primary Sources C.2.

44 See Primary Sources C.3.

45 See Primary Sources B.3.

46 See Primary Sources C.2.d.

47 Wappler, *Stellung Kursachsens*, 148.

48 See Primary Sources C.2.d.

49 See Primary Sources C.2.d.

50 See Primary Sources B.4.

51 Alberto Melloni, ed., *Martin Luther: A Christian between Reforms and Modernity (1517–2017)* (Berlin: de Gruyter, 2017), 469.

52 See Primary Sources B.6.

53 Oyer, *Lutheran Reformers against Anabaptists*, 59.

54 Franz et al., *Urkundliche Quellen zur hessischen*, 261–62.

55 Philip sent Tasch to Rinck at Birbach. This location cannot be identified with certainty. Geldbach ("More Ample Biography," 383) considers several possibilities and concludes that this is the most likely.

56 Geldbach, "More Ample Biography," 383.

57 Glebe, "Anabaptists in Their Hearts?," 50.

58 Packull, "Early Hutterite Account," 61–62.

59 Stayer, *German Peasants' War*, 80.

60 These articles were demands by the Swabian peasants' movement following a meeting in Memmingen in March 1525. They called for various economic, political and ecclesial reforms.

61 See Primary Sources C.4.c.

62 See Primary Sources C.3.

63 *Chronicle of Hutterian Brethren*, 126–28. See also Oyer, *Lutheran Reformers against Anabaptists*, 84.

64 See Primary Sources C.5.

65 Stayer (*German Peasants' War*, 118) gives examples of these positions from various testimonies during this process of interrogation. *Gelassenheit*, roughly translated as "yieldedness" and derived from the teaching of medieval mystics, appears frequently in Anabaptist writings.

66 See Primary Sources C.4.d.

67 See Primary Sources C.3.

68 Oyer, *Lutheran Reformers against Anabaptists*, 64.

69 See Primary Sources B.9.

70 Williams, *Radical Reformation*, 663.

71 Quoted in Gerhard Neumann, "Rinck, Melchior. 'A Newly Discovered Manuscript of Melchior Rinck,'" *Mennonite Quarterly Review* 35 (1961): 197. Source not provided.

72 Oyer, *Lutheran Reformers against Anabaptists*, 52.

73 Oyer, *Lutheran Reformers against Anabaptists*, 64.

Chapter 3

1 The text is reprinted in Neumann, "Rinck, Melchior," 197–211.

2 The text is reprinted in Neumann, 211–17.

3 The text of Rinck's letter to Eberhard von der Tann and his tract are preserved in the Saxon-Ernestinian Archive and reprinted in Wappler, *Stellung Kursachsens*, 167–70. There is a translation of the tract (but not the letter) in Friesen and Klaassen, *Sixteenth Century Anabaptism*, 55–58.

4 The letter and tract were both translated by John Wenger and published in the *Mennonite Quarterly Review* 21 (1947), 282–84. They are also included in John Howard Yoder, *The Legacy of Michael Sattler* (Scottdale, PA: Herald Press, 1973), 135–37.

5 Oyer, *Lutheran Reformers against Anabaptists*, 59. Yoder was less certain about Rinck's authorship but did point to some internal evidence.

6 The existence of this document is noted in Werner Packull, "Early Contacts between Anabaptists in Hesse and Moravia," in *The Contentious Triangle: Church, State, and University: A Festschrift in Honor of Professor George Huntston Williams*, ed. Rodney Petersen and Calvin Pater (Kirksville, MO: Truman State University Press, 1999), 184.

7 Unlike most of the other letters listed here, this letter appears in the Primary Sources under Interrogations. See Primary Sources C.2.a.

8 The latter two letters appear in the Primary Sources under Interrogations. See Primary Sources C.2.c and d.

9 Schowalter, "Menius, Justus, (1499–1558)."

10 Oyer, *Lutheran Reformers against Anabaptists*, 181.

11 Justus Menius, *Der Widdertauffer lere vnd geheimnis, aus heiliger Schrifft widderlegt* (Wittemberg, 1530). Available online.

12 Wappler, *Täuferbewegung in Thüringen*, 52. Translation by Leonard Gross. "Christus hette nicht gesagt, 'das himmelreich ist ihr,' nemlich der kinder, sondern es ist solcher, talium, nicht illorum, das ist: deren ists himelreich, die den kindern gleich sein."

13 Wappler, *Täuferbewegung in Thüringen*, 54. Translation by Leonard Gross. "Alle bucher des newen Testaments in allerlei sprachen Griechisch, Lateinisch, Deutsch etc. weren allzumal falsch und kein rechtes auf erden mehr."

14 Justus Menius, *Von dem Geist der Widerteuffer* (Wittemberg, 1544). Available online.

15 See Primary Sources C.1.a.

16 Glebe, "Anabaptists in Their Hearts?," 50.

17 Geldbach, "Lehre des hessischen Täuferführers," 119.

18 If Rinck's family name, as has been suggested in relation to his university matriculation record, was actually Schnabel.

19 Oyer, *Lutheran Reformers against Anabaptists*, 103.

20 See Primary Sources B.9.

21 Hammann, "Lindenborn," 69.

22 Hege, "Early Anabaptists in Hesse," 165.

23 Stayer, *Anabaptists and the Sword* (Lawrence, KS: Coronado Press, 1973), 193. This apparently irritated the Moravian missionaries working in Hesse in the 1530s.

24 John Oyer, "Luther and the Anabaptists," *Baptist Quarterly* 30, no. 4 (October 1983): 165.

Chapter 4

1 Goertz, *Anabaptists*, 21.

2 Examples are given in Grete Mecenseffy, "The Origin of Upper Austrian Anabaptism," in Stayer and Packull, eds., *Anabaptists and Thomas Müntzer*, 153.

3 For these statements from the Marburg debate, see Primary Sources C.1.c and d.

4 See Primary Sources A.1.

5 See Primary Sources A.6.

6 See Estep, *Anabaptist Story*, 116.

7 For these and other statements in this chapter from the Marburg debate, see Primary Sources C.1.

8 Williams, *Radical Reformation*, 168.

9 Oyer, *Lutheran Reformers against Anabaptists*, 75.

10 Oyer, *Lutheran Reformers against Anabaptists*, 107.

11 Oyer, *Lutheran Reformers against Anabaptists*, 182–83.

12 Oyer, *Lutheran Reformers against Anabaptists*, 210.

13 See Primary Sources C.2.b.

14 Friesen and Klaassen, *Sixteenth Century Anabaptism*, 82.

15 See Primary Sources A.4.

16 See Primary Sources A.1. See also George Williams, "Sanctification in the Testimony of Several So-Called *Schwärmer*," *Mennonite Quarterly Review* 42 (1968), 13.

17 Oyer, *Lutheran Reformers against Anabaptists*, 76–77.

18 Raidt appears to have changed his mind on this, at least with regard to Rinck's followers, writing to Landgrave Philip some years later: "as far as the conscience and the soul are concerned, they [the Anabaptists] are new monks and 'saints of good works,' who partly understand the law, but they have no awareness of Christ, for they want to fulfill the law and satisfy it with their own works and performance." Quoted in Glebe, "Anabaptists in Their Hearts?," 355. Franz et al., *Urkundliche Quellen zur hessischen*, 300: "soviel es die conscienz und ire sele betrifft, so sint es neue monche und werkheiligen, die das gesetz verstehen zum teil, aber vom erkentnis Christi wissen sie nichts, den sie wollen das gesetz stillen und im gnungtuen mit iren eigen werken und erfullung."

19 See Primary Sources A.2.

20 Glebe ("Anabaptists in Their Hearts?," 352–55) suggests Hessian Anabaptism represented "a carryover of medieval Catholic soteriology" and that it "rested on a theological base fundamentally different than that of Protestantism." Rinck's statements do not support this analysis.

21 Oyer, "Luther and the Anabaptists," 165.

22 Oyer, *Lutheran Reformers against Anabaptists*, 83.

23 Oyer, *Lutheran Reformers against Anabaptists*, 164.

24 Michael Baylor, ed., *The Radical Reformation* (Cambridge: Cambridge University Press, 1991), 153.

25 Menno Simons, *Complete Works, 1496–1561* (Scottdale, PA: Herald Press, 1956), 445.

26 Cornelius Dyck, William Keeney, and Alvin Beachy, *The Writings of Dirk Philips* (Scottdale, PA: Herald Press, 1992), 209.

27 See Primary Sources A.6.

28 See Primary Sources C.2.b.

29 See Primary Sources A.4.

30 Harold S. Bender and Paul Wappler, "Thuringia (Germany)," Global Anabaptist Mennonite Encyclopedia Online, 1959, last modified May 13, 2021, http://gameo.org/index.php?title=Thuringia_(Germany).

31 Geldbach, "Lehre des hessischen Täuferführers," 124.

32 Oyer, *Lutheran Reformers against Anabaptists*, 86–87.

33 Neumann, "Rinck, Melchior," 214.

34 See Primary Sources A.1; A.2.

35 See Primary Sources C.1.e.

36 See Primary Sources C.1.c.

37 Wappler, *Täuferbewegung in Thüringen*, 54.

38 See Primary Sources A.3.

39 Both Angersbach and Ot used this phrase in their testimonies.

40 Wappler, *Täuferbewegung in Thüringen*, 54. Ironically, Menius later accepted this interpretation, although not with the implications taught by Rinck.

41 See Primary Sources C.2.b.

42 See the third article in Primary Sources C.1.a.

43 Oyer, *Lutheran Reformers against Anabaptists*, 100.

44 Franz et al., *Urkundliche Quellen zur hessischen*, 23.

45 See Primary Sources A.2.

46 Oyer, *Lutheran Reformers against Anabaptists*, 187.

47 See Primary Sources A.1. below, 113ff.

48 See Primary Sources A.3.

49 See Primary Sources A.6.

50 See Primary Sources A.2.

51 Geldbach, "Lehre des hessischen Täuferführers," 127.

52 See Primary Sources C.1.

53 See Primary Sources C.2.b.

54 Hill, *Baptism, Brotherhood, and Belief*, 125.

55 Hill, *Baptism, Brotherhood, and Belief*, 120.

56 See Primary Sources C.3.

57 Quoted in Oyer, *Lutheran Reformers against Anabaptists*, 164.

58 Quoted in Thomas A. Brady Jr. and Ellen Yutzy Glebe, eds., "Protestants and Radicals—Martin Bucer's Debate with Hessian Anabaptists (1538)," German History in Documents and Images, http://germanhistorydocs.ghi-dc.org/pdf/eng/Doc.50-ENG-MartinBucer_en.pdf, 10.

59 Quoted in Hege, "Hesse (Germany)."

60 Hill, *Baptism, Brotherhood, and Belief*, 123.

61 See Primary Sources C.1.c.

62 See Primary Sources C.2.b.

63 See Primary Sources A.5.

64 Oyer, *Lutheran Reformers against Anabaptists*, 78.

65 Dyck, *Introduction to Mennonite History*, 102.

66 See Primary Sources C.2.b.

67 Glebe, "Anabaptists in Their Hearts?," 203.

68 Oyer, *Lutheran Reformers against Anabaptists*, 83.

69 See Primary Sources A.4.

70 See Primary Sources B.3.

71 See Primary Sources C.1.a, b, and c.

72 *Zue widerlegung des vermainten Euongelisten Glauben*, mentioned by the Hutterites.

73 See Primary Sources C.3.

74 See Primary Sources C.2.b.

75 Glebe, "Anabaptists in Their Hearts?," 6.

76 Littell, "Anabaptists at Marburg," 265.
77 See Primary Sources C.3.
78 Dyck, *Introduction to Mennonite History*, 114.
79 Oyer, *Lutheran Reformers against Anabaptists*, 64.
80 See Primary Sources A.4.
81 See Primary Sources A.2.
82 Oyer, "Luther and the Anabaptists," 165.
83 See Primary Sources A.4.
84 Oyer, *Lutheran Reformers against Anabaptists*, 90.
85 See Primary Sources C.2.b.
86 See Primary Sources C.1.a.
87 See Primary Sources C.2.b. Geldbach ("Lehre des hessischen Täuferführers," 121) regards Angersbach's testimony as "quirky" and unrepresentative, but there is ample evidence that Rinck did teach about *Gelassenheit.*
88 See Primary Sources C.3.
89 Glebe, "Anabaptists in Their Hearts?," 149–50.
90 See Primary Sources C.4.
91 Stayer, *German Peasants' War*, 118.
92 See Primary Sources C.4.c.
93 Stayer, *German Peasants' War*, 118.
94 Stayer, *German Peasants' War*, 11, 18.
95 See Primary Sources A.6.
96 See Primary Sources C.2.b.
97 See Primary Sources C.2.d.
98 Friesen and Klaassen, *Sixteenth Century Anabaptism*, 82.
99 Oyer, *Lutheran Reformers against Anabaptists*, 193.
100 See Primary Sources A.3.
101 See Primary Sources A.5.
102 See Primary Sources C.1.b.
103 See Primary Sources C.2.b.
104 See Primary Sources A.4. This assumes that the accepted view of the marriage is correct and that Anna did not eventually join her husband.
105 Stayer (*Anabaptists and the Sword*, 332) writes that Rinck "took an obscure apolitical position on the Sword," but his writings on the subject actually set out very clear views on the role of the civil authorities. Similarly, Goertz notes that his erstwhile revolutionary colleague Thomas Müntzer "did not develop a firm teaching about government but preserved for himself full freedom to approach the government with direct demands according to the situation." "The Mystic with the Hammer: Thomas Müntzer's Theological Basis for Revolution," in Stayer and Packull, eds., *Anabaptists and Thomas Müntzer*, 124. Rinck exhibited a similar freedom, although he had a more positive view of the role of civic authority than Müntzer.
106 See Primary Sources B.3.
107 See Primary Sources C.2.c.
108 See Primary Sources C.2.d.
109 Stalnaker, "Anabaptism, Martin Bucer," 614.

110 See Primary Sources C.2.d.
111 See Primary Sources C.2.d.
112 See Primary Sources A.2.
113 Quoted in Goertz, *Anabaptists*, 21.
114 Geldbach, "Lehre des hessischen Täuferführers," 125.
115 Stayer, *German Peasants' War*, 117–18.
116 See Primary Sources A.3.
117 Williams, *Radical Reformation*, 665.
118 Oyer, *Lutheran Reformers against Anabaptists*, 164.
119 Friesen and Klaassen, *Sixteenth Century Anabaptism*, 79, 110–11.
120 See Primary Sources C.2.b.
121 Stayer, *Anabaptists and the Sword*, 194–95.
122 Stalnaker, "Anabaptism, Martin Bucer," 613.
123 See Primary Sources C.2.b.
124 See Primary Sources C.3.
125 Glebe, "Anabaptists in Their Hearts?," 151.
126 Stayer, *Anabaptists and the Sword*, 195.
127 See Primary Sources C.4.
128 Glebe, "Anabaptists in Their Hearts?," 211.
129 Oyer, *Lutheran Reformers against Anabaptists*, 166.
130 Friesen and Klaassen, *Sixteenth Century Anabaptism*, 85–86.
131 Glebe, "Anabaptists in Their Hearts?," 211–12.
132 Friesen and Klaassen, *Sixteenth Century Anabaptism*, 86.
133 Goertz, "Mystic with the Hammer," in Stayer and Packull, eds., *Anabaptists and Thomas Müntzer*, 123.

Chapter 5

1 As in Article 6 of the Schleitheim Confession.
2 See Robert Friedmann, "The Schleitheim Confession (1527) and Other Doctrinal Writings of the Swiss Brethren in a Hitherto Unknown Edition," *Mennonite Quarterly Review* 16 (1942): 82–98.
3 Leonard Gross, *The Golden Years of the Hutterites* (Scottdale, PA: Herald Press, 1980), 165.
4 Friedmann, "Schleitheim Confession," 91–92.
5 Hill, *Baptism, Brotherhood, and Belief*, 7.
6 Glebe, "Anabaptists in Their Hearts?," 2.
7 Franz et al., *Urkundliche Quellen zur hessischen*, 148. "Einichen menschen aber umb des willen, das er unrecht glaubt, zu toidten, haben wir nie getan, wollen auch unsere sohne ermanet haben, sollichs nicht ze tun, dan wirs, dass es widder gott seie, halten, wie das im evangelio clar angezeigt."
8 Christopher Ocker, "Between the Old Faith and the New: Spiritual Loss in Reformation Germany," in *Enduring Loss in Early Modern Germany*, ed. Lynne Tatlock (Leiden: Brill, 2010), 250.
9 See Primary Sources C.3.
10 Glebe, "Anabaptists in Their Hearts?," 145–46.

11 See Primary Sources C.4.d.

12 See Primary Sources C.4.c.

13 Hill, *Baptism, Brotherhood, and Belief*, 15–16 (dissenting from the views of Goertz and Glebe).

14 James Payton, "Reformation Ecumenism Reframed," *Post-Christendom Studies* 2 (2017–18): 26.

15 David Wright, *Martin Bucer* (Appleford, UK: Sutton Courtnay Press, 1972), 32.

16 David Wright, ed., *Martin Bucer: Reforming Church and Community* (Cambridge: Cambridge University Press, 1994), 46, 68. Some of these references were deleted from his 1550–51 commentary on Ephesians, perhaps because he no longer regarded Anabaptism as such a threat.

17 Klaassen and Klassen, *Marpeck*, 178.

18 John Oyer, "Bucer Opposes the Anabaptists," *Mennonite Quarterly Review* 68 (1994): 36, 44.

19 Max Lenz, ed., *Briefwechsel Landgraf Philipps des Grossmutigen von Hessen mit Bucer*, 3 vols. (Leipzig, 1880–91), vol. 1, no. 20, quoted in Stalnaker, "Anabaptism, Martin Bucer," 628.

20 Oyer, *Lutheran Reformers against Anabaptists*, 61–62.

21 Oyer, *Lutheran Reformers against Anabaptists*, 105.

22 Hill, *Baptism, Brotherhood, and Belief*, 7.

23 See Martin Bucer, *Concerning the True Care of Souls*, trans. Peter Beale (Edinburgh: Banner of Truth Trust, 2009), ix.

24 Amy Nelson Burnett, "Martin Bucer and the Anabaptist Context of Evangelical Confirmation," *Mennonite Quarterly Review* 68 (1994), 96, 110.

25 Quoted in Hege, "Hesse (Germany)."

26 Quoted in Wright, *Martin Bucer: Reforming Church*, 124–25.

27 Burnett, "Martin Bucer," 107.

28 Glebe, "Anabaptists in Their Hearts?," 347.

29 Wappler, *Täuferbewegung in Thüringen*, 117.

30 Glebe, "Anabaptists in Their Hearts?," 341.

31 For example, Hochhuth, *Mittheilungen aus der protestantischen*; Wilhelm Diehl, *Martin Butzers Bedeuting fur das kirchliche Leben in Hessen* (Halle, 1904), 54, quoted in translation in Stalnaker, "Anabaptism, Martin Bucer," 602; Walter Sohm, Territorium und Reformation in der hessischen Geschichte 1526–1555 (Marburg: N. G. Elwert (G. Braun), 1915); and Franklin Littell, *The Anabaptist View of the Church* (Boston: Starr King Press, 1958), 36.

32 Quoted (in translation) in Hege, "Hesse (Germany)." The quotation is from Eduard Becker, "Zur Geschichte der Wiedertäufer in Oberhessen," in *Archiv für hessische Geschichte und Altertumskunde* (Neue Folge X: Darmstadt, 1914).

33 Stalnaker, "Anabaptism, Martin Bucer," 606–7.

34 Stalnaker, "Anabaptism, Martin Bucer," 642.

Index

Studies in Anabaptist and Mennonite History Series

The Studies in Anabaptist and Mennonite History Series is sponsored by the Mennonite Historical Society. Beginning with volume 8, titles were published by Herald Press unless otherwise noted.

1. Harold S. Bender. *Two Centuries of American Mennonite Literature, 1727–1928*. 1929.
2. John Horsch. *The Hutterian Brethren, 1528–1931: A Story of Martyrdom and Loyalty*. 1931. Reprint, Macmillan Hutterite Colony, Cayley, Alberta, 1985.
3. Harry F. Weber. *Centennial History of the Mennonites in Illinois, 1829–1929*. 1931.
4. Sanford Calvin Yoder. *For Conscience' Sake: A Study of Mennonite Migrations Resulting from the World War*. 1940.
5. John S. Umble. *Ohio Mennonite Sunday Schools*. 1941.
6. Harold S. Bender. *Conrad Grebel, c. 1498–1526, Founder of the Swiss Brethren*. 1950.
7. Robert Friedmann. *Mennonite Piety Through the Centuries: Its Genius and Its Literature*. 1949.
8. Delbert L. Gratz. *Bernese Anabaptists and Their American Descendants*. 1953.
9. A. L. E. Verheyden. *Anabaptism in Flanders, 1530–1650: A Century of Struggle*. 1961.

10. J. C. Wenger. *The Mennonites in Indiana and Michigan*. 1961.
11. Rollin Stely Armour. *Anabaptist Baptism: A Representative Study*. 1966.
12. John B. Toews. *Lost Fatherland: The Story of Mennonite Emigration from Soviet Russia, 1921–1927*. 1967.
13. Grant M. Stoltzfus. *Mennonites of the Ohio and Eastern Conference, from the Colonial Period in Pennsylvania to 1968*. 1969.
14. John A. Lapp. *The Mennonite Church in India, 1897–1962*. 1972.
15. Robert Friedmann. *The Theology of Anabaptism: An Interpretation*. 1973.
16. Kenneth R. Davis. *Anabaptism and Asceticism: A Study in Intellectual Origins*. 1974.
17. Paul Erb. *South Central Frontiers: A History of the South Central Mennonite Conference*. 1974.
18. Fred R. Belk. *The Great Trek of the Russian Mennonites to Central Asia, 1880–1884*. 1976.
19. Werner O. Packull. *Mysticism and the Early South German-Austrian Anabaptist Movement, 1525–1531*. 1976.
20. Richard K. MacMaster, with Samuel L. Horst and Robert F. Ulle. *Conscience in Crisis: Mennonites and Other Peace Churches in America, 1739–1789*. 1979.
21. Theron F. Schlabach. *Gospel versus Gospel: Mission and the Mennonite Church, 1863–1944*. 1980.
22. Calvin Wall Redekop. *Strangers Become Neighbors: Mennonite and Indigenous Relations in the Paraguayan Chaco*. 1980.
23. Leonard Gross. *The Golden Years of the Hutterites: The Witness and Thought of the Communal Moravian Anabaptists during the Walpot Era, 1565–1578*. 1980. Rev. ed., Pandora Press Canada, 1998.
24. Willard H. Smith. *Mennonites in Illinois*. 1983.
25. Murray L. Wagner. *Petr Chelcický: A Radical Separatist in Hussite Bohemia*. 1983.
26. John L. Ruth. *Maintaining the Right Fellowship: A Narrative Account of Life in the Oldest Mennonite Community in North America*. 1984.
27. C. Arnold Snyder. *The Life and Thought of Michael Sattler*. 1984.
28. Beulah Stauffer Hostetler. *American Mennonites and Protestant Movements: A Community Paradigm*. 1987.
29. Daniel Liechty. *Andreas Fischer and the Sabbatarian Anabaptists: An Early Reformation Episode in East Central Europe*. 1988.
30. Hope Kauffman Lind. *Apart and Together: Mennonites in Oregon and Neighboring States, 1876–1976*. 1990.
31. Paton Yoder. *Tradition and Transition: Amish Mennonites and Old Order Amish, 1800–1900*. 1991.
32. James R. Coggins. *John Smyth's Congregation: English Separatism, Mennonite Influence, and the Elect Nation*. 1991.

33. John D. Rempel. *The Lord's Supper in Anabaptism: A Study in the Theology of Balthasar Hubmaier, Pilgram Marpeck, and Dirk Philips*. 1993.
34. Gerlof D. Homan. *American Mennonites and the Great War, 1914–1918*. 1994.
35. J. Denny Weaver. *Keeping Salvation Ethical: Mennonite and Amish Atonement Theology in the Late Nineteenth Century*. 1997.
36. Wes Harrison. *Andreas Ehrenpreis and Hutterite Faith and Practice*. 1997. Copublished with Pandora Press Canada.
37. John D. Thiesen. *Mennonite and Nazi? Attitudes among Mennonite Colonists in Latin America, 1933–1945*. 1999. Copublished with Pandora Press Canada.
38. Perry Bush. *Dancing with the Kobzar: Bluffton College and Mennonite Higher Education, 1899–1999*. 2000. Copublished with Pandora Press U.S. and Faith & Life Press.
39. John L. Ruth. *The Earth Is the Lord's: A Narrative History of the Lancaster Mennonite Conference*. 2001.
40. Melanie Springer Mock. *Writing Peace: The Unheard Voices of Great War Mennonite Objectors*. 2003. Copublished with Cascadia Publishing House.
41. Mary Jane Lederach Hershey. *This Teaching I Present: Fraktur from the Skippack and Salford Mennonite Meetinghouse Schools, 1747–1836*. 2003. Published by Good Books.
42. Edsel Burdge Jr. and Samuel L. Horst. *Building on the Gospel Foundation: The Mennonites of Franklin County, Pennsylvania, and Washington County, Maryland, 1730–1970*. 2004.
43. Ervin Beck. *MennoFolk: Mennonite and Amish Folk Traditions*. 2004.
44. Walter Klaassen and William Klassen. *Marpeck: A Life of Dissent and Conformity*. 2008.
45. Theron F. Schlabach. *War, Peace, and Social Conscience: Guy F. Hershberger and Mennonite Ethics*. 2009.
46. Ervin R. Stutzman. *From Nonresistance to Justice: The Transformation of Mennonite Church Peace Rhetoric, 1908–2008*. 2011.
47. Nathan E. Yoder. *Together in the Work of the Lord: A History of the Conservative Mennonite Conference*. 2014.
48. Samuel J. Steiner. *In Search of Promised Lands: A Religious History of Mennonites in Ontario*. 2015.
49. Perry Bush. *Peace, Progress, and the Professor: The Mennonite History of C. Henry Smith*. 2015.
50. Rich Preheim. *In Pursuit of Faithfulness: Conviction, Conflict, and Compromise in Indiana-Michigan Mennonite Conference*. 2016.
51. Anita Hooley Yoder. *Circles of Sisterhood: A History of Mission, Service, and Fellowship in Mennonite Women's Organizations*. 2017.

52. Jo Anne Kraus. *Holy Experiment: The Warwick River Mennonite Colony, 1897–1970*. 2021.
53. Stuart Murray. *The Legacy of Melchior Rinck: Anabaptist Pioneer in Hesse*. 2022.

The Author

STUART MURRAY spent twelve years as an urban church planter in Tower Hamlets (East London) and has continued to be involved in church planting since then as a trainer, mentor, writer, strategist, and consultant. For nine years he was Oasis Director of Church Planting and Evangelism at Spurgeon's College, London. In 1997 he founded *Urban Expression*, a pioneering urban mission agency with teams in several cities in the UK and other countries.

Since September 2001, he has worked under the auspices of the Anabaptist Network as a trainer and consultant, with particular interest in urban mission, church planting, and emerging forms of church. In 2014 he became founding director of the Centre for Anabaptist Studies, based at Bristol Baptist College.

He has written several books on church planting, urban mission, emerging church, the challenge of post-Christendom, and the contribution of the Anabaptist tradition to contemporary missiology. Publications include *Post-Christendom: Church and Mission in a Strange New World* (2004), *Church after Christendom* (2005), *Planting Churches: A Framework for Practitioners* (2008), *The Naked Anabaptist* (2010), and *A Vast Minority* (2015).

He lives in Canterbury, is married to Sian, who is a Baptist minister, and has two grown-up sons and three grandchildren

CPSIA information can be obtained
at www.ICGtesting.com
Printed in the USA
BVHW051726280722
643269BV00002B/9